PRINCIPLES OF POWER

The Art & Wisdom Of Badassery

ERIC SCHLEIEN

CONTENTS

Foreword

Principles of Power can be related to as an advanced Coaching Handbook for Leaders.

If you are a leader, an aspiring leader, a coach, consultant, or program facilitator, this book is designed for you. The material is well and thoughtfully organized. The book is written in plain, easily accessible English, and delivered inside of a modern leadership context of service and contribution

The ideas are logically presented, although some may be personally challenging. If you can successfully set your existing belief structures to the side, you will experience a number of rich and useful insights. You might even find yourself saying the occasional Aha, Duh, and maybe even a few Wows'.

It is useful to separate management from leadership for clarity in a conversation about either subject. Too often, management and leadership are conflated, to the detriment of both. Let us distinguish management from leadership in order to point out that the two actually exist in different realms.

Leadership is messy, filled with mistakes and corrections and is an art form. Leadership is about effectiveness.

On the other hand, Management is neat and orderly and has structure and rules. Management exists in Time and everything is measured. Management is about efficiency.

Leadership = Effectiveness. Management = Efficiency. There is a profound gulf between the two realms.

The current management operating principle is, 'if it can't be measured, it doesn't exist'. This is nonsense and, unfortunately, is widely taken as gospel. The sunk costs of this well-intended rubric from a past era are unhappy workers and any access to extraordinary results.

People do not appreciate being related to as a 'thing to be measured', and are exquisitely sensitive to being commoditized to forward another's (the manager's) agenda. If you have ever experienced your reports 'digging in their heels' and exhibiting passive resistance to the company program, especially Strategic Initiatives, then you know exactly what I'm pointing to.

"Culture eats strategy for breakfast every day."

— Peter Drucker.

This. 'if it can't be measured...' heuristic and other mistaken notions have served to justify egregious management practices masquerading as leadership. Just think about it. Many things exist which cannot be measured.

In fact, virtually everything qualitative that human beings prize, like the love of family, compassion for those less fortunate, art, ethics, morality, and cultural expression cannot be measured. However, they are vital to life and real in the face of the obviously incorrect platitude. Leaders today recognize that the human factor is critical to the success of any enterprise anywhere in the world.

So, this book is not about that. It's about you and your leadership.

Eric features many partnerships in *Principles of Power*. His inclusion of useful quotes from Warren Buffet, Charlie Munger, Werner Erhard, Nassim Taleb, Seth Godin, and many other leaders attests to the thinking and the research that went into the writing of this book.

It is now undeniable that the understanding and implementation of powerful Listening, authentic Relationship, and a recognizable Permission to Lead, are cardinal distinctions of effective leadership.

The word, 'cardinal' has a Latin root and means 'hinge' – like a hinge on a gate. So, like a hinge, cardinal distinctions are connected to every nuance of leadership. You will see these distinctions in action in the background of Eric's many leadership conversations.

Authentic Relationship, for example, is essential to the effectiveness and empowerment of the participants and the leader. If authentic Relationship is missing, any outcome or result devolves to the result of domination or force, and is not an outcome of effective leadership.

Consider this: Leadership is granted by the permission of those being led. Take a moment and allow that to sink in. We are well launched into the 21st Century. We now live in a 'digital' era.

In the previous 'analog' era, leadership was commonly considered to be the exclusive preserve of a 'Strong Man'. Archie Brown, Professor Emeritus at Oxford and one of the leading voices on Political Leadership, in his, *The Myth of the Strong Leader'*, took this notion to task and pointed out that 'Strong Leader is an obsolete notion.

Seth Godin also pointed out in his wonderful book, *Tribes*, that the old 'broadcast' model was one in which the leader, standing up front, orders people around. It's like your TV broadcasting content to you with zero interest in your feedback. No more, says Godin. He points out, correctly, that in this age of the Internet, we are all nodes waiting to be connected. The digital age leadership is a communication game we all get to play.

This is the basis of what is called 'Triads' in the book, *Tribal Leadership*.

Lt. Col. Wayne Pollard, USA (Ret) describes this phenomenon as *'Leading From Your Current Position'*. Even the Army gets this now, having spent the past two decades transforming to meet the leadership demands of a modern world.

Here's the latest. The emerging leadership model is radically altering from analog to digital. The new model is widely distributed and self - managing. This model will usher in the Block Chain era – it is here and it is the wave of the immediate future.

So, here's a clue:

If you do not have permission to lead, you are not the leader. Period.

Whereas the authority of the manager can force output, no one will follow when the heart is not engaged. The leader is in a position to make a big difference for the group, but only if those with her/him *grant permission* to lead.

If the reader is paying close attention, Eric speaks to this in his chapters about *Vulnerability* and *Surrender*.

This is also why another of the cardinal distinctions of leadership is *Listening*. An overwhelming proportion of organizational failures are a result of the leader not listening to their constituency. Shining the workforce on and ignoring what they are really saying is fatal. 'Out of touch' is how it is usually explained. Underneath that, it's really a case of not engaging and enrolling the permission of the followers.

Permission is the key to taking people to the next level of accomplishment. No permission/ no movement.

Another clue:

Leadership is about effectiveness and exists in Space.

The job of the manager is to drive the result or outcome, regardless of the human cost. Management is a 'no matter what' environment, and managers tend to relate to the worker as a 'cog in a machine'. This is the source of ineffectiveness, low output, and employee turnover. Ask any HR Director, when people quit a job, they actually quit the manager.

The job of the leader is that of an environmentalist, providing the Space for people to collaborate, flourish, and create. These two different activities, management and leadership are often commingled, especially in business schools and in the workplace. They are distinct and operate under different rules and measures. It's like Checkers and Chess – Same game board, different games with different rules and outcomes.

Disentangling and distinguishing the two arenas of activity grants power to both managers and leaders.

So, the fundamental exercise of *listening for people's greatness* is in the background of every sentence in this book. And there is much more...

Principles of Power is strongly influenced by the transformational work of Werner Erhard. Much of the author's thinking is also grounded in the classic distinctions of *Tribal Leadership* and the thinking of Warren Buffet and his partner, Charlie Munger.

Those, plus Eric's own extensive practical experience renders *Principles of Power* to be an extremely useful 'go to' resource, filled with useful, implementable information, sprinkled liberally with memorable quotations from intelligent diverse sources – all apt and worth adding to YOUR leadership lexicon.

All learning is a function of Surprise. Allow yourself to be surprised and take what you get.

Enjoy!

—**John King**, co-author of *Tribal Leadership*

Introduction

When I began writing, I never intended for my work to develop into a book. I started writing for the love of expressing my ideas and getting real-time interactions and feedback from social media. The vast majority of what's written in this book was merely a means to communicate my insights, ideas, and contribute to others.

Over the past several years, I have received countless private messages and emails from people expressing to me the difference I've made in their lives through me sharing on social media. Occasionally, someone would tell me that I should write a book. However, I wasn't inspired to do so and was content with merely sharing principles and ideas I was using in my life and contributing them so others in my community could use the ideas for their own lives for how they saw fit.

I became inspired to write this book while on a road trip. I was at a used bookstore in the middle of Iowa. There was a terrible snowstorm, and I was forced to get off the highway. I ended up stumbling across a used bookstore, which to my surprise, actually had an excellent selection of books I'd read. It wasn't one of those used bookstores with mostly junk. I stumbled upon a book by one of my favorite authors, Seth Godin, which was called "Whatcha Gonna Do With That Duck? : And Other Provocations." The book was a collection of his writings that he had posted on his blog.

At that moment, I realized I had an attachment to what a book "should" look like. Through letting go of my attachment to what a book should look like, and, consciously choosing to focus on what I was committed to through writing a book, I had the experience of being freed up to just simply write and enjoy the process without having to worry about everybody "getting it." I decided I'd rather write authentically and not hold back, knowing I may only be speaking to 2-5% of the population who will "get it," as opposed to writing in more general concepts and holding back a bit to attract more people. I think both models have their place; I just know I'd have no interest in holding back to appeal to more people. It's just not something I'm interested in, and I have tremendous respect for those who choose that path. It's just not for me.

This book isn't mean to be read as some guidebook or book of advice. I'm more interested in sharing ideas, frameworks, and principles (hence the name of the book), that leave people with more power and effectiveness in their lives.

This book is also not meant to be intellectualized where you walk away just knowing more facts and information. That's not what impacts performance and effectiveness in life. What I'm committed to with this book is to leave you with, hopefully, a few new insights and breakthroughs that can be naturally applied to your life, and, lead you to be pulled towards taking new actions and producing new results.

What it will take from you, the reader, is an open-mindedness, a sense of curiosity, and a willingness to try things on that may feel or seem counter-intuitive at first. I can assure you that if you read "Principles of Power" from a space of agreement, you'll most likely be left with no new insights, and, this book will have been a complete waste of your time. What I mean by reading this book from a space of agreement is reading through the lens of what you agree with and what you don't agree with.

This book will provide the most value for you when it's read from a space of actively looking for how this book can contribute to actual areas and circumstances in your life. Where the magic happens is when you see for yourself how these frameworks and principles impact your life, in real time, when applied, and, not just thought about or intellectualized.

With that being said, you could have 100 people read this book, and

100 people would get different things out of it. Whatever new insights you get out of reading this book are yours to have. Anything I say that, even when you make an effort to apply it, just doesn't resonate with you or work for you, just toss it aside.

My conversations also work a little bit like grenades. And, if you know anything about grenades you know that there's a delay between when you pull the pin and when the grenade explodes. A lot of these ideas and principles that I'll be sharing with you work a bit in that way. I've come to discover that after having shared many of these ideas and principles with thousands of people over the past decade.

It's quite common for me to share something with someone and it doesn't click for them until much later. Sometimes days and sometimes years later. So it's possible, and even likely, that something you read in this book will have an impact on you at a later time, and, it will just naturally click when it's meant to click.

Also, these ideas and principles aren't where the power lies. The power of these ideas and principles lie in the thinking and the inquiry you engage in these principles for yourself in your own way. It's one thing for an idea to be understood intellectually. It's an entirely different level of knowing when something is gotten viscerally, and, something shifts inside of you. These principles gotten at an intellectual level, while perhaps interesting, won't add much value to your life. So, whatever you get at the level of your core, where something shifts, that's where the power is.

I think of this book like an arrow. If you take an arrow and it points you to a destination, you getting to the destination is what matters. If you were to spend twenty years over-analyzing the arrow and just stand in front of staring, what you would get is lots of thoughts about the arrow which would defeat the purpose of the arrow's function. If you just think about the ideas in the book, it will add nothing to your life aside from perhaps some interesting factoids you can talk about at a cocktail party.

However, if you really do the work, really start inquiring and looking to see how you can apply these ideas to your own life, then the insights and breakthroughs you get through inquiring into these frameworks and principles are the tangible results you'll have after reading this book.

And, because you did the thinking for yourself, and, you discovered whatever there was for you to discover, it's not something you memorized; hence, you can't ever forget it. It's something that is yours to keep for the rest of your life. If you try to memorize the ideas in this book, you'll forget them over time, and it will make no difference.

I take the position that if you're reading a book on frameworks and principles, you're probably already more open and at a higher level of intelligence than the average person. You're also someone that perhaps has a commitment to growth and expansion in your own life which takes a willingness to see beyond what you already understand.

You're also probably more curious and interested in learning new things than the average person as well. The person who is hardest on yourself is also probably you. That's good news for both you and me because I can't be there to coach you. You're just reading a book, and you very likely don't even know me personally. However, I have found that people who are intelligent, coachable, and, are already hard on themselves, don't need much coaching. They don't need to have someone be very aggressive with them either. They actively look to see what there is to see for themselves, and, they'll coach themselves and just do the work. When someone discovers a principle or framework for themselves, smart people tend to coach themselves, and you don't have to intervene much other than just to hold space for them to engage in that kind of high-level thinking.

This book is simply here to hold the space for you to engage in the ideas and principles laid out in the following pages. Whatever you discover out of them is what you discover. Whatever doesn't contribute to you, either at this moment in time or forever, doesn't contribute to you. I also write this book from the point of view as viewing you, the reader, as someone who is already whole and complete, not broken, and that there is nothing that needs to be fixed about you. I take the position that any area of your life where you feel a loss of power, a loss of your Self-expression, or you experience lacking a sense of aliveness, vitality, or a connectedness to others, that it isn't a function of who you are, but a function of something that's in the way that you just can't see. And, if what's in the way was brought into view, you'd be able to free yourself from it, as opposed to taking actions on top of it, which is about as useful as painting over a canvas that already has a painting on it to create a new painting. It just doesn't work nor does it create anything new. Instead, it only produces more stuff on top of the old canvas. Like I say several times in this book: "whipped cream on shit is still shit."

I'll take the analogy even further and say that whipped cream on a delicious cake just adds to the delicious cake. Unless of course, you don't like whipped cream, and then you can substitute that for some other topping you like.

Intended Outcomes

There are three intended outcomes for anyone reading this book.

1. To discover things in the way to get at the heart of what's not working.
2. To see what's in the way that's preventing you from taking life to the next level in areas of your life that are working well.
3. To see new actions and ways of being that you can take on and apply to what's already working to enhance further what you're already up to in life.

Lastly, there is no general rule to any of this, and, however you use this book that actually adds value to your life is fine by me. I'm simply sharing how I see things and how I believe you can use this book to provide yourself with the most value and efficient use of your time.

While writing this book, there were terms mentioned rooted in a body of work known as "Tribal Leadership" which weren't always explained or distinguished out. Therefore, I decided to interview John King who developed many of the principles and mental models discussed in this book. John is a dear friend of mine and someone whose work I admire. He's also a genius even though he probably would say that I was wrong about that. He's just humble, and I'm right. John is known best for developing the "Tribal Leadership" methodology and as the co-author of the book, "Tribal Leadership." There are terms he uses when I quote him later on in the book such as "The Cultural Map" or "Stage 4" that don't have any inherent meaning in the English language. Therefore, I interviewed John and put the interview transcript at the beginning of the book so you'd already be familiar with those concepts and understand them within the context of what I'm sharing later on.

I am beyond blessed to have the opportunity to share ideas and principles, some my own, and many that I've learned from others. I hope you enjoy and get a lot of value from this book.

My Interview With John King

CO-AUTHOR OF THE NEW YORK TIMES
BESTSELLER, TRIBAL LEADERSHIP

ERIC SCHLEIEN (ES): All right John, so thank you for taking the time to do this interview. I wanted to talk with you about some of the frameworks and principles that are brought up in "Principles of Power." Some of these principles are principles and frameworks that you invented, and, [I] wanted to take a deeper dive into them so that when they're brought up later in the book, readers will have a better understanding of what I'm talking about. Does that sound good?

John King (JK): That sounds great.

ES: Ok perfect. Let's start with the cultural map. In the book, I mention things like *Stage 2*, *Stage 3*, [and] you're quoted a few times where you talk about that and its relationship to *givers and takers, push and pull*, and *flow*. Can you give us a little sense of that world and what you mean by the different *cultural stages* and how that interacts with some of the other models that you've invented?

JK: Sure. The *cultural map* is a diagram that shows how people group together and how they talk when they are working together. It's designed for groups, [and], it's designed for looking at culturally how people work together. The backup on that is how they connect or clump up together. What I noticed was that we live in a culture where it's pretty much about your individual effort, and therefore, people are not very good at forming partnerships. When they do form partnerships, they form them in a hierarchical manner, that is to say as a junior to senior in the partnership, which is in my world, is not actually a partnership. Mostly what we're trained to do when we work is we work inside of what is called a zero-sum environment. A zero-sum environment is where somebody wins and somebody loses. The purpose of the *cultural map,* and the structural map that goes with it, is to show people exactly at which point things tip-and-change to the next level of the zero-sum game, and, then where the zero-sum game becomes bankrupt if you're trying to accomplish something at the level of group, and, at which point there needs to be a mental shift into something called a *non-zero-sum positive outcome.* In a zero-sum game, there's a winner and there's a loser. I win you lose and we can kind of count it. I win by 3 points you lose by 3 points, the sum is 0. In a non-zero-sum game, it's actually a participation in which we're all in the same game together and we all win together or we all lose together. My purpose was to have people look at this, see how they talked, and how their language actually impacts whether they're in a zero-sum or non-zero-sum game, and, what level or stage—I called it a stage—of the game that they're playing it—and at which point—if they happened to find themselves in a non-zero-sum game, what level they are there. And what we noticed—I didn't know this going in—what we noticed was when people go from a *Stage 3 zero-sum game* which most everybody knows how to do it to, and go into a *Stage 4 non-zero-sum game,* their productivity goes up by a factor of about three times to five times.

And so, I became interested in that because I'm interested in productivity. I'm interested in partnership and I'm interested in "how does partnership affect productivity", and, I'm interested in the role that language and structure play in productivity and partnership.

ES: You mention there are five stages of culture, five ways that people organize themselves in groups.

JK: Yes.

ES: Can you say a little bit more about that?

JK: Yes. In ascending order, people are more effective, that's the first part of this. At *Stage 1,* there's only about 3% of the people that are organized at *Stage 1.* It's a kind of a place where criminals are, and, it's an area that we call undermining. People who are in an undermining [relationship to their environment] and alone [in their environment] because it's a very alone sort of thing are at *Stage 1.* The next level up is something like— we experience this on a bad day—at *Stage 2*. *Stage 2* is ineffective. When I notice that I'm not really being effective at what it is that I'm committed to, one of the things that I notice is that I am not really well connected. In fact, not connected at all to the people around me. I'm kind of there and I'm amongst them. But, I'm not connected to them. So at *Stage 1*, one of the things people at *Stage 1* say is: "life sucks". At *Stage 2* —it's a big change—it's "my life sucks." I mean, I could see that your life works. I can see that the things you do work well. I can see it's a great life. I just don't have an access to participating in it. I'm not connected in a way that I can participate in it effectively, so I'm being ineffective, and "my life sucks."

ES: To make a further distinction, most people, when they say "life sucks", what they actually mean is "my life sucks."

JK: That's actually what they mean. We tend to speak hyperbolically. And for the most part, very seldom, do people actually get into the true "life sucks" unless they're in wartime or [involved in] criminal activities, or, they're trying to bring down the whole structure. But the truth is, that "my life sucks" is kind of the place where you feel ineffective and then we kind of dramatize it.

ES: Right.

JK: *Stage 2* is connected by the way, kind of like I say joined at the hip to *Stage 3*. *Stage 2* and *Stage 3* have a symbiotic relationship. *Stage 2*, is ineffective, or you could say "a loser", at least in this particular point [of view]. They have a point of view that "my life sucks." *Stage 3* is the winner. Think of sports. The person who is the champion is the *Stage 3* and what they say is, "I'm great, you're not, and I have the statistics to prove it." So they are organized around winning. And if you're organized around winning, in this particular way, it's a *zero-sum game*. The people that you are winning over are the people who are at *Stage 2*. The trick about this is that *Stage 3* does not exist without *Stage 2* nor does *Stage 2* exist without *Stage 3*. They live in a comparative world. This is where we form partnerships. But the partnerships are definitely senior and junior. *Stage 3* is senior and *Stage 2* is junior. What you have is a relationship where *Stage 3* is dominating a *Stage 2* and *Stage 2* is avoiding the domination. It's a relationship from [Stage] 3, "I'm great, you're not and I have the stats to prove it", to [Stage] 2, "my life sucks." If you think about it just a little bit, you can actually see, when you're being ineffective and then somebody is actually driving you, managing you, dominating you, what comes along with it is a kind of a glee, a sense of I'm better than you. So how we build our self-image quite often, particularly when we're young, is we build ourself at *Stage 3*. It is not just a small thing, it's a big thing. If you extrapolate this out to companies, it's: "our company is better than your company", which is a *Stage 3* to *Stage 2* sort of saying. "General Electric is better than Westinghouse", or, you can say politically, the United States often represents itself as better than Canada. And so if you're a Canadian, you're in a *Stage 2* relationship to most Americans and nobody realizes it because it's all sort of in the background. So that's Stages 1, 2, and 3.

There is a shift that occurs at *Stage 4*. At *Stage 4*, there is a realization that if I'm going to do something, I need to actually be generating leadership, effectiveness, or empowerment of other people around me. So what I need to put together is, I need to put together a small group or a team. Often it's 3, 4, 5, or 6 people who are all in the same boat, and, we're all—you know—paddling towards the same goal. So at *Stage 4*, it becomes "we're great", and, we begin to look at ourselves socially. For the first time for human beings they look at themselves socially. This is where leadership starts. This is where empowerment starts. This is where interesting results begin to occur. This is the beginning of something. This is a partnership. This is, literally, where people form effective partnerships and whereas *Stage 1* was called "undermining", *Stage 2* is called "ineffective", *Stage 3* is called "useful", it's a useful place, however, *Stage 4* is called "important", and, important at the level of stable partnership and inside of a common languaging of "we're great."

Then, if you've done the work and put yourself solidly at *Stage 4*, then opportunities come along. They only come along for groups that are operating at *Stage 4*. And usually they're the kind of opportunities that will make history, it will change the game completely. This is what we call a "vital stage" or *Stage 5*. At *Stage 5*, this is where *team* really shows up. Because your little group begins to connect up with somebody else's little group and somebody else's little group with somebody else's little group to form a team. And when we form a team, the language around is generally "life is great", and what we're doing is accomplishing off-the-charts sort of results. Most people at *Stage 3* think they're doing *Stage 5*. Not accurate. When you get to *Stage 4*, and you do

4

the work around building yourself at *Stage 4*, you have that *Stage 5* opportunity. You actually get to see the remarkable difference between a *zero-sum/Stage 3/"I'm great, you're not"*, and, a *non-zero-sum/ "life is great"/ Stage 5*. But in order to do this, you have to do the work, and you have to do the work with other people. Human beings are social creatures. In fact, they're ultra social creatures. And so we work best, not when we're alone, we work best when we work effectively with other people. So *Stage 4* is all about effective stable partnerships, and, in *Tribal Leadership*, the whole name of the game is getting people stable at *Stage 4* so that they are ready for the opportunity when it shows up. And it will for people who have done the work at *Stage 4*. It does not show up for people at *Stage 3*, and, they end up missing the opportunity and then—I don't know—be weird about it.

ES: When you say *getting people stabilized at Stage 4,* do you mean, essentially, having people have their environments be conducive to *Stage 4* as opposed to these peak *Stage 4, oh we had a moment of partnership then it goes back to the old ways again?*

JK: Yeah. Thank you, that's actually really well thought through Eric. It's about environment. See the thing is at Stages 1, 2, and, 3 it's all about *me, me, me*, and, it's only about *my survival*, and it's all about *me winning, you losing*, and *me getting ahead*. However, at *Stage 4*, there's a consciousness that: *how I win is by making sure that other people win*, so, what should become at *Stage 4*—and this is the beginning of leadership—you become not someone who is out for yourself, but someone who is out to create an environment for other people to perform well. So, it's about being an ecologist. It's about being an environmentalist. It's about really providing an environment. It turns out, generally speaking, if you base your relationships with people properly, which is on merit, it turns out that people are probably pretty good at what they do and don't need a whole lot of managing, but, they might need some leadership. Leadership—being kind of a code word for: *a great environment to work in.*

ES: Right.

JK: Google is a great example of it. Because what Google does is hire really smart people and then creates an environment for them to work well together. And as a result, they get off-the-charts kinds of results. This is also happening in our other programs that we see that are the flashy splashy great ones going on. The ones that seem to be passing away are the ones where they are still operating of the old version of "I'm great, you're not."

ES: Right, which isn't that conducive to having stabilized—

JK: Right. Rather than actually having stabilization—it actually presents bullying to say it brutally.

ES: Right, interesting. Can you explain how someone would actually apply these principles—I'm very interested—if you could talk a little bit more about the principle of the *triad* and how that impacts—and how you can use that principle to impact the environment around you.

JK: Well that was really at the heart of it—I love this question—and it's one I'll have to create a little bit with you. But because it's a little bit abstract here—I could draw it and it would be a little bit different perhaps—but one of the things that I—shock, shock, shock—one of the things that I realized at a certain point in time was that there was a limit to what the individual could actually produce. Then there was something the individual could produce if they were to, in a sense, enslave other people and dominate other people and make other people do it. We call that management. But when I saw—and started looking at extraordinary results at the level of team—when I started that, what I saw was that people had radically shifted their attention from their own survival to the success of the other people they were working with. And when I saw that, I began to look at *how do we work together*. I asked this question: *what's the minimum number of people in a relationship that has it be stable?* I've asked that question several thousand times. And the answer that I almost always get is two. But when I ask people where they learned that, for the most part, they don't know. They point to maybe their parents or they point to some sort of something. But the truth is, it's a myth, and it's a myth that we've been fed by the social sciences: Sociology, Cultural Anthropology, Psychology. We've been fed that it's about two [people].

ES: How did you discover that [it] was a myth?

JK: I discovered it in a way that was very touching to me. I have a friend who had a beautiful talented son who was being scouted to go to Notre Dame University and he was an athlete and a scholar—very stunning young 15-year-old boy—and, I got a call one day—and it turned out that the boy committed suicide. Shot himself in the head. And, it was such a shock to me because this kid had such a life in front of him—that I began to—I couldn't get my mind around it—so I went to a whiteboard and started drawing out—I knew him fairly well, and so, I started drawing out every significant relationship that the young man had. And when I drew them out, they came out as triangles, and, I began to look at that and consider that the only way that we are truly stable is when we are in some kind of triangulated relationship. I looked physically across the room—and I have a camera on a tripod—and looked at the tripod and I went "oh! *The fundamental structure for stability is at least three anchor points, not two, and maybe I could think from that.*" So, I looked at this diagram of triangles, and, I saw that what had happened for one reason or another over a course of several months is that every single triangle that this young man was in—as his network of relationships had broken —they had gone away, they had stopped, they had literally dissolved. And here was a young man who was standing alone—but it looked like he had his family—and his friends, and his school, and everything else—I got everything looked cool but it turned out that it was not so. He had shifted from one school to another school, and, when he shifted from one school to another school—his best friend who had been his friend for life and his girlfriend who he loved—decided they were in love, and, they abandoned him. So his mother and father had kind of gone away from [him], his sister kind of gone away from him, his friends—he gone to a new school—his friends were missing, he was at *Stage 2* to begin with, and then all of a sudden, the straw that broke the camel's back for him was that his best friend and his girlfriend decided that they were in love. Now people don't take teenagers very seriously in the matter of being in love. They say it's puppy love. But for them, this is love. This is the real deal. He didn't have any way to deal with it. So what he did was he stole his parent's car—you know—hijacked the car and got a couple of buddies, and, went over to his ex-friends house and beat him up. And then the roof fell in on him and everybody around him, including his parents, the boy's parents, and so on like that, just landed on him. And he was forced to shame himself or humiliate himself in front of the family—both families—to the guy who had been the guy who stole his girlfriend. At least that's the way it looked in his life. And he was forced to shake his hand. When he did, the guy whose hand he shook—who was 15-years-old also—smiled because he won. And he literally kind of rubbed it in. Then he went home and he was still in trouble because he'd stolen the car, and he'd lied, and he'd done this and he'd done that, and, then a couple of days later, he was found in his parent's bedroom closet, and, he had blown his brains out. And this was totally shocking. But what it got me to was—that when I drew out the figures on the white-board, what I saw was, *we are stable when we are in triangulated relationships*, and so that became the basis of the way that I look at networking and it became the basis of something that I called *triads*. Then I saw that when you move from *Stage 3* to *Stage 4*, if you took a couple of people with you, and you did it in such a way that everybody in the triangle was committed to the success of the other two rather than worrying about their own survival—the thing about it is that the building of a *triad* is a mutual thing.

ES: Right.

JK: In other words, it won't just work for me to pick you and some other random guy and then be committed to your success unless I've got you in a *non-zero-sum game* with me in which you realize that my success is your success and the other person's success is your success. The rule is: *the one person in the triad is accountable and responsible for the success of the other two*. If you looked at it like a triangle, you would say the vertex is accountable for the success of the opposite leg, and, it requires that all three people in the *triad* are actually on the same boat. And the reason this is good is because it starts to bring up stuff that we start hearing a whole lot about. But we hear it discussed in an ineffective way. For exam-ple, this is where values come in. If I take you and another person, we have to be very clear that our values are aligned with each other, and so, if somebody has significantly different values, this is probably not going to work. This is where generosity comes in. Leadership is a generous space. This is where the idea of having the permission of the others comes in. Leadership is a distinction that operates or is granted by the permission of the people being led. So what you've got to have is you've got to have an environment in which all can succeed and that what you're there [for], is you're there for the success of the others in the group. Some people are extraordinarily good at this but not very many— maybe 20% of the population—if they wake up to it. So if I took the numbers and I said 3% are at *Stage 1*, about 20% is at *Stage 2*, roughly 50% are at *Stage 3* at any given moment—and it's a very fluid in-and-out thing—*Stage 4* is 20%—its an enlightened 20% of people who are inter-ested in the success of something that's bigger than me—bigger than them. So something that comes in at *Stage 4* is something called a *noble cause*, something that makes it bigger than me, bigger than the three of us, and something that is worthwhile for us spending our time, and our effort, and our money, and our ingenuity on to make happen. This is the —I don't know—the golden egg I suppose or the Holy Grail of organizational culture thinking. If we can get everybody working, and working happily together in a respectful and honoring way with each other, inside of the same kind of value set, and working on something together that is worth accomplishing together, that's bigger than us, then we have a good chance of putting ourselves at *Stage 4*. Otherwise, it just devolves into: *I won this round* or *I lost this round*.

ES: Right. So if someone is part of an organization and they notice that the culture is at either *Stage 2* or *Stage 3*, how can they start to begin building *triads* to move to a stable *Stage 4*? What are some things to start looking for?

JK: Well, for one thing, listen to the way that people talk and you will find that in some way, shape, or form, people in these particular environments—along the lines of "my life sucks" or "I'm great and you're not"— and they're that way with each other—in other words, there's all kinds of internal competition and a lot of putting people down—it's often pretty snarky—so one of the things is—if you listen to the language, that will give it to you. Another is, if you take a look at how they organize, at *Stage 2*, people are disconnected. There in and around the group but they're not really connected to the group. If you take a look at someone who is sort of drifting and they don't really seem to have people—except maybe people who talk like they do, which is "my life sucks"—but other than that, they're not really well connected, that'll be somebody at *Stage 2*. *Stage 3* is at the center. *Stage 3* is the person who considers themselves to be the leader and they may have had five or six people around them that depend on them. They form a hub-and-spoke. So if you think of the "so-called leader" at the hub and you think of the people at *Stage 2* as being the spokes—that's what they do—they're smart: they put people around them, they lie to them, they tell them that: "I'm going to take care of you," but ultimately, if you take a look over time, their practice is not to take care of people but to take care of themselves first. And then, if there's anything left over, maybe take care of a few of the people that are the spokes.

ES: Could you say that those kinds of relationships are more transactional or commoditized?

JK: Yeah absolutely transactional. This is something that, *I want to win this game*, or, *I want to win this account*, and, *I'm going to do what it takes in order to beat you to do that*. Very transactional. The long-term kind of relationships are the ones where we decide: *we're all in this together—and in all of us being in this together—I have to support you—and I'm expecting your support—so that we the three of us, the five of us, the seven of us—think—you know—some more than one—that what we're doing is—we're working on something that's going to be of benefit to each and every person, and if it's not of a benefit to all of us, we don't do it.*

ES: If you want to move your organization from *Stage 2 or 3* to having it be stable at *[Stage]* 4, you essentially are looking for those people that could be your partners in building those *triads*. Is that the sense of it? What has been your experience?

JK: Yeah it's a good question because you would think that you would look at the *Stage 3* [people] because they're a little higher on the food chain. But the truth is, when people are at *Stage 3*, and they're winning, there is basically no incentive for them to change. So they're very difficult to change. What we're looking for are people who are at *Stage 2*, but who are bright and who are open and willing to make a change. So—*my life sucks—but I could see that it could be better if I was—you know—working with you and you—and we were actually up to something that was going to be a benefit to all three of us.* Where you look is you look at the *Stage 2's* and you put together—what I'm going to call *awake* or *enlightened Stage 2's* who see that—*I'm sick and tired of being in survival*, and, *I'm sick and tired of being the loser and on the bottom end of this deal*, and, *what I want to do is I want to actually work my way out*, and, *the way that I work my way out is in a true authentic partnership with at least a couple of other people.*

ES: I would add to that—and tell me your thoughts on this—that there's going to obviously be some people who are hanging around talking about how "my life sucks" in that environment. They're not really awake, but you could say, that if you're in a *Stage 2* or *Stage 3* culture, that people who are *awake*—and maybe you could even say—have a commitment to partnership, a commitment to *Stage 4*-ness in a culture—they're inherently going to be at *Stage 2* in that kind of environment.

JK: Yeah, it's true. There's an ontological rule that: *you have to have a breakdown before you can have a breakthrough. Stage 4* is a breakthrough place. It's a breakthrough in several ways. It's a breakthrough because it's no longer a survival place. It's a place where you're actually generating abundance. It's a breakthrough because it's no longer singular, it's social. And it's a breakthrough because, I have this realization of: *working with people is actually going to work for me*, so that's a breakthrough. And when human beings went from—*the one individual* to *the team player, the collaborator*—that's when the whole conversation called *human being* began to move forward rapidly. For example, you take other primates—chimps haven't learned this. So they live in a hierarchical world and they're brutal. It's a brutal world, a brutal competitive world, and it's all about survival. So what we're looking for is—we're looking for *Stage 2's*—who while they may be in a survival-based relationship—*Stage 2/Stage 3*—they actually can see that if they were thinking about it differently—that there's actually a different, more powerful, and more effective way to think about *the way that I work with people*. At *Stage 2*, the way that people work with people is they work in a way where they're disconnected. If I work in a way that I am profoundly connected to other people—and what I mean by profoundly is: *you're connected at the level of some sort of resonance of your values*—then you're more than: *we're not just manufacturing widgets here—this is an honest person who does things in a way that I admire and I want to work with that person.*

ES: Right.

JK: I was working once in a utility years ago—they were very good at working with each other once they understood that they could drop the bravado and the machismo of *Stage 3/Stage 2*—and all of a sudden, they started working in a way that was uplifting to the company. I asked the class—I said: "I don't know quite why I like working with you guys." And this guy says, "I know why"—because he was one of the ones who was a leader in this area—and I said, "why is it, Tony?" And he said, "we cut square corners." And it hit it right on the nail head for me. We like people who are honest, effective, generous, and they're willing to work with other people, and it's not based on their likes or dislikes, it's based on their commitment to what it is that they're doing together.

ES: Right. Now I want to further distinguish something. When you say *someone at Stage 2*, you don't mean someone is inherently *Stage 2*, you mean they're at *Stage 2* in relationship to their environment.

JK: Yeah, that's really a good and important point. The truth of it is there are tons of ways you can participate in life. You participate at work, you participate with certain people at work, you participate in your family, you participate maybe in your community—and you know—you may well be operating at *Stage 4* in your community—think like maybe you're a Scoutmaster or something like where you're doing something for other people—and, at work, you're maybe just surviving. And at *Stage 2*, it's not uncommon for people to be in one of those stages and then to leave that stage and go somewhere else and then come back. And quite often, people don't notice it and that is why I actually articulated the vocabulary. The vocabulary is very clear. As you speak, that will actually define the stage you're in. And then if you take a look, a close look, [at] what your physical structure in relationship with others is: *am I amongst the group and floating?* That's *Stage 2*. In effect: *am I connected but I'm in a hub-and-spoke but I'm either the hub or the spoke?* That's a *Stage 2/Stage 3* kind of relationship. Or am I in some sort of triangulated network kind of relationship where—*wow this is kind of easy and we're getting a lot done, and, we like each other, and, we're enjoying the work because we're doing it for some greater cause, some greater reason than just to turn out the work.*

You take a look at championship teams. All the teams meet at the beginning of the season and they all decide whether they're going to go to the Super Bowl. Are they going to win the Super Bowl? Are they going to make it to the playoffs this year? And in that meeting is where they actually design whether they're going to be a *Stage 2/3* team—which most teams are—or a *Stage 4* team that occasionally rises to the occasion of *Stage 5*. In football, *Stage 5* is winning the Super Bowl.

ES: Yeah.

JK: And by the way, teams meet in the Super Bowl competition—and when we get to the end of the competition—for one of them: *"life is great"/Stage 5*—and for the other "my life sucks", which is *Stage 2*.

ES: The pitfall for some people when they first get introduced to the *Tribal Leadership* work is they hear the principles through an overarching context of *the individual* which your work is not really about. Right? So, *I am Stage 2/I am Stage 3.* Or—*I need to use language in order to be Stage 4 so I'm going to use a lot of we language*—there are all of those things that people could hear at the beginning which I think—and tell me if you think I'm wrong—but I think it's shaped by the context of our society as a whole.

JK: Well, particularly around business, we live in a management-driven culture not a leadership-driven culture. And as a result, we often see that leadership is a subset of management, and, it's not true. That's backward. Leadership comes first and then management occurs afterward. *Management Is granted by authority.* If somebody tells me I'm the manager I come in, I go, *Hi I'm your new manager.* There's no voting and we are now automatically put in a state of: *I'm Stage 3 and you're Stage 2* and I'm managing you. *Leadership is granted by permission of those being led.* So it's a collaborative/cooperative kind of space. But you're not going to collaborate/cooperate with me unless you are somewhat inspired by what I'm offering to you—as you know—what we're going to be working on together. Management is pretty much saying the way things work is by domination, however, we're going to make it a little nicer. B-schools teach people: *oh what you need to do is you need to think about people, you need to take them into consideration, you need to listen to them.* They give you all kinds of tips and all kinds of strategies so that you can get more out of these poor god-forsaken *Stage 2's.*

ES: Yeah.

JK: But that's not how it happens. How it happens is by having authentic relationships with people where there is *authentic give-and-take* in the relationship and where we are literally collaborating and cooperating with one another in order to get something done. That's not the way we think when we're in *survival*. When we're in *survival*, we think about saving our own case and it doesn't matter what happens. We have a point of view in *the movie of our life* because we're not related to reality, we're related to some kind of story that we've got going on in our life.

ES: Almost like a belief about your life?

JK: Belief—and it's like a bad movie, Eric—like—I am the writer, producer, director, and star of the *movie of my own life.* And everybody else in my life is supporting cast, at best. So that means your mother, that means your mate, that means the people you work with—they're there to support you—the hero in the movie I've called *the life of Eric.* And until we get that *the life of Eric* is actually a low-level sort of game that everybody is playing—I mean everybody is playing—until we understand that until I can actually combine my movie with your movie, and, a couple of other movies—and strip out the drama so that we can work together where we're in a pragmatic realistic working relationship—

we're going to be inside of a whole bunch of people bumping up against each other doing nothing other than *the movie of their own life* and it's a movie that really needs better writing, better directing, better producing, and better acting.

ES: Yeah. Can you explain the relationship between—in the personal development and and the consulting world, there's a lot of emphasis on being in this peak performance state, on being in what they would call a *flow* state—can you explain the relationship between *flow* and *Stage 4* and *culture* in general?

JK: Yeah. *Stage 4* is a *flow* state. So, when we get it going, when we get everybody going, we're in *flow* state. Well, what is *flow* state? *Flow* state is part of a cycle. There's a four-part cycle and the first part of the cycle is something where we're learning a whole lot, where it's called *loading* and we are becoming overwhelmed with the information that we need and the adjustments we need in order to work effectively. So there is the learning part. Then, there is a formal part called *the release*. And *the release* is a place where maybe we do something socially together, we do something to kind of get away from what it is that we've been working on, and then coming back, what has happened is we have bonded in such a way that we go into *flow*. So if you think—I can look back and look at the military—so basic training was brutal. But after basic training, you got to a point where you really were able to kind of release the energy of all of that and bond with your buddies. And you came back—and you came back as: *wow, we're really bonded as a platoon*—so it happens on every sort of level. A smart leader teaches, teaches, teaches, teaches, teaches—watches the frustration—and then at the right point—provides something quite often—it's a place where they can laugh and they can have a good time and even poke fun at the person who is the leader—and then they come out of that and they are connected together and they go into *flow*. And *flow*—your productivity is just off-the-charts. People think *flow* is a place that feels good. It's not [about] a place that feels good, and it might, but it's not about feeling good. *Flow* is a place of accelerated learning. So what you've done is you have *loaded up*, you have got *the release*, you're now working with the other people, and now you're in a state of accelerated learning. You're learning about what they can do, you're learning about what you could do, and you're applying the principles that you're learning really fast. So accelerated learning leads to accelerated performance. And that gives us an access to the cycle of *flow*.

ES: There's a model that you developed that actually breaks down that principle of *flow*. Can you talk about that a little bit?

JK: I'm not sure, tell me what you're thinking of in this model—

ES: With the four quadrants.

JK: Yes, well this is something that I developed for managers based on the work of Mihaly Csikszentmihalyi who is the guy who distinguished-out flow and he's the genius who talks about it all the time. I'm just a guy who borrows from people smarter than I am. But if you look at a four stage matrix, and you look in the lower left corner, this is an area where you're not performing well at all. So that's an area of where it's of low energy, it's of low commitment. So nothing really happens here. There are two measures. One is the area that measures how difficult something is and your skill-set in being able to do it. The vertical access is how difficult things are. The horizontal axis is your skill-set. What it's saying is low skill and low performance. However, quite often, we get people who are overwhelmed, they are in a state of anxiety, they are scared to death. If you take a look at it, you could see in the matrix that they're in the upper left. And in the upper left there at a level of high expectation of their productivity. But if you look down on the horizontal axis you can see that their skill set is still very low. So, people who are are like that are in a state of overwhelm. And if you're a smart manager, what you do is you provide training for those people so that they can actually do what it is their tasked to do. So if you give high training and high competitiveness, the productivity goes up immensely. If you take a look at the bottom right quadrant, this is a quadrant where people have an enormous amount of skill but they have very little incentive to do anything because they're not challenged. So if you take a look at where the challenge is low and skillset is high, then they're in a state of boredom. So the three states are:

low skill/low challenge: apathy
high challenge/low skill: anxiety or overwhelm
low challenge/high skill: boredom

[The fourth state would be *flow*. This is high skill/high challenge and would be in the upper right quadrant of the 4 stage matrix]

anxiety

flow
apathy
boredom
CHALLENGE
SKILL

And where we want to get is where they're in a state of *high skill*, and at the same time, *high challenge*. *Flow*—and there's been an enormous amount of work done on this since 1991—I mean literally tens of thousands of case studies on this—where we find that if we want to get the best performance out of people, we've got to give them the highest skill set and the highest challenge and make it available to them.

This is why in sports—we say that you can take a look at what happened in some sports like track and field—you know 40 years ago—and we could see that the food is better, the actual activities that they're doing is better understood, and so on like that. But ultimately, the coaching is better and the coaching is what has made—forget that they've got better shoes, and better surfaces to run on—all of that was going to happen with technology.

So technology is a part of it but the biggest part is that we have more *aware* coaches. We have people who are coaching who understand that: *if I'm going to train and develop these world-class athletes, I have to get them into flow, and, the only way I could get them into flow is by high challenge and high skill set, and, so that's what we work on.*

ES: Yeah. Speaking of being action-oriented, one of the brilliant things about the *Tribal Leadership* work is that the principles are all applied, it's not just theory and being intellectual about things.

JK: Yeah.

ES: And it only works when you actually apply it to situations. That leads me into strategy—and I know you have a strategy model that you developed.

JK: Yes.

ES: And I think it's brilliant.

JK: Thank you.

ES: Any corporate strategist would tell you that strategy is very hard, there's a very high rate of failure. Your strategy model has a very high success rate on average. One of the things that you figured out—which I think is incredible—is you saw the connection between taking on a strategy [and taking on a strategy] that was actually conducive to the culture that it was in. So if you have a team-based strategy in a *Stage 2* culture, it's not going to really work very well.

JK: Not at all, won't work at all.

ES: Can you explain a little bit about—

JK: Here's a little bit of my thinking about strategy. For one thing, I personally think that five year strategies are fine, two-to-five year strategies are fine. And I think that people should have an idea of where they're going in two-to-five years. But I think that if you're going to put that out as your strategy, you're going to end up somewhat like [what] China does and Russia does with their five year plans because all kinds of things happen between here and the next five years including that we forget what we're doing and we have to be driven to do it. So earthquakes occur, floods, famines, hurricanes, divorces, deaths, births, all these things are things that alter an individual's strategy. So for myself, I began to just look at myself and I began to see: I *can hold an idea powerfully for 90 to 120 days.* So I thought to myself: I *wonder what it would be like if I devised a strategy model that was only 90 to 120 days long.* And then I re-strategized and I built a series of strategies on top of each other like people set pancakes on top of each other to get to the top one. But rather than going for what's going to happen in five years, because it's a lie, I'm going to go for: *what can I do by the end of the quarter?* So I like to set the strategies on a quarterly basis and then every quarter we visit them—even often during the quarter—to see how we're doing on the particular strategy we're working on. And at the end of the quarter, we have a report card day, and we set the strategy for what's going to happen in the next quarter, and we go through the process again of visiting it, and doing what I call *spin the plates* during the course of the quarter. The strategy is simple. And, the strategy is simple because I was a strategist and I was failing as a strategist. I was doing the *Blue Ribbon Strategy* which is Michael Porter's strategy from Harvard Business School. Michael Porter is a genius and he did put together a very complex and articulated strategy which ultimately became Singapore. You can't say anything but good about Michael Porter and Porter's strategy. However, I found that it was not practical for the individual, not practical for a lot of people, so I decided that I would go somewhere else to look for what would be my strategy. The trouble with Porter's strategy is that it's only successful 30% of the time and it requires a lot of tending to. And I thought to myself: *we should be able to devise something that is more effective than 30% of the time.* And I did. And in my searches, I found a strategy model that was simple [and] was effective about 80% of the time. And so I took that model and adapted it. At the time, it was not a strategy model that was useful for people. It was actually useful for moving heavy machinery around. It was a strategy that was used by the United States Army. I took that strategy—and over the course of about a year of working on it and proofing it on a beta group of about 300—roughly 12-year-old girls—like they're the smartest people on the planet and they will tell you immediately and get immediate feedback whether this is working or not—and you will also be able to see: *can they teach this strategy to others?* The strategy is of no real value if you can't not only implement the strategy but [aren't able to] teach it to others so [that others] can implement the strategy for themselves.

The strategy model that we do is a simple. Basically, [a] Y-shaped strategy with 3 moving parts and three challenging questions. If you can unlock that strategy yourself, you will devise yourself a strategy for the next 90 days that is doable assuming you do it.

ES: Right. Now, have you noticed—so what I think is very interesting —one of the first experiences I had to being able to *shift the environment around me* wasn't through *Tribal Leadership*—but then I started seeing all these connections—it was when I was doing a program through Landmark [referring to the personal training and development company, *Landmark Worldwide*, formerly *Landmark Education*]: The Self-expression and Leadership Program [commonly referred to as *the SELP*].

JK: Yes.

ES: And one of the distinctions I remember my program leader saying was that: *your Self-expression is a function of the listening of your environment* and that projects are an access to shifting that listening. Can you talk a little bit about how taking on projects can actually impact the *Stage 4*-ness, impact the amount of leadership versus management in a given environment?

JK: Sure. So first of all, that's actually accurate and it's a brilliant insight. The Self-Expression and Leadership Program actually is a senior part of the curriculum, which is called *The Curriculum for Living* for Landmark. The beginning of it is [The Landmark Forum], it's all about you and getting you out of *survival*. Once you've done that, you go into the Advanced Course and you begin to see through the Advanced Course that your full Self-expression is going to be in the way that you interact with your communities.

And then you go into the SELP program, and in that, you design a project which does several things. It teaches you how to do projects. It shows you that if you can bring people into a project, and have it be a worthwhile project, something is going to bring a benefit, or in the language of that particular program, *create a possibility* for a group of people that you are touching—and the term that they say is *touching, moving, and inspiring*—that if you could do that one thing, what you will end up [having] out of that is a profoundly heightened sense of effectiveness. So there is lots to be said of the Self-Expression and Leadership Program in terms of your engagement with a project that gets you out of it—actually gets your nose out of your own navel—out of the way of your own *Self*—gets you into a conversation that is about designing effective and useful futures for other people, and as you do this, you will you will experience more success in your life.

One of the things I like about that program is that it's about starting a program and that at a certain point of the program letting it go, just turning it over to the other people and going and finding another program. [In this sentence, John uses the word *program* instead of the word *project*]

Because you as a human being—see, in your case Eric, you're a young man and I would guess that between now and when you die—if you live a normal lifetime—you will probably do 200 or 300 projects in your life. And one of the things that particular program does, and one of these things that I'm concerned about is: *teaching people how to be effective and successful in doing whatever the projects are that they bring up.* I'm a huge fan of the SELP program that Landmark provides.

ES: There was something else I wanted to ask you regarding *survival*. You said that—you talk about *taking yourself out of survival*, you have a term—and I don't know if you're the one that coined it or if you just use it—but you talk about the *capital S Self* versus the *lower case self*—and these two *selves*. Right?

JK: Yeah.

ES: *Self*, as an expression of who you are—and then this sort of this automatic identity—this kind of automatic machinery running in the background—

JK: Yeah.

ES: Can you go into how that plays into the environment that you're in? If there is a correlation—

JK: Yeah, It's the *capital S Self*. I think is something I came on—probably when I was about 17 or 18-years-old and I was reading Alan Watts—or it was that point in my life where I began to see that there was a difference between *who identified myself as,* what's called *my persona* or *the mask that I wear* or constructed, or, *what's really at the heart of the matter for me as a human being.*

And so that is what I call my *capital S Self.* The distinction that I like to look at is the difference between *excellence* and *greatness* because it gives me access to this. See, *excellence* is what other people say about you. You do something and you do it well and they say that is excellent. *Excellence* is something that is like a jacket that you put on, and, it looks excellent on you. *Greatness* is something that is deeply and profoundly inside of you, it's not an external thing, like how you appear to the world. It's actually your relationship to your inner—what I say *capital S Self*—and how do we nurture that?

Now both of those are going on all the time at the same time. And as a matter of fact, in the world of survival—to get back to your question—in the world of survival, mostly all we're concerned with is:

How do we appear from the outside-in?

How do we appear to our peers?

How do we appear to our culture or community?

It's all about, in the coinage of some people [in the Landmark community], it's all about *looking good*—and people will sell their soul—I don't think that's much of a reach to say—people will sell their soul to *look good.* And when I say soul—you might want to say that people will sell out on their *Self,* they will sell out on their dreams, they will sell out on their values, they will sell out on the things that they truly stand for in the interest of *looking good* in other people's eyes.

So when I say *excellence* versus *greatness* or when I say *identity* versus *capital S Self,* that's just another way of how I look at it.

ES: Interesting. So I think that covers the models and principles in "Principles of Power" [here I am referring the models and principles that

John developed specifically, not every single model and principle in the book].

Is there anything else that you think you'd like to add to this conversation or contribute to this conversation?

JK: Not so much. You know it's kind of like—I had a friend say to me the other day, it's not like eating an apple, it's more like peeling an onion, and I like that. It's kind of like as we talk about these things, and we're sort of peeling it away, or peeling it away to see that which is underneath what that which is underneath—what is the *source* or the *cause* of something—and if you've eaten an apple all the way down, you're left with a core. There's something right there in the middle. But if you peel an onion all the way down, and you peel it all the way down, there's *nothing* at the center. And *nothing* is your area, your soul, your *Self*, the place where you generate your creativity, the place where you access your true power. It's never going to be *outside-in*. But *outside-in* is the way you're going to always be perceived. It's always going to be you as a human being and how you generate from the inside-out *from nothing*.

ES: That's great. Well John, I really appreciate your time.

JK: Well, thank you. And, I appreciate the questions Eric. And I appreciate the opportunity to talk about something that I love a lot.

What gets in the way of connection

WHAT STOPS people from experiencing love, connection, and feeling connected to another is the illusion that they need to find it, or work towards it. Consider that taking on this view perpetuates merely an experience of not being related or connected.

When something is in the way of our natural connection to others, all there is to do is to distinguish what's in the way and give it up.

Some possible things in the way:

1. Resisting what's so
2. Thinking something should be another way
3. Resenting something or someone
4. Needing to prove something or validate yourself
5. A belief that goes against being true to yourself
6. A judgment about yourself, the situation, or someone else
7. An outcome you're trying to force
8. Something you're trying to manipulateAn ulterior motive
9. A point of view and you believe that it's the only point of view
   —regardless of whether you're actually right or not

When you can distinguish what's in the way, you have the opportunity and the choice of whether or not to simply give it up and get it out of the space.

Disempowering stories around "no"

It's amazing how the word, *no,* stops so many people. The disempowering stories people come up with around failure, being told no, or being rejected in some way are absurd.

You apply for a new job; you get rejected.

You seek to raise capital for your new business; someone isn't interested.

You ask someone out; they're not interested.

People can get all crazy about not producing the result they want, and it has nothing to do with the circumstances. Instead, it's the stories or interpretations that people make up about not getting the results they want at any given moment that shapes one's experience of that failure to produce a given result.

Who knows where the life of probably most of your heroes, who are insanely successful, would be today if they made a no at-the-moment mean a no forever, and came up with some story about how they failed.

For example, before starting the investment firm I currently run, I had failed to produce this result twice. The first time was when I was in college, and I was managing money with a partner. He decided he wanted to work at a firm that was more in line with what he was interested in, the quantitative value approach, as opposed to what we were doing, which was in the realm of fundamental analysis of individual securities. After he left, I could have easily told myself that I should just quit and work for a larger firm, and not have my own company anymore. However, I didn't let that moment of someone not wanting to work with me anymore give me an excuse to stop going after what I want and resign myself to settling for that outcome. If I had done this, deep down, I would have felt like I was selling myself short.

A few years later, I came up with a new model for shareholder activism and found two people who were trained in changing the culture at organizations. After about a year of them training me, of them *"not being ready yet"* to start a company with me they flaked on the project, and I was left with feeling like I had just wasted another year of my life trying to build a new investment firm. Like I was failing at it again due to my supposed partners not actually being committed to the project. I was so angry at myself due to the fact I had felt that I allowed myself to get strung along by empty promises and false hopes.

However, I learned a valuable lesson for myself and continued to press on. I realized that the only reason I was hanging onto people who weren't serving me was due to the fact that I was operating out of scarcity and was trapped inside of a mindset where I thought that if I cut my ties with them, there wouldn't be anybody else who could help me. I was convinced that because this skillset was so specialized, it may be true.

What's true is that there are indeed very few people who can impact organizations in this exact way. However, what's also true is there is almost always many ways to skin a cat even if it's not the way you initially envisioned. The attachment to *my way* of skinning the cat as opposed to being committed to skinning a cat without cutting corners or sacrificing my integrity in the process was actually what I should have been after. Lesson learned.

After this second failure, I decided that I would let go of my attachment to doing the shareholder activism and just continue to commit myself to starting a firm where I could manage money for others.

Out of that commitment, I went ahead and started an LLC. I spent a year asking people to give me money to invest. It took lots of trial and error and I kept having people not be interested and giving me their reasons why. I just let them know I got it, didn't resist it, and used each *no* as an opportunity to continue to find and seek out investment partners. And after a year of doing this, I finally got my first investor.

It took hundreds of rejections over several years to get to that first investor in my own firm. If I had let any one of those prior circumstances stop me and make it mean that I should just resign myself to a lifestyle I didn't want, I never would have produced that result.

It's the difference between having someone not being interested in giving you that job, in investing in your project, in being romantic with you, or allowing any form of rejection to provide you with an excuse to put some kind of disempowering meaning to it as opposed to using that rejection as an opportunity to continue to create what you want for yourself and your life.

Someone declines your proposal to go on a date with them. Use that as an opportunity to create a future of what it takes to have the love of your life (or whatever dynamic you're interested in creating for yourself and your life).

You don't get the job you want. Use that as an opportunity to create your dream job or dream lifestyle.

It's actually not complicated when you approach life like this. Operating from this space gives one the opportunity to be larger than their circumstances as opposed to simply having to *"make the best of it"* and resign themselves to what's *"realistic."*

One of my mentors John King would say, *"There's no such thing as failure, just correctable results."* This principle of failing to produce a result in any given moment, and, using it as an opportunity to continue to take actions to get the intended result applies to all human beings. This principle applies to someone who is homeless to someone who has a relatively great life and is looking to take their life to the next level, or, contribute at their highest level at an even larger scale.

One thing a lot of people need to get with this commitment to *not getting stopped in the face of very little support or agreement* towards your goals is that you're not getting a result isn't personal, and posturing yourself as a victim to the circumstances around the result you failed to produce is an asinine way to behave in life.

There is no limit to how this principle can be applied. If someone isn't interested in hiring you at their organization, then you can apply for 100 more jobs that would also give you what you're looking for. If the job you want requires a particular skill set, then you can go out and learn the skill as opposed to resisting the reality of the situation regardless of whether you personally believe it's fair or not for the world to operate in a certain way.

To use that job example again—you can make yourself even more competitive next time around and create a future for yourself where in 2 years you are applying again to the same company where, this time, you give that employer no chance in hell they can say no.

That's not motivational bullshit, something to hype you up, or a guarantee of success. It's simply that life truly is that simple regardless of what your current circumstances are.

However, if you take no action or start mentally masturbating about it, and, get stopped by some disempowering story you tell yourself, then, you nearly *guarantee* the results you're getting already. At the end of the day, it's your actions that matter and it will often take several thousand micro-actions and micro-failures to produce the results that you are committed to.

Playing big

WHEN YOU PLAY BIG, not everybody is going to get you. You can spend your energy trying to justify and prove yourself, but that rarely makes a difference. People will think what they think. Often, even if you show them all the evidence in the world why what they think about you is an inaccurate view of you, their point of view about you will remain the same, and even be further solidified. Consider that the more you resist how someone thinks of you, the more ingrained their thinking of you will be. Your efforts are much better served creating what there is for you to create and focusing on what matters internally.

You could be the most successful person at what you do in the world, accomplish things bigger than most people ever dreamed possible, and there will *always* be someone who thinks you don't care, who thinks you're selfish, who thinks you're unkind, who thinks you're unloving, who thinks you lack compassion, and who thinks you're not good enough.

Whatever you do, don't try to be something you're not in order to have others think a certain way about you. They won't, and, you'll do it at the expense of your own natural Self-expression and aliveness in life. When you're settled about who you are and what your mission in the world is, people can call you the nastiest of things, and it won't matter to you anymore because you're so settled about what your life is about.

Dealing with people's bullshit

THERE IS NEVER a need to deal with bullshit. Anytime you complain about it, what you're not being responsible for is the fact that you're the one choosing to engage with it in the first place. Simply, just don't engage in people's crap and continue to engage with people's greatness. The very nature of taking a stand for someone or something often revolves around giving space to the bullshit and only dealing with the awesomeness of another.

Being responsible for the occuring

WHEN I REALIZED that nobody had the power to make me feel a certain way whether it be uncomfortable, upset, angry, etc. and it was, in fact, *me* who chose to bring those ways of being into a situation—my integrity and personal responsibility *had* to be taken to a whole new level.

When I realized these other people weren't responsible for my own internal state, something shifted. Now, anytime I would complain about someone making me feel upset or uncomfortable, I would feel gross to my very core because, deep down, I knew I was out of integrity with myself.

When I say out of integrity with myself what I mean is that there are specific commitments I have to myself that I am dishonoring. One of the commitments I have now in life is to be 100% responsible for how I feel and not blaming others for how I choose to be in the world. I know that anytime I'm being anxious or angry or any other way of being that isn't very empowering for me, that I am the one doing the choosing of that.

Being a victim to my internal state and blaming others for me choosing to be anxious in the face of my anxiety or choosing to be angry in the face of my anger lacks personal integrity for how I'm committed to living my life. Anytime I am out of integrity with myself it has a negative impact on the general quality of my life. That principle doesn't just apply to me by the way; it applies to all human beings.

When I'm out of integrity with myself—that lack of integrity, diminishes my own freedom, Self-expression, and power in my life. Coming clean about where I'm bullshitting myself is how I get all of this back. What's downright terrifying is that when this is missing for long periods of time and one is out of integrity for years around something as simple as this, it can lead to you not even remembering what you're missing and your baseline for what's *normal* just becomes *fine*.

You could say that the people who have the deepest relationship to the principle of integrity are the ones with the most integrity issues. There was a time where saying something like, *"this person makes me sad"* or *"this person makes me angry"* did not resonate with me as an integrity issue.

Now I can't get away with that anymore for myself. There's immense power in that.

Misery loves company

WHEN WE PLAY huge in our lives, we will inherently threaten people's identities. Be great with people and simply do not entertain their machinery. Give them full and complete space for them to kick, cry, scream, and whine. Don't resist it, don't defend it, just give it all total space. The people who don't get threatened, and instead, become inspired by who you are and see your extraordinary greatness – those are the people you want to play with. As the saying goes, "misery loves company." Don't entertain that crap. Don't allow yourself to be run by other people's crap. It will only cost you your life.

The more you try to *fix it*—the more it stays around. Reality exists through conversations/language and the more *"fix it"* conversations you have—the more whatever you're trying to *fix* will stay around. The human mind often goes into a state of *"there's something wrong here, I need to fix it"* or something along those lines. However, once that becomes the context for a situation, you're already stuck in the trap.

I'll give you a silly little example. Let's say you were supposed to have a business meeting. The person doesn't show up. Your mind may go into a space where you think, *"there's something wrong here, I need to fix it."* If that's the context in which you're thinking and acting from, just imagine how the experience of yourself will be, and, how effective you will be in handling the situation. That disempowering mindset often ends up creating a self-fulfilling prophecy. And, the more times you do that, the stronger that feedback loop becomes in which *there really is something wrong here*, and, the more energy you start devoting to learning how to *fix it*.

The *fixer* way of being can be a very tough one to give up, especially if a lot of your success has been associated with that way of being.

The experience of *needing to fix something* may not ever go away. However, the freedom lies in noticing how *automatic* that mindset is. Notice the bodily sensations, thoughts, emotions, and mental attitudes that come up for you when you feel you need to *fix* something. Now, get you aren't those emotions, thoughts, attitudes, and bodily sensations, but merely the one who observes them.

Getting that gives one space for creation and something to put into place. So perhaps when someone doesn't show up for a meeting, all that's missing is accountability, and, putting in some kind of accountability system is what's needed to restore workability. Or perhaps, it's just communication and giving the person a call to check-in and see where they're at (without invalidating them) that's called for. Use your intuition on that.

Fixing is in the realm of reacting. It lacks power. Yes, you can be good at that game. But even if you're only half as good at *the creation game* as opposed to the *game of fixing and changing*, you'll be on average more effective at producing results while at the same time exerting less energy.

What gets in the way
SHIFTING THE WORLD AROUND YOU

IF YOU'RE someone who is out to change the world in some way and you have a keen and unique awareness of the world around you, it's very easy to get upset, to get angry, and to put others down when we feel rightly justified in doing so. I am also clear that to allow yourself to worry about such things, and, to become vile and cruel towards others robs you of your aliveness, your vitality, your happiness, and your own Self-expression. It'll also make you less effective in shifting the world around you. As soon as you allow yourself to become hooked by extrinsic circumstances, you've already lost the game, and you've diminished your own power in life. When you find yourself needing to justify or being righteous about a point of view (even if you know you're actually right), and, when you find yourself feeling the need to invalidate others (yes, even if they're totally asinine and stupid ignorant fucks)–this all gets in the way of actually having the things you want to see in the world become reality.

Transforming Mental Health

THERE IS a huge missing in the mental health field. What I see is missing (DISCLAIMER: I am not a doctor or psychologist, and none of what I say here is medical advice) is that clients/patients are often treated from a space of being broken as opposed to being whole and perfect just how they are and how they aren't. I've observed (completely non-scientifically and anecdotally) that more and more therapists are starting to wake up to this and are starting to treating their patients from this space with *much* more effectiveness and a more significant impact. I also am clear that anyone who doesn't explore these ideas and refuses to read up and study the latest research and innovation going on around the world in the realm of making an impact on the mental well-being of human beings is being a righteous know-it-all.

I think righteous know-it-all may even be an understatement due to how influential a therapist or psychiatrist can be over someone's life. When any scientist, doctor, or anyone who impacts people's health and well-being is more committed to justifying their own point of view than treating their patients, it really pisses me off and I find it really fucking sad. The root cause behind what gets in the way of our aliveness is perfectly described by Werner Erhard who is one of the most influential people in the field of transformational learning.

"The only two things in our lives are aliveness and patterns that block our aliveness. As patterns are experienced out, our lives become clearer. Things begin to make more sense. What we do makes more sense. It's funny, but when the alive you emerge from behind the smokescreen of all those patterns and begins to participate in life directly, life really does a have purpose. It all somehow makes sense, in a fantastic way. When you get rid of the blocks, what you have is aliveness, and when the blocks are gone, purpose emerges. There is no use searching externally for a purpose, or trying to 'pull it in.'

It is already there. Just focus on clearing out what is between you and aliveness, so every time we create greater aliveness, the purpose is being served. Aliveness and purpose are practically the same thing. The purpose is greater aliveness, so every time we create greater aliveness, the purpose is being served. As more and more of us get to see that the purpose is greater aliveness, it happens that all of us start to do the same thing – we start serving the purpose. Life comes on to us in our own terms, and so does the opportunity to serve.

That everyone is serving the purpose in a different way does not mean that everyone is doing something different. That's the illusion. We do the same thing in different ways. As each of us makes our part of the whole really work, the purpose is being served. The purpose is life and that it be, completely. The commitment is: aliveness."

— WERNER ERHARD

Transformational learning is incredibly powerful when the principles of the field are synthesized with the field of mental health and psychology. In February 2018, I attended the Daily Journal Annual Meeting in Los Angeles, California. Charlie Munger, who is Warren Buffett's business partner and is also the Chairman of Daily Journal. The meeting has a bit of a cult following, and there were about 1,000 "groupies" there to see Charlie and hear him speak and take questions. At the meeting,

Charlie was sharing how useless psychology is when it's only understood academically, and on the contrary, how powerful it is when the principles of psychology are synthesized with other fields of study. This Werner quote is a perfect example of how one could impact and make a difference in the field of psychology through an understanding of principles from an entirely different field.

People will judge you regardless

GO WHERE YOU'RE CELEBRATED, not tolerated. And for those who throw their judgmental crap at you—just remember it has nothing to do with you. Who you're *being* can be a threat to some people's identities, and almost unconsciously and automatically, they'll take sides, get positional, go to *I agree/disagree conversations*, and look for some way to kill off anything you're committing to contributing or creating.

Shine your greatness in the world and always focus on giving your gifts as deeply and at the highest level possible. Essentially, sharing and contributing from a space of your authentic Self-expression and what makes you feel alive and purposeful as opposed to doing something because you think you should, or, because it validates some aspect of your identity is crucial. Never diminish yourself by trying to fix yourself and going into the *"there's something wrong"* mode.

People will judge you regardless.

"Your playing small does not serve the world. There is nothing enlightened about shrinking so that other people won't feel insecure around you. We are all meant to shine, as children do. We were born to make manifest the glory of God that is within us. It's not just in some of us; it's in everyone. And as we let our own light shine, we unconsciously give other people permission to do the same. As we are liberated from our own fear, our presence automatically liberates others."

— MARIANNE WILLIAMSON

Being energy efficient

IT TAKES LESS energy to be open and keep an open heart regardless of your circumstances as opposed to holding on in a state of emotional closure in order to protect or defend something. There will *always* be people who don't see you for you, and they're tainted by their own lenses and interpretations for reality that absolutely have nothing to do with you. Just give yourself away in each moment and commit yourself to service and contribution without attachment to what comes from it. Don't do it because it's morally right or because you think you should. Do it because of what it brings to your own satisfaction in life. That's a choice in each moment.

Be on your deathbed knowing you gave every ounce of your core that you had to give. I'm truly committed to the idea that people get to experience themselves authentically at the level of Self without thinking about it and are able to share that part of themselves even with those who won't see it in them.

I'm so committed to this idea that we all authentically and intrinsically are able to experience ourselves and express that part of us no matter who we're with, and no matter our circumstances. When we come from fear—*looking good, avoiding looking bad, trying to dominate, trying to avoid being dominated, defending, surviving, manipulating*—it diminishes our power, our effectiveness, our happiness, our vitality, the amount of authentic love in our lives, and the results we're committed to producing in the world.

Don't get attached to people
COMMIT TO THEIR GROWTH INSTEAD

SOMETIMES DISENGAGING from someone is the best way you can make a difference with them when it comes to having them be more connected to who they really are at their core so they have the opportunity to contribute their deepest gifts to the world. Don't get attached to people. That doesn't serve them or you. Commit to their growth. You literally can't fail with that commitment. It's actually impossible.

"When we leave someone who is feeding off of our energy, blaming us and giving nothing in return we offer them the opportunity to find themselves and share those gifts with the world. Until then, we enable them by permitting them to use us for our energy while their real gifts remain hidden. Giving away our energy to someone who complains or criticizes us denies them the pressure required to create 'purpose' out of their 'potential'."

—Graham R. White

Fixing yourself is an asinine game

PEOPLE WHO SPEND their whole lives trying to fix themselves, change themselves, and trying to get all their ducks in a row are almost certain to be stressed and miserable. It's an asinine game that is not winnable. Stop worrying about fixing your problems. It's exhausting and doesn't do shit. It just makes your problems bigger and perpetuates the very neural connections you're trying to change.

Focus on solving a world problem, investing your time in something awesome, building some dream fairy-tale relationship, building an amazing family, or whatever it is that you're passionate about. You can create your future regardless of your circumstances or you can find reasons why you can't do something due to your circumstances, or, the story you have about yourself aka *the way you are*. It's that mindset that leads one not to take action and leads one to tell themselves something along the lines of, "*before I can do X, I first need to fix something about myself or my life.*"

People with money issues, relationship issues, Self-esteem issues, anxiety issues, fear issues, etc.—that concept of always fixing and changing just leads to more of the same old bullshit and feeds more into the disempowering crap you're trying to *compensate for and overcome* in the first place.

A much more effective approach is to distinguish all the bullshit stories you have and all the bullshit reasons you have justifying them. Have a day where you're feeling really sad? Okay, first get that you aren't that emotion and simply *notice* it. Then, determine what *stories* or *interpretations* you do have about that feeling of sadness. When *stories* are distinguished, you cease to be disempowered by them. Some people will fight tooth and nail not to get that because it's such a fucking threat to their *identity*.

Tell someone who is depressed that they just need to distinguish some *story*. Unless they're insanely highly conscious or it's not part of their *identity*, they'll probably get reactive and tell you that it's "*just the way they are*." Go tell someone who has cancer that there's been a cure found and they would *not* say, "*well I'm a cancerous person, it's just who I am*." Observe how the word, *I*, is used in that context. It's a lie and describes the *identity*, not the Self.

Create some new empowering stories for yourself that you get present to once you've naturally transcended the old bullshit.

When you start committing to the things in life that really light you up, the petty bullshit stops being fed energy. Over time, brain patterns change. It can take years. However, results are instant.

The importance of supportive webbed networks

FOR EVERY SINGLE person that has had the courage and the audacity to live a life so true to themselves that they tapped into aspects of the human spirit that we don't necessarily always have full language or understanding for—there are many more people who have tapped into those aspects of humanity at some point and stopped because they simply lacked an environment that would support them. They either put constraints on themselves or society just did it for them.

I cannot stress enough the importance of building a connected web of people around you who will always seek to have your flame burn brighter and brighter.

When people see something outside of their box of awareness—they'll often want to kill it off in any way they can. So in those moments where people try to box you in (and if you put yourself out there in huge ways, it *will* happen)—having the support of the people around you to help you remember who you are when you might lose your awareness a little bit is one of the greatest gifts to our spirit.

Without that kind network, some people lose that awareness and not only never regain it—as more and more time goes on, and, as more and more blocks get put in place—those people will become ever more disconnected from their own natural aliveness, purpose, and Self-expression.

The trap of half-commitments

HALF-COMMITMENTS TO STAY FREE KEEP one trapped. Essentially, pretending you're committed to something, when really, you're always keeping one foot out the door so to speak and never really fully giving your all.

People who don't fully commit aren't fully showing up for life. They lack freedom. Their word lacks power. What's sad is that people are afraid to commit because they think they'll be at a loss of freedom. In fact, it's that very lack of integrity and their weak relationship to their word which is at the source of it.

And the truth is, you're always committed to something. Not being committed to something is a commitment in and of itself. If you're committed to doing things with one foot out the door, what you're *really* committed to producing are results that will reflect that. It's horrible.

Being with darkness

THE MOST BEAUTIFUL people I've ever met in my life have also had some of the most intense darkness, the most intense "*black swans.*" I've also learned that by loving people through their darkness, it creates the opportunity (not the guarantee) that their own light will be brought out into the world that much more. It creates the opportunity for them to be freed up at an expanded level. I've also learned that when I become afraid and try to run away from and suppress the dark sides of someone —all the beauty, goodness, and light that first had me feel connected and inspired by them in the first place also dulls.

If you can't be with and hold space for someone's darkness, you'll always end up stuck with dullness.

Two risks

THERE ARE two types of risk in the game of sharing.

There's always a risk that when you share yourself freely that you'll offend the wrong person, that you'll make yourself look bad, that someone will think poorly of you after hearing what you shared.

The bigger risk is not sharing. The bigger risk is withholding and losing the opportunity to inspire, connect with others serendipitously, and impact the lives of others. Giving up aliveness, power, and simply not sharing your core for fear of being judged is a losing game over the long haul. You lose all of those things and what you get is to look good, which by the way, doesn't even look that good. It's a pretty shitty deal yet people dupe themselves into taking this deal against their own *Self*-interests all the time. It's a deal rooted in survival.

There will always be someone judging. At least let them judge you for you.

Don't micromanage people's reactions

STAND for people's greatness even when they fight tooth-and-nail to argue for their smallness. It's not your job to micromanage the reactions of others.

Pleasure and aliveness

IF YOU ARE LIVING ACCORDING to what others think, you will never truly feel confident or happy inside. That's simply because you're out of integrity with your core and that destroys aliveness. If you aim just for certain results without taking the experience of aliveness into account, you'll probably experience low levels of pleasure and low levels of aliveness via a diminished sense of purpose. If this experience of purpose, aliveness, and vitality gets reduced enough, we call it burnout. However, most people don't get the *source* of their exhaustion and approach it from an action-oriented lens as opposed to an *ontological* one. Some people stay in this space their whole lives as their solutions are rooted in a *context* that doesn't take purpose into account. So no matter how hard they swim, they stay trapped in the fish tank while their soul longs to swim in the ocean.

If you commit to both having a pleasurable life and a life filled with the experience of aliveness, success is not guaranteed, but it is maximized on the probability scale. I believe we as human beings are designed for pleasure and aliveness where we are flourishing and thriving, and, not just surviving.

The one pitfall to this way of thinking is that not everything that feels pleasurable makes you feel alive which then in and of itself is not very pleasurable. And not everything that makes you feel alive is pleasurable.

Resisting machinery creates more garbage

EVERYONE HAS their own internal struggles, their own battles, and their own darkness that they deal with. Yes, every single human being. In others, you can resist, fight, and judge that side of someone else. However, it will only leave someone with the experience of being judged, dominated, or made wrong. Furthermore, they will almost certainly meet you with resistance, judgment, and their walls being up.

You will be re-activating the very part of their *automatic machinery* that left you wanting to resist or fight something about them in the first place.

If you want to drive out the darkness from this world, don't match it with darkness. Match it with your unconditional love. Get their experience as opposed to resisting it. Getting one's experience doesn't equate to condoning one's behavior nor does it enable it. In fact, resisting that side of someone else has a much higher chance of enabling any kind of disempowering or undermining behavior.

Surrendering

SOMETIMES WE WANT to surrender to love. Sometimes we simply want to penetrate through people's closed off bullshit until their heart is completely surrendered. And as they open and surrender, you continue to open deeper as well. And when they're tight and closed off, you have the opportunity stand tall not backing down until they are completely open and surrendered because you will not tolerate anything less.

1. Both expressions make a difference for humanity
2. Both expressions have their time and place of being authentically appropriate

However, there is one thing that is certain regardless of circumstances. When someone is standing for love and does not waver and someone is standing for fear...It's love that wins out.

The phrase *"love conquers all"* has degraded in the culture into some bullshit motivational phrase that typically makes no difference to the quality of one's life or is used as a coping mechanism when you aren't feeling very loving. However, getting this concept authentically at your core would leave one with the natural insight that *"love conquers all"* as opposed to a nice sounding belief system.

And speaking of belief...

When we start believing people's bullshit, then our hearts close too and we act less from our natural Self-expression and more from our reactions. The vast majority of human progress has come from human beings acting from a space of authentic Self-expression and not from a space of automatic reaction.

Never let anyone ever give you an excuse to stop *standing* for them which diminishes your own Self-expression in the process. *How you do anything is how you do everything in life.* Keep your heart open no matter what. Play the game of life with every fucking ounce of your being. Be on your fucking deathbed knowing you gave every ounce of love you had to give and that you gave all of yourself.

You had others be forwarded around you,

freer around you,

more alive around you.

If you've thrown people out of your life out of reaction—

If you've ever closed your heart—

Apologize.

Say sorry.

Give up your points of views, opinions, and justifications, if that's what it takes.

It only costs you your aliveness.

Manipulation and control
THE EVER CONSTRAINING PRISON

IT'S possible to get what you want using force, manipulation, and control. However, it becomes an exhausting existence. To keep your life looking the way it does, you need to keep controlling and manipulating to keep it going. Some people don't know they have a choice to take any actions otherwise. I think that's sad. It's an ever constraining Self-imposed prison. And, the more time goes on, the harder it psychologically becomes to free yourself.

The freedom in surrender

SURRENDERING yourself over to someone and giving up all boundaries completely is a scary thing for a lot of people. Oftentimes, it's also not something that people consciously want, especially if they have never experienced it before or if something in their past made them close off that part of themselves. In fact, to those people, it often sounds stupid and pointless or "unhealthy," "immature," "unrealistic," or "disempowering."

There's a difference between *needing someone for your own completeness,* and then *when being complete isn't good enough, and you need to go even deeper.* In this case, the access to this is through giving up all boundaries, sharing freely, and *surrendering* fully.

While that can feel scary as shit, the other side of that is ever-increasing freedom and a deepness and oneness that can only be understood through experience, not through intellectualizing it.

And to top it all off, our generation has it even harder due to the fact that our mothers learned the importance of *having a voice, taking a stand,* and being an *empowered* woman. This consciousness shift was a positive in that it gave many women the opportunity to go from being in a space of *needing someone* to *being whole and complete* to being in a space of experiencing themselves as *whole and complete on their own.* However, what was sometimes lost in this elevation of consciousness was the natural ability to *surrender* to the moment with another human being and dive deeper with someone than one could on their own. This collapsing of the principle of *surrender* with the notion that you were *needing someone to be complete or* somehow disempowering yourself through needing someone else to feel whole led to more separation and boundaries. Those same boundaries that brought one from *needing someone to feel whole* to being whole on one's own gets in the way.

If one wants to dive endlessly deeper with another human being, the same boundaries that got them to the *consciousness of wholeness* on their own now get in the way and stop being appropriate to elevate their own consciousness even more. Yesterday's insight become tomorrow dogma, degrades into a belief system, and then undermines growth in the future.

Surrendering to the moment while in a contextual or ontological space of *needing someone to be complete* looks very different than *surrendering* and letting go of all boundaries while in an ontological and contextual space of being whole on your own.

Being with the naysayers

THE MORE YOU put yourself out there, the bigger you play, the more naysayers you'll have, the more you'll inspire, the more of a difference you'll make, and the more you'll start connecting with others through serendipity. However, if you're not willing to handle the nay-saying part, don't expect the other shit to happen either. It's all just part of the game.

How to kill aliveness

IF YOU WANT someone to trust you and feel they can be fully themselves around you, then let them be as emotional around you as possible. The moment you shut down when people are being irrational, emotional, and angry—you'll simply teach them to suppress themselves around you. If you want to kill off the aliveness and radiance of the people around you, that's a perfect way to do it!

A commitment to freedom

REACTION WITH REACTION only perpetuates whatever you're resisting.

When you have a commitment to love or a commitment to freedom or whatever you're committed to with others—that doesn't mean be that way when it's convenient. It's easy to love when you're being loved. It's easy to be committed to the freedom of others when you're in an environment that calls for it.

However, the people that change the world *stand* for something bigger than themselves even when their environment doesn't call for it. It's being loving even when your environment doesn't support it. It's standing for the freedom of other human beings when all around you there is coercion and force. Meet reaction with creation. Meeting reaction with more reaction only perpetuates whatever you're resisting.

The integrity of integrities

ALLOW yourself to get pulled by your mission and your purpose. It's your deepest truth at your core. Follow it. Don't resist it. Don't deny it. As you become more present to what there is for you to do—you can either choose it powerfully and do it, or, you can take action out of line with that truth. The more you follow it, the stronger that pull becomes and the easier it is to feel. The opposite is true as well. And as you continue to widen the gap between what there is for you to do and what you're currently doing—you will continue to feel more constrained, more miserable, and your vitality, aliveness, and Self-expression will diminish. It's highest level of being out of integrity with your core. And maintaining this integrity is the most empowering context for everything else. It's the integrity of integrities. Follow your core. Own your greatness. No motivation or plowing through life required (as long as you honor your word throughout the process). Things unfold naturally.

People who are suffering

WHEN PEOPLE HAVE to attack you every time they feel threatened—they're merely projecting their own suffering onto you. Understanding that gives you access to a tremendous amount of freedom. You never need to apologize for your own greatness, for your own goodness, and, some people will feel threatened by that for whatever reason.

It's not your responsibility to control or dictate other people's reactions, and you can still apologize for how something came off to someone else. Then all there is to do is share what your intention was. If they *still* don't get that, then explaining yourself is a trap that will never have a conversation be workable. At that point, the person actually has a commitment to not hearing you. That's *very* different and distinct from miscommunication.

So when people spew venom on you—do not give it an ounce of energy, just give it space. Allow people to animate their own suffering and continue to create and be awesome.

The more someone suffers internally, the more likely they are to attack the people who are creating amazing things and amazing possibilities for the world.

Some people are more committed to their views. Committed to being the victim. And it doesn't matter how great you are with them, how respectful and honorable you are with them—they'll look for some reason to spew their own shit on you. Let it be. Give it space. Be great. Love them regardless.

The unwillingness to explore
THE IMPACT AND THE HARM

I'VE ALWAYS BEEN the kind of person to explore ideas regardless of whether I condoned it or not. I've visited the Westboro Baptist Church hoping to meet some members even though nobody was around when I was able to take a side detour to Topeka, Kansas twice. For those who aren't familiar with the Westboro Baptist Church, they're considered the most hated family in America and they're the ones who picket funerals of dead soldiers saying "*God Hates Fags.*" I have spoken to Shirley Phelps-Roper who is one of the leaders of the Westboro Baptist Church and the daughter of Fred Roper, the churches founder on the phone before, and, I've always had a fascination with wanting to talk to leaders of countries that were committing acts of human rights violations.

I have a curiosity to explore different ideas. I always find it amazing how often people take that as me endorsing something. That's insanely lazy thinking.

What's even more common are people who resist a willingness to listen to a new idea. That kind of stubbornness and intellectual dishonesty speaks more to willful ignorance than anything.

As Charlie Munger of Berkshire Hathaway puts it:

1. "I never allow myself to have an opinion on anything that I don't know the other side's argument better than they do."

2. "We all are learning, modifying, or destroying ideas all the time. Rapid destruction of your ideas when the time is right is one of the most valuable qualities you can acquire. You must force yourself to consider arguments on the other side."

3. "The ability to destroy your ideas rapidly instead of slowly when the occasion is right is one of the most valuable things. You have to work hard on it. Ask yourself: what are the arguments on the other side? It's bad to have an opinion you're proud of if you can't state the arguments for the other side better than your opponents. This is a great mental discipline."

It's truly amazing to me how many people *do* pride themselves on having an opinion they are proud of, yet have not explored other possibilities. In some professional fields such as psychology, medicine, and politics: science often degrades into dogma and belief.

Consider that people who close off that easily just show they don't even understand their own viewpoint, meaning it's almost definitely in the realm of a *belief system* and not grounded on anything other than an *attachment to being right* as opposed to an underlying commitment to getting to the *heart of the matter*.

When there are huge breakthroughs to be had in professional fields, that if achieved, would most likely cause a radical difference in society, and instead, industry leaders look the other way and willfully ignore new possibilities—I'd make the argument that those people do great harm to not only themselves but to the other people their field impacts. It also harms the integrity of their field.

If you're already living powerfully

1. Your *authenticity* will scare a lot of people, and it will also attract a lot of very powerful people to you.
2. You will end up being a mirror for many others where they will learn a lot about themselves through seeing themselves through being around you. That's a gift you are to those people.
3. People who are scared and not willing to look at themselves often won't be able to see your gifts without any added lenses to it.
4. People who are committed to their own integrity will naturally be very powerful around you. They know they can share anything, totally let go, and there's real power that shows up in that space. Those people will find you very easy to talk to. It just flows.
5. People who are petrified to look at themselves, who won't be on the hook for anything, who will say whatever is convenient at the moment, and, who literally put their integrity on the back-burner, won't last long around you. They'll be uncomfortable: call you pushy or get squirmy in their own way. Those are relationships centered around *unworkability*. You simply won't have space to show up in their world without

having to diminish your own power to fit into their own *reasonableness.*

6. You often show up early to avoid being late due to unforeseen circumstances, call people back, and fulfill on what you say you're going to do. When you don't, you honor your word and get the impact. It doesn't mean you never fail to produce the results you're committed to, it doesn't mean you won't act in ways that are inconsistent with the kind of human being you're committed to being in the world—it simply means you go the distance to make it work (and making it work without cutting corners which would be a lack of integrity like trying to play football in a field with a huge hole in it).

Being grateful for every circumstance

WHETHER YOU BELIEVE everything happens for a reason or not is irrelevant. What I am clear about is there's always something to be *grateful* for regardless of the circumstances.

However, the moment that a gratitude practice becomes some kind of *positive thinking technique,* it loses its power and just becomes another intellectual piece of bullshit that makes no difference.

Where people get fucked up and start suffering is when they create a disempowering *interpretation* of what happened. Without sorting that out and having the kind of clarity and completion that comes out of that—one will always be *grateful on top of suffering* or something bad or negative underneath it which will *always* diminish the power of any kind of gratitude practice this.

Most of the people who have changed the world have had tough backgrounds where they had "forced personal development" to get to where they are today.

If you're poor and grew up in a troubled home, you had to be bigger than that. If you've been bullied or were sexually abused as a child or teenager, you had to learn to keep your heart open and love when every ounce of your *automatic machinery* or *identity* was pulling you towards fear.

If you grew up physically unattractive, you had to learn to build character because your looks wouldn't allow you to get by. If you never went to school or didn't have a degree, you had to make it work without one.

If you're a free-thinker, you've had to learn to share in a way where people could hear you because sharing unfiltered—the way you would in your own small circle—would be like not speaking at all. Challenge, adversity, and unfavorable circumstances are gifts.

Because when you do become bigger than those things—you get to look back and look at all the people that have never had to go through what you went through.

And you know what? Without any dire need, without any forced societal pressure—they most likely won't. The people who change the world the least, the people who are the least lit up by life—their comfort is more important than what their true Self-expression would take a stand for in life. Their comfort becomes more important than their *aliveness*. And that's really sad.

It's only when it's more painful to stop being in your position that causes massively radical new action. And it's that massive action out of the radical new insight that alters what's possible for humanity.

The ovarian lottery

YOU HAVE WON the ovarian lottery which is harder to do than winning the state lottery. Treating the gift of life as a dress rehearsal for the real thing and waiting for someday is about as demented and beyond stupid as someone taking their lottery winnings and spending 100% of the winnings on shaving cream bottles.

Where are you holding back in life?

What are you waiting for?

Naysayers

EVERYONE WHO IS up to huge things in life has *naysayers* in their life. These *naysayers* may be people you share your visions with, and they may be your family or friends who just want the best for you but don't see what you see.

There are three insights that I discovered which have shaped my interactions with *naysayers*. I don't claim these to be universal principles, so if this doesn't resonate with you, then just push it aside.

1. When you are making huge waves in life and not just going through the motions, you will most likely have people tell you that what you're up to is not possible, not realistic, that it's *not the right time*, or they will have some kind of circumstantial reason or evidence about why it cannot be done or should not be done. Then they will look to *justify their point of view at all costs* and will often be willing to destroy a relationship with you in order to *be right* if you start resisting their point of view.

2. You can use these objections as an opportunity to who will *listen for your greatness* and not fill your head with disempowering garbage. When I started intentionally taking this on, it took me about three years before I could honestly

tell myself I had this kind of environment that supported *conversations for possibility* vs. *conversations for reasonableness*.

3. Being committed to new possibilities without having an environment around you that supports this is stupid and just makes the game that much harder.

9 principles to be highly disconnected and dysfunctional

IF YOU WANT to experience being disconnected to others and experiencing general dysfunction in life, then I *highly* recommend taking on these nine principles:

1. Start getting obsessed with loving yourself and tell yourself mantras like I can't love others until I love myself and all that crap. This will help you focus inwardly and create lots of boundaries that won't let people contribute to you. Then, you'll have less love in your life, and that will reinforce your ever-expanding need to love yourself even that much harder. If you want to get that you are the source of love than *be* love. Love yourself but expand that to include others as well. This is in contrast to the mindset of: "I have to love myself and *then* I can finally be complete and love others."

2. Make sure you try to survive better and interact with your circumstances in a way that's about your survival and trying to stay afloat. People who are just generally happy and living life fully and freely will occur to you as delusional people who aren't dealing with "*reality.*" Your reality will be the *right* one, and you'll reinforce this by finding others to confirm your

reality of how hard and tough life is. Then you can battle it together! Oh yeah, baby!

3. Out of that *survival* and *scarcity mindset*, when you see the things that aren't working in your life, make sure you come from a place of thinking there is *something wrong* and then try to *fix it*. Make sure you remind people that you just need to make things better and that you really need to start loving yourself harder.

4. As your soul continues to rot, your heart continues to harden, your body gets tenser, your *aliveness* diminishes, and as you become ever more disconnected—just remember: you just need to give yourself more self-love and make things better because *there's a lot wrong*! The struggle is real but be "proud" of all the hard work you do. You're "strong" and "independent" so you can do this!

5. Make sure you're always *reacting* as opposed to *creating*. Make sure you're looking to *get something out of others* vs. *looking for opportunities to contribute and make a difference*. Make sure you complain a lot and make sure you put others *in the wrong* and establish that you come from a space of how things *should be another way*.

6. Make sure you're *at the whims of your thoughts and emotions* (the 60,000 or so automatic thoughts you have a day) and make sure that you think you are those thoughts. Make sure you try to figure out why you're having those thoughts too.

7. To *cover all this up*, get very "independent" and "strong" and use that as a way to not deal with any of what you're covering up. So instead of *being* independent and strong, you're *doing* independent and strong while *being someone* who is suffering, disconnected, or fearful which perpetuates everything you're trying to compensate for or *fix* through doing strong and independent. Make sure you make lots of *demands* instead of *requests*, or, because you don't want to rock the boat, just don't ask things from others because you *know* how pushy and needy you'll come off. And hey!—you're independent and strong—so you can just do it yourself anyway. Duh! And of course, as this increases the chance of sickness manifesting

physically, well, you can handle it because you're a trooper and you work hard! One way to combat this is to make sure you do lots of *positive thinking* when something isn't working. Maybe just tell yourself how strong you are? And really believe it and put some magnets up on your fridge with lots of positive affirmations! Make sure you muster up motivation and positivity and put on a happy face! Or just go to a club and start dancing and drinking to not think about this so much. *Whatever you resist, persists.*

8. Make sure you just put more energy into what's not working and hopefully if you continue to press harder and push harder it will all work itself out.

9. Make sure you go back on your word the moment you have a *state change* and your *automatic machinery* starts acting another way. Your heart told you so; therefore, it's true. Then, you'll *find evidence* and create an environment conducive to you *being right* about how true it is. So in that sense, you actually do get to *be right* about that point of view! That's a sure fire way to produce the outcomes in life you truly desire inside which makes your soul come alive...*not*. And then you'll die one day, and the opportunity of playing the game called being a human comes to an end.

The fear of being negatively judged

EVERYBODY LOVES to talk about how they love being around someone who they can just completely let go around without the fear of being negatively judged.

However, it's often those same people who judge others or hold back out of fear people won't do that with them.

Consider that one way to access creating a kind of environment that naturally pulls for this kind of space around you is to simply be that for others and don't be a judgmental asshole around someone feeling safe enough to be themselves around you.

Simple.

Being hooked

NOTICING YOUR ACCESS TO FREEDOM

THE EASIEST WAY TO tell if someone has been brainwashed by their culture isn't by how they live. One thing you can look for is how they judge others and where they get hooked or triggered by something and start operating automatically in reaction.

You can apply this to yourself as well, which is where it has power. The moment you *get hooked* or become in reaction to something—start *noticing* what your mind does. The more you *notice* and see the automatic patterns, the more you become free of them and have space for *Self-expression* vs. the *automatic machinery* of your mind doing the expressing.

There's no freedom in being a *slave to your mind*. The moment *you're hooked* you've already lost the *game called what I'm committed to as a human being*.

Actions rooted in fear

THE MORE YOU take actions out of a fear of something/from a place of *survival* (to avoid something, resist something, defend something, protect something)—the more you create the very thing you want to avoid.

Here are seven examples:

1. *The people who avoid confrontation* tend to have the most of it.
2. *The people who tend to avoid being dominated by money* are the ones screaming about how money is the root of all evil or how they never have enough money, and it impacts their life, and they become a victim to it.
3. *The people who are afraid of people not liking them* and then take actions to avoid people not liking them typically end up having more people dislike them.
4. *The people who need to control situations*, so they start taking actions of control. The more they try to control the things around them in life, the more they lose control. It leads to a very vicious and rather exhausting cycle.
5. *The people who are afraid of doing business with friends* and end up losing some of their friends in the process, or, become closed

off to people who care about them in their life supporting them and being a contribution to them.

6. *The people who are afraid of failing*, therefore, take no action or hesitant action in line with what they're committed to and then fail to get what they want.

7. *The people who are afraid of being judged*, so they shut down their Self-expression, and in the face of it, are less powerful, and then people judge them for that. Now they're being judged for something they're not.

Be the 3%

I ONCE HEARD SOMEWHERE that 97% of people don't change until their circumstances force them to do so. I have no idea if that's true but what matters is what it points to about the current state of the human condition. Stop waiting. Stop making excuses. Be the 3%.

The noticing model

THERE'S a tremendous amount of freedom in simply getting that you're not the *little voice in your head*, but that instead, you're merely the observer of that little voice. Imagine what becomes possible for humanity as more people begin to wake up to that.

Credit goes to John King, author of the New York Times bestseller *Tribal Leadership*, for this *noticing model*. The *noticing model* is the first part of a four-part model belonging to John's *model of transformation* which I won't go into here.

1. *Notice* that you are opinionating.
2. *Notice* that you have an opinion of your opinionating.
3. *Notice* that you try to control your opinionating.
4. *Notice* that your opinions don't care, and keep flowing anyway.
5. *Notice* that you are not running the show, your opinions are.
6. *Notice* that you are not your opinions, but rather, you have opinions.
7. Or, *notice* that your opinions have you.
8. *Notice* that this is going on 24/7 in the background.
9. Do not attempt to correct or *fix* the condition—simply *notice*.

Vulnerability

OUR CULTURE DOESN'T MAKE much space for *vulnerability*.

If our culture truly made space for others to be vulnerable, it wouldn't be a topic of interest for so many, and, Brené Brown wouldn't have given a TED talk about it.

Instead, *"being vulnerable"* would be the natural and predominant space that human beings operated inside of in all areas of their life. *Vulnerability* wouldn't be something we had to think about or practice.

So, what's in the way? It's simply a learned/conditioned behavioral pattern based in your brain reacting to *something that happened in your life in the past* where you were shit on for simply sharing yourself and then it became unsafe somewhere along the line. Literally, for someone aiming to invalidate you simply for you being you.

If you want to make it safer for people to share themselves—don't shit on them when they're taking that "risk" in completely letting go and sharing themselves authentically. You make the world work just that much more by simply *creating the space* for others to be that way around you without fear of being shat on.

Freedom from anxiety

ON JANUARY 16, 2016, I checked myself into Urgent Care as my body was experiencing vertigo for two straight days.

Here is what happened when the doctor walked into the room and what was the start of the conversation between my doctor and I that day:

Doctor: *For someone whose blood pressure is high right now and high levels of anxiety right now you seem very calm.*

Me: *That's because I have a freedom from anxiety, so it doesn't run me.*

Doctor: *What do you mean?*

So, what do I mean?

When someone says, "*I am anxious,*" they confuse *who they are* with the emotional, mental, and physical experience of anxiety which they are actually just *noticing*.

At that moment my body had high blood pressure and there were anxious emotions due to my body being in some kind of fight or flight mode. However, I am clear that: *who I am is anything I cannot distinguish.*

What the fuck do I mean by that? Simple.

I have a hand. I can look at my hand. I can put my hand in front of my face and see that I have a hand. However, I am very clear, and most of you are very clear that while you *have* a hand, *you are not your fucking hand.*

How that principle applies in this situation is simple. Who I am is something that can *notice*. I can *notice* my surroundings. I can *notice* the emotions I have inside my body. I can *notice* my body. I can *notice* the bodily sensations inside me as well. I can *notice* all of that; therefore everything I can *notice* I can distinguish. And because *who I am is anything I cannot distinguish—the logical conclusion is that* who I am is that thing doing the *noticing*. Therefore, *I am not* my emotions nor my body sensations...nor my hand!

So when I *notice* that I have anxiety vs. *being* an anxious person (which is a *linguistic constraint* that perpetuates the *identity*)—at that moment, I get unstuck from a *belief system* called *I'm an anxious person* (in that moment), and get to choose to *be* something other than anxious in the face of my anxiety. At the doctor's office that day, I had a choice of who to *be* in the face of those emotions and bodily sensations, and I *chose* to be peaceful and calm around it as distinct from letting my anxiety *decide* for me which gives me no *choice*.

This way of living life will actually lead to more emotions and thought patterns correlating to who you're *being* over time. The human brain indeed is that elastic.

For instance, I used to *identify as* someone who was depressed and suffered from depression. I was *resisting* my upsets and sadness. *You become what you resist.*

I start *being* my depression, or another way of saying it, chose a *depressed way of being* as opposed to someone who felt shitty in a moment and resisted it enough that it became my default brain patterns. When people are suffering, they never realize they are choosing it. If they realized they were choosing it, they wouldn't consciously choose it.

All of that could have been dealt with in a matter of minutes (yes, that's not a typo) which had been taking me years to "*work on*" and "*get better*" (both are *inauthentic* fronts to avoid being responsible for something and are *rooted in the past* which inherently perpetuates the very past you're trying to *fix* or *overcome*) when, instead, I could have simply just stopped resisting it, made space to allow all my automatic thoughts, emotions, and bodily sensations, and, I would have experienced *being the observer* all of that vs. *being* it. That's the shift from *having brain patterns* vs. *your brain patterns having you*. Same brain patterns, different context.

It took about two years for my brain patterns to change naturally as I wasn't giving charge, even remotely close to, the level of my old brain patterns anymore. So while my brain patterns took a while to change biologically, getting this distinction *transformed* my happiness instantly as opposed to trying to *change* it. I went from *someone who suffered from depression and anxiety* to someone who occasionally *had feelings of sadness or anxiousness come up for me* and then they'd disappear again because I was giving space to them and not resisting them. On a side note, giving space to something is accepting something or choosing what's already do, not ignoring it. Ignoring something is a form of resistance. *What you resist, persists. What you give space to disappears.* I'm interested in the game called *freedom from anxiety*, not the game called *learning how to cope with anxiety*.

As long as I continued to allow all of the disempowering thoughts and feelings and opinions to be there about my anxiety and depression, and then in the process, creating a new way of being in the face of it vs. on top of it (where whatever is on top of it is just another form of resistance), my biology continued to shift over time. Whipped cream on shit is still shit.

"Somehow, at least in our culture, we find relief when others are anxious too. So we spread our anxiety, stoking it in other people, looking for solace in the fear in their eyes. And thanks to the media, to the microphone we each have, to our hyper-connected culture, it's easier than ever to spread our anxiety if we choose. And when someone who seeks power offers to hear our anxiety in exchange for attention or a vote, it gets even worse. It's worth noting that there's no correlation between the real world and anxiety. In fact, it's probably the opposite—when times are good, people with a lot to lose start to get that itch. Absorb the anxiety if you wish, spread it if you must, but understand that it's an invention, and it's optional."

— SETH GODIN

Giving your energy where your gifts can be received

It's easy to tell someone not to take things personally. However, just like most things in life, it's easier to *preach at someone* vs. *creating a conversation for someone,* so they have the space to *get it and discover it for themselves,* so it's real for them and not just a belief system or a positive mantra to say.

However, when you are living life from a place of *offering your greatest gifts to the world* aka living from a place of *Self* as opposed to your *identity,* it becomes almost easy and natural to not take things personally without having to think about it. If you don't know the difference between your Self and your identity, who you are is the thing that can *notice* the aspects of your identity.

When you're living from that space vs. a space of *survival,* you'll see that even when you're giving your all and contributing fully, there will *still* be people and environments where you will not have space to contribute.

Then it becomes kind of funny you cared about people's opinions all along. Contribute to 50 different environments. Maybe just a few fully receive your contribution. Then you spend your energy on those and just give space and let the other people or environments be where they're at and where they're not, be gracious and generous, and continue being great in the world.

Possibility vs. ordinary

THERE ARE two prevailing worlds that human beings traffic in. Neither is good or bad or right or wrong. However, one tends to lead to greater results in life and general connection to aliveness and purpose.

1. *The World of Ordinary* (your identity prefers this world).
2. *The World of Possibility* (living a transformed life).

Ordinary: fear; looks like the past; rules; jealousy; looking good; boundaries (something in between you and I); expectations; disappointment; judgments; assessments; doubt; track record (the past provides the numbers); blame; fault; resignation; cynicism; good/bad communications; avoiding; resisting; acting from your strong suits; acting from your complaints; acting from your identity; comfort zone/safer (the illusion of safety).

Possibility: love; inspiration; passion; commitment; empathy; trust; being larger than your circumstances; not being run by reasons; being powerful in the face of no agreement; creating new futures that were not going to happen by default; aliveness; community; flow; Self-expression; transformation/something shifts or new becomes possible.

Most people have very little muscle in the *world of possibility* with it often being experienced as *peak moments* vs. a baseline experience for being alive.

Insecurities

WHO YOU'RE BEING about your insecurities is your choice. You either have insecurities, or your insecurities have you. Your insecure thoughts and emotions and bodily sensations have nothing to do with you. You are the observer of them, not them. They are out of your control. What you can control is who you're being about those insecure feelings and thoughts and bodily sensations. You can *be* insecure about your insecurities, or you can be confident and Self-expressed in the face of them, your choice, moment by moment.

If you're someone who says, *"I am insecure,"* then you're choosing to *be* insecure about your insecurities.

You don't say, *"I am a hand."*

You say, *"I have a hand."*

You don't say, *"I am an eyeball."*

You say, *"I have an eyeball."*

You don't say, *"I am the sky is blue."*

You say, *"I see the sky, and it's blue."*

You have insecure thoughts. Cool. So does every other human being on the planet. You have approximately 60,000 thoughts a day. Some insecure. Some funny. Some weird. Whatever! None of them have anything to do with you.

Waiting to give your all

ONE OF THE biggest traps I see people fall into is that they are *waiting to give their all*. They are waiting to share themselves fully because they are afraid of being "too much" for someone.

I have some terrible and wonderful news for you. That person, that organization, that business connection, that potential relationship, that "whatever who you are waiting to share yourself fully with"—

Guess what.

If they are scared to go as deep as you and match where you're at now, they most likely always will be. I've seen people literally wait years to finally set the conditions that are perfect in their head and hope that person they're *waiting to give their all for* shows up to the party. They often never do, and then, you have to diminish the party to keep the other person at the party. The other option is you can just set the conditions on your own terms, and that may lead to new people showing up for the party. It also gives people who you have shitty dynamics with to rise to the occasion on their own time. The result of doing this is that you get the results you intuitively (if you were honest with yourself) knew you'd get all along. Furthermore, all that waiting and "being where someone is at" nonsense was a literal waste of time.

Being where someone is at is a powerful concept. It loses its power when its used as a tactic to get people to change or a coping mechanism for yourself to stay inside disempowering relational dynamics with others.

Set the conditions and see who shows up to the party, seriously. And you know who practices this principle better than anyone I've ever seen?

Billionaires. Warren Buffett, Charlie Munger, Jeff Bezos, Steve Jobs, Elon Musk, Richard Branson. They literally all do this.

You get what you tolerate in life.

Black holes of possibility

IF THE CONVERSATIONS around you are unenlightened then simply find some new people to play with vs. trying to alter how you speak to people. You'll end up feeling drained and having a natural intuitive knowing that there are inauthenticities in the space. It's a waste of your time and energy, period.

Some people get weird about high-level conversations especially when it comes to things that threaten their own point of view about the world. I'm naturally into personal development, into growing myself, and with just even the smallest amount of research, it is obvious what stuff works and what doesn't work (i.e., motivational speaking in corporate environments—huge money drain).

So, for instance, if someone is threatened by personal development and you're committed to growing yourself—then don't be fucking friends with that person, it's pretty much that simple.

Like anyone who actually shies away from their own growth, anyone who resists expansion—I just don't play with those people. Those are the people that will break their word with you, who will continuously try to micromanage your speech and get offended easily, those are the kind of people who are either politically correct about everything OR completely resigned and cynical about life. Those are the people that will have reasons and excuses about everything and often be really nice about it.

It's an energetic black hole as you can't change people.

When people live life constantly breaking their agreements and commitments with others and as opposed to take responsibility for the impact they just ignore it or get "sincerely sorry" or "feel bad" about it, what they get is lack of result, an excuse, and a diminished sense of aliveness, purpose, confidence, and a diminished relationship to themselves.

To these people—"life happens" and they come up with a new excuse of the day. If you look at the people in your life who act like righteous little assholes with you about taking on big shit—the people with all the nice sounding reasons (or whatever their version is)—well, you can bet your ass they're also the people who are going to be the most out of integrity with things too.

Speaking in concepts, having reasons for everything, breaking their word with you, manipulating, lying, and all the other weird and dishonest/inauthentic shit they may do in that space.

You get what you tolerate. It's that simple.

I don't have friends who get weird about big shit. My friends thrive off that energy.

Find people who will play big games and empower you with what you're up to. Once you take that mindset, they're not that hard to find. For example, right after you buy a new car, you start seeing them on the road everywhere!

The more you're attached to people committed to mediocrity—the more you'll stay trapped in those social patterns around you. Additionally, it'll occur as the people up to big shit are *rare and scarce* while people coming from *survival* are all around you. Total scarcity mindset. People up to big things in life are not *scarce*. And for the people who become black holes. Let them dig themselves out of the hole.

Living your life for others

꧁꧂

SOME PEOPLE OBSESS over what their social media looks like. They obsess over what they should wear when they are out in order to impress random people walking down the street. Here's the truth: nobody fucking cares about that. And if they do, they most likely aren't the kinds of people that you'd want in your life anyway. If your life is centered around being validated on social media as opposed to using social media as a way to express yourself or pursue networking opportunities, then you should probably delete your social media accounts or put limits on your use.

Do you think anybody has ever been on their deathbed thinking to themselves, "If only I had done more to impress more random people"? Yeah, nope.

If you're buying a cool new piece of clothing, accessory, car, house, or phone—make sure you are doing it because you actually enjoy it yourself. Sure, some people may get impressed by it for a few minutes or a few hours but then right after they will go back to their lives and really not give a shit about it.

How do I know? Think about all the random people who have tried to impress you subconsciously (probably in the hundreds or thousands) and think about how many cool phones, jackets, wallets, cars, and

94

clothing you remember and how much that impacted how much you liked them or thought of them over time. Probably not many.

Random people don't give a shit about you for more than a few minutes. That neighbor, the person at the gym, the person at the coffee shop, the person walking down the street, the person who sees your tag on Instagram.

Living your life for others is not only moronic, it's also pointless. Why? Because nobody cares enough anyway for it to actually yield a result.

Revenge

THERE'S A SAYING THAT GOES, *"The best revenge is massive success."* It's also wrong. If you care about revenge, you've already failed. The best revenge is not caring about revenge. Focus on being great with others and providing value to the world. The rest has a way of taking care of itself.

Positive thinking keeps things stuck

EVERY TIME you engage in positive thinking, what you are doing is keeping stuck or keeping around anything you're trying to overcome through the doing of positive thinking. Whatever you resist, persists. Whipped cream on shit is still shit. As long as you hold a negative association with what you refer to as *yourself,* it is actually impossible to authentically think positively about it.

Universal intelligence = fuel; car = action

EVERYBODY HAS unique gifts to share on the planet. There are four distinct mindsets people have around this conversation:

Mindset 1. People who hear that and think it sounds like woo-woo bullshit (skeptical and closed off which is also known as being cynical).

Mindset 2. People who are disconnected to their gifts but can see others aren't.

Mindset 3. People who have some sense of what their gifts are but their circumstances don't align with their authentic Self. They internally feel a bit trapped in their circumstances or simply have resigned themselves to the reality that their gifts will just stay inside of them and that their mission will be lived out in a diminished way.

Mindset 4. People who are in the truest sense living life to the fullest. Living life from their highest integrity at their core. People whose internal gifts and truths are playing out externally in reality.

For people in the first three points, what I'm about to say is especially important.

There are 4 rules to getting to the fourth mindset authentically.

Rule 1. You have to continuously be willing to look and not just have it be a one time deal where it's: *"this didn't work" waiting to happen,* but a real willingness and 100% commitment.

Rule 2. There is nothing to get, nothing to seek, and nowhere to arrive. It's already all inside you.

Rule 3. When you do experience that deep truth—you have to trust it and listen to that deep core knowing intuition.

Rule 4. Patiently determined. Meaning you go full force while also allowing the results to unfold for where you're at. How things unfold may not happen how you expected so you can't be attached to the way your mission or path unfolds, just committed to keeping your integrity to the process.

When you keep acting from that place, beautiful things happen and there's a flow to life. There's a simple natural unfolding process.

The author Napoleon Hill referred to this deep knowing as *universal intelligence.* So if *universal intelligence* is the fuel, action is the car. Both are vital, as there're no results without action.

Comfort zones

WHEN I WAS a junior in high school, I made a promise to myself that for the rest of my life I would do at least one thing every day that made me uncomfortable. Fast forward about a decade and my comfort zone now is unrecognizable to what it was back then. Like the lobster dying in boiling water, the slow expansion of our comfort zones sneaks up on you. When you look back, the growth is actually incredibly amazing.

At the same time, I still have a comfort zone and always will. As long as you're human, you have a comfort zone.

There are people who are resigned in life and have zero desire even to explore their comfort zones. If that's you, then I'm not sure why you are still reading this book.

I would assert that—because you, the reader, chose to read a book like this—that you either already explore and look to expand your comfort zones or have a commitment at the very least to explore and expand your comfort zones regardless of whether you take actions in integrity with that commitment.

Expanding a comfort zone can be a habit. Some questions I believe are worth exploring first for yourself are:

1. How willing am I to expand my comfort zones in the first place?

2. Am I more committed to expanding my comfort zone or more committed to the feeling of comfort?
3. If answered that I'm committed to comfort over expanding my comfort zones, then what disempowering thoughts or emotional associations do I have around expanding my comfort zones?
4. What incredible outcomes could I produce if I was fearless and authentically comfortable in all situations?
5. How can I attempt to make it as painful as possible for myself to see how not living that life and continuing down the road of comfort will lead to certain regrets I will have on my deathbed?

The more painful you can associate staying in the same position and not expanding, the psychologically easier it will be for you to break-through and create new brain patterns.

If you answered *more committed to expanding my comfort zones*, then look at question 3 and apply it to one area in your life, right now, where you are currently holding back or not living fully. If there's nothing there, then look to see what you can take to the next level and what you'd need to let go of (circumstantial attachments, disempowering thoughts you've been believing about yourself or your circumstances, etc.), and what actions you could immediately take to get to that next level.

Once comfort zone expansion becomes a habit, it will be uncomfortable to stay "comfortable" as you'll see the impact of your Self-expression in the world being diminished, and it will not be a pleasant experience.

It's worth exploring a few questions:

1. Why am I committed to expanding my comfort zone?
2. Why am I willing to feel uncomfortable?
3. Am I clear that I am not my discomfort, but I am merely the one who notices it?
4. Who am I choosing to be in the face of discomfort?
5. What actions can I take that are correlated to who I'm choosing to be in the face of my discomfort?

The answers to these questions will point to the underlying commitment. Staying present to that commitment will make those times when you've fallen asleep at the wheel psychologically easier to wake your Self up from.

That game is a mountain with no top. One illusion in life is that you're staying in the same spot. Treading water is akin to *slowly* falling down the mountain. You're either climbing or falling. You're either spiraling upward or downward. There is no stagnation. The illusion of stagnation is a trick that our minds play on us. The automatic machinery of our minds (which we can *notice* by the way) compares everything we are familiar with to what's right in front of us. This pattern recognition that our brains are hardwired to perform have been great for our evolution and survival but have also lead to the experience of *sameness*. When we are unconscious of our minds doing this, we become a slave to this experience and over time we are left ever more entrenched in layers upon new layers of resignation in our lives.

Being grateful for resentment

❦

PERHAPS IT'S AN AMERICAN THING, or maybe this mindset trickles into many cultures, but many people have some kind of negative context for what is considered "negative" emotional experiences such as anger, sadness, or resentment. Resentment, in particular, is very interesting because so many people commit to living a life free of all resentments. I would argue this to be a lie or more politely a half-truth.

Yes, I get it. It's not healthy to go around being resentful all the time. I think most people understand that both intellectually and viscerally. However, while I believe noticing resentment and not being run by it is healthy, I have seen it also do extreme harm. One very powerful lens to view resentment through is gratitude. To view resentment as a gift. And no this isn't me telling you to cover it up with positive thinking. That would just be another form of lying. What I'm saying is the opposite and getting to the truth about resentment.

While perhaps not all the time, I would assert that most of the time resentment is a form of valuable intuition. It shows up when a need of ours is unfulfilled. I've met people who like to tell themselves they aren't needy people and it was out of having intimate conversations with enough people like this that gave me this realization. One thing I discovered was that all of these "non-needy" people were all resentful in some area of their lives. That gave me the idea to take a look for myself at any areas of my life where deep down if I was brutally honest with myself, I was having the experience of being resentful show up for me. 100% of the time, there was some unmet need not being fulfilled.

So consider that resentment most if not all the time is a cue to address an imbalance or an unworkability if you will. Where there's a need (regardless if you want to tell the truth to yourself about it or not) that hasn't been fulfilled.

Once you distinguish the unmet need you can either fulfill the need yourself, or if it involved other people, to be able to ask for what you need without any kind of guilt, shame, or scarcity.

And yes, you can control the space from where your communications come from, in this case, the space in which your requests come from.

Empowering Space: You can make requests from a space of confidence, abundance, and clarity.

Disempowering Space: You can make requests from a space of guilt, shame, and scarcity.

Action combined with a disempowering way of being is usually better than no action at all. However, what's even more powerful is taking responsibility to come from an empowering space. Taking action that's aligned and integrity with who you are at the level of Self will yield more positive results for your life, and you'll have an advantage over your peers who don't operate in this way. You can live a life filled with lots of resentments. However, it's your choice whether you are being resentful about whatever you feel resentment towards. You can choose gratitude and enjoy the gift that resentment is. That's not to be woo-woo about it but merely because the impact of being resentful, ignoring resentments outright, or covering them with positivity has a real negative impact on our lives.

For me, the experience of resentment is a gift. It's an opportunity to fulfill an unmet need through either making the request for it or just taking it on yourself to satisfy that need.

The downward spiral of scarcity

It's easy to tell when someone is operating from scarcity or operating from abundance. Neither is right or wrong or good or bad; however, this framework for living can have huge impacts on one's life.

Scarcity is the predominant societal mindset. This societal mindset is what you could call the average baseline for being for human beings.

Notice I didn't say that the mindset is the average baseline for thinking. The reason is that our culture actually does have space for this kind of thinking today. There are now enough coaches, consultants, and leadership books out there in the popular culture that a lot of people, especially in the workplace, are trained in higher levels of thinking. However, if the state of being doesn't change, the thinking combined with the old ways of being will just lead to more of the same, and there won't be many breakthroughs to be had. And that is why I say baseline for being and not thinking because the mental awareness, especially amongst the business world is already there.

When people in some kind of scarcity way of being are able to get beyond something they know to be possible, they'll tell you reasons why they can't do something or why something isn't possible. If something is too much money, they'll give you all the reasons why they can't afford it vs. creating structures to create affording something. I use the money example because the relationship people have to money is a common scarcity conversation that goes undistinguished for most people.

Scarcity is this mindset that there isn't enough of something. Scarcity is based in survival. This is purely evolutionary as dealing with threats for most of human history was more important than creating something. Yes, you can be great at building huts, but it's even more important to avoid being mauled by a tiger. Not staying on guard for most of human history got you killed. Our minds are still wired like that, even though we live in a very different world.

When you operate from scarcity there's usually never enough: resources, love, people, friends, money, time, etc.

Scarcity is all about protecting, surviving, and defending. It's about taking action out of fear of what could happen. It's very limiting of the Self.

And scarcity creates a downward spiral.

If you asked someone whether they would rather live in scarcity or abundance, most people would say abundance. However, the truth is most people really don't know what they want as most people still operate from a space that who they are is their identity and all the automatic stuff that comes with that. Therefore, their life is constructed around their problems and if they actually had everything they said they wanted in their lives, they'd be literally fucked. It would literally kill off who they thought themselves to be. Just look at the countless stories of people who became famous and went batshit insane or child actors whose identity was predicated on them being a child actor.

If you were to ask the average person whether they'd rather drink an elixir that produced the following outcomes: made their skin glow, made them age slower, made them feel amazing, made them physically more attractive, and then based off emotional and physical health were more likely to make more money—and then with all that positive self esteem —their circles of influence kept growing and growing and they kept bringing in really high-quality people into their life which then allowed them to stay more grounded and motivated and make even more money which led to a higher quality of life emotionally, physically, spiritually, sexually, and financially—and then—you offered them another elixir that would make them age quicker, shorten their lifespan, make them emotionally worse off which then increased their probability of attracting lower quality people in their life, made them overall less physically attractive, less emotionally healthy, and reduced their energy levels—

One would assume that almost everybody would say they wanted the first drink. However, if you asked the average person if they wanted a kale, spinach, celery, ginger, turmeric juice OR a can of Coke, most people would ask for the Coke! They said they wanted one thing, but their actions said otherwise.

There's this distinction that the hungry don't get fed. Essentially, when you're attached to something—your attachment gets in the way of you getting the result. At the level of neuroscience, you're literally creating more wiring in the brain of what you don't have. That's always operating from the framework or context of scarcity. This leads to more scarcity which then further validates your shortage of resources, love, people, friends, money, time, etc.

There's a well-known phenomenon called *the poverty-cycle* which has been documented not just through anecdotal observation but through statistical analysis and extensive data analytics. Without getting too deep into it, if you're born poor and have a scarcity mindset around your own poverty, your actions have an increased chance of leading you to more poverty instead of taking you out of it, and that cycle can last not just a lifetime but over many generations. It's mental patterns created in language passed on from one generation to the next.

This literal scarcity mindset is at the root of a lot of what goes on in the world that doesn't work. And I'm not just talking about big things but often tiny things that just seemingly go unnoticed in the day-to-day minutia matters of the world. Consider the clingy girl who is so afraid to lose her man that he ends up breaking up with her due to her constant demands of attention with those demands of attention coming from a place of scarcity. Demands of attention from a space of abundance create an entirely different experience.

Consider the guy whose girlfriend has just broken up with him, and he's decided to immediately go to the bar to meet another girl to get his mind off things. Then he goes to the bar really fucking desperate to meet someone, and he ends up having a hard time "getting" anyone to hang out with him and just pushes women away as they can feel the neediness and desperation in who he's being.

Now think about the person who nails an interview for a job or college. I got into Babson College (a prestigious business school on the East Coast) while having one of the lowest SAT scores and GPAs amongst my peers. I got in because of my interview.

When I was interviewed, here I was in high school with no money, no business experience, really low self-esteem at the time, and didn't really like who I was. However, for this interview, I decided I was going to *be* someone who already got into the school. I shared about my business ambitions, what I wanted to create around building an investment firm. I shared about my love for Warren Buffett. Not once did I give a reason of why I should be accepted, I just *knew* I should, and it came out with every ounce of my being.

For those of you who have interviewed applicants for a job: who is more likely to get the job assuming their skillset is roughly the same? The one who gives off that needy and desperate way of being or the one who is being grounded, secure, and calm, and is naturally excited to share about the value they would love to add to the company.

If you look at desperation or neediness, it's always coming from a space of scarcity.

There's some concern in the background:

"If I don't get this job I won't be able to feed my family."

"If this girl doesn't go out with me, I'll never find another girl like her."

"My looks aren't good enough; therefore, I need to compensate."

"My skills aren't good enough; therefore, I need to compensate."

There's something either insufficient, not enough, or knowing your world will fall if you don't get the outcome you want. People can sniff out that attachment a mile away and operating from that space leads to an ever-increasing probability of creating a continuous self-fulfilling prophecy.

To use one of the examples from before and expand on it: *"My looks aren't good enough; therefore, I need to compensate. Then whatever I compensated for didn't work so I need to adjust again and compensate for what's now not working. Do this for many years, and you'll be trapped in inauthentic layer upon inauthentic layer of survival rooted in some scarcity conversation you probably made up many years ago."*

Abundance works the opposite. Operating from a space of abundance is amazing. Knowing that you're already whole and complete.

Knowing that there's no such thing as failure, just correctable results. Trusting your Self and operating from that space vs. reacting to some sort of circumstance most likely leads to more enjoyable outcomes than had you been coming from a place of scarcity.

When you run into an issue thinking about ways you can create a solution vs. get reactive and start letting a circumstance give you the excuse to play smaller. Abundance leads to an increased probability of an upward spiral in life of wonderful outcomes in life.

This isn't rocket science. It's also not about fake positive thinking either and being one of those obnoxious *fake it 'till you make it* people.

There's what I call fake spiritual growth or fake growth. It's some weird form of positive thinking where your growth is literally meditating and isolating yourself somewhere and pretending all the issues in the world don't actually exist. Now there's nothing wrong with meditating or having alone time—that's not what I'm saying. What I'm saying is doing that as a way to avoid reality is just as spiritually stunted as the cynic who sees all the ills in the world and is resigned and cynical about it.

To me, growth is being unwavering and tackling life. Letting the big things you're up to shape you and make you stronger. Being a truth seeker. Having an insatiable learning for trying to understand the way the world works and the nature of being human and the human experience. That's a conversation worth devoting a lifetime to.

I want to go back to the clingy girlfriend example for a moment—

Now if you took one of those people whose growth was their identity and who was living a life hiding behind their mantras, meditation practices, and positive affirmations while pretending the world didn't exist— and then you took another person who was resigned and cynical about the world and in constant survival—and then you took someone who really loved taking life by the horns and letting it shape them—you could say the following are three possibilities of what could happen with those three kinds of people as related to the'd interact with the hypothetical clingy girlfriend. Let's call her *Clarissa the Clinger.*

Fake Spiritual Identity. He'd invalidate Clarissa. Then give her some New Age spiritual advice as a way to *fix her* which would really just be his way of not being able to hold space for her. It would be his way to resist.

The Cynic. He'd invalidate Clarissa and would not be polite about it. Then he'd complain about how psychologically fucked up women are.

The Truth Seeker. He gets the nature of Clarissa and understands the importance of validation and honoring someone's core regardless of where they're at. He would love her where she's at and would not try to change a thing about her. He'd give her some validation, not from a place of trying to get a reaction or some kind of validation but would simply be coming from a space of really worshipping her heart at her core while at the same time not sucking up to her or completely falling apart to giving into her shit. This doesn't mean he wouldn't break off the romantic relationship if that's what was an authentic expression of his love.

Your access to that kind of grounded-ness is through simply not resisting things. It's the difference between allowing yourself to feel good vs. trying to feel good and exerting force with positive thinking and a fake personality. Owning where you're at gives you access to creating something new and creating in it of its very nature isn't rooted in reaction. It's in a space of abundance where you naturally have the opportunity to create authentically; you're operating from a space of limitless possibilities vs. your limited box of beliefs which are based in the past.

Closure is a choice

ANYTIME YOU FIND yourself feeling closed off to a situation or an individual you can choose to *be* open in that moment regardless of your bodily sensations, thoughts, and emotions related to *closure* and *disconnect*. That doesn't mean to ignore it. It means to embrace and feel it all fully and choose who you're *being* around it.

What I do—and consider trying this out for yourself for a few weeks and see how it works for you—*have your feelings of closure be the trigger in choosing to be open.*

And over time, that depth of openness will continue to expand. It's what John King calls *expand to include.* Over time, your discomfort will become minimized. However, if you choose to resist, react to how you're feeling, and choose to essentially try to *fix something*, go into a mindset of *there's something wrong here*, or allow yourself to *be in survival* around your feelings, bodily sensations, and thoughts in the realm of survival—all you will do is strengthen those neural networks and strengthen those patterns of survival.

Being in survival around your own internal automatic survival state works very well if you're trying to avoid some kind of physical threat or avoid getting into a car accident by being a good defensive driver. However, it's a terribly irrational way to think and be in life if you're committed to creating possibility and living from your deepest purpose. It's actually just plain stupid and asinine once you realize you have some choice about it.

Access to freedom

PEOPLE WHO AREN'T CONSTANTLY SHARING and speaking up for themselves around others will always almost find themselves feeling disconnected and closed off emotionally from others.

As long as one continues to think the source of their experience of not being connected to others has something to do with anyone outside of themselves, they lack personal responsibility in that situation, and that will always correlate to less freedom, less peace of mind, and less aliveness in their lives.

Freedom comes from taking 100% responsibility for your life, your experiences, your emotions, your thoughts, and your actions.

Blaming others (even if justified in your view) will lead to a lack of freedom, aliveness, love, vitality, and being powerful with whatever you're up to.

THE VICTIM MENTALITY = CHAINS.

The problem about problems

THE BIGGEST ISSUE with problems is that people think they shouldn't have them or they should look differently. That's literally insane. If you want no problems in life, choose to commit to nothing and spend the rest of your days on a couch or a park bench.

However, when you're up to something and have a commitment, you will have inevitable problems to deal with.

The pitfall is when we experience a breakdown in our commitments and our vision and we go into a mindset of *"there's something wrong"* and then go into automatic fixed ways of trying to fix it such as: rationalizing, justifying, avoiding, beating ourselves up, blaming others, working hard and plowing through it, analyzing, and using positive thinking to cover up what doesn't work.

Fixing and changing gets you more of the same. Shifting what's possible for people's lives give people a whole new paradigm NOT based on the past to step into and all new actions and possibilities become available vs. reacting to something which occurs as bad or wrong.

Stinginess

STINGINESS IS DELIBERATELY HOLDING oneself and one's contribution *close to the vest* and without generosity. This is literally a way to destroy the Self-expression of the people around you. You can also be stingy with how you allow others to contribute to you and you'll soon find out that that creates a space for others to be stingy with you as well. Self-perpetuating cycle. Of course, the inverse is also true and way more fun.

Cutting out the bullshit

PEOPLE WANT to be around people with good vibes. Not positive thinking bullshit to cover crap up, but authentically great vibes. Do you want to constantly be around people who are always complaining, negative about stuff, in survival about the world and their circumstance? Fuck no, you don't.

Sometimes people get so weird about shit. Why don't you like me? Why don't you text me back faster? Why did you just look at me like that? They tell jokes then wait to see if others laugh and feel bad if they aren't.

Cut that shit out; people hate that shit. Girls hate it. Guys hate it. Everybody fucking hates it. People like authentically positive people because good vibes just make others feel better too. Duh!! Positive people are active, enjoy doing things, operate from abundance and not scarcity, they talk to people because it's fun vs. trying to impress them, don't go around not trusting others and being all cynical or cynical disguises as skepticism, they have goals and dreams and not just to look good but because it's a natural Self-expression and lights up their soul. They don't complain about little shit. They have their own lives and enjoy living them. They don't cling and latch onto people which is some disgusting bullshit in order to fulfill something they feel is missing inside. However since that void they are trying to fill is actually made up and not real, it'll never be enough, they'll go harder and harder, and they'll keep doing what doesn't work and suck the energy out of people in the process.

They don't try to control others as control freaks always have underlying shit. If you're smiling and having fun, you'll instantly be way more awesome to be around than if you're not doing that shit. And again, not in order to manipulate or create a reaction but because life is fucking fun. If you fake having fun, you'll just look like an inauthentic tool. Just enjoy what you're doing. And if you don't enjoy what you're doing then why the fuck are you doing it and wasting your life? Probably some scarcity conversation you're living inside of. No, I'm sure of it.

Don't just listen to someone because you want to get something out of them. Listen to them because you enjoy the conversation, take an interest, and learn from it. Like the guy who is out on a date and is only listening to his date in order to fuck or the car salesman that pretends to enjoy what you're saying because he wants to make the sale and then he wonders why he occurs to others as a slime-ball. Totally idiotic.

If you don't give two shits about what the other person is saying, then steer the conversation to something you authentically enjoy talking about. Again, all simple shit that people complicate and then read books for ten years on "how to be more confident and positive." Waste of time and energy.

The risk of not being committed

PEOPLE WHO ARE afraid of making commitments take a bigger risk than those who don't. If you're committed to not committing, your life will reflect that. More turmoil, more flakiness, just all around less effective. The more you're committed to something intentionally, the more your life works. The illusion of safety, *really*. It's asinine *not to commit* even if it feels comfortable and not risky.

The most generous gift

ONE OF THE most generous things you can do for another human being is grant them your listening. When we listen for people's greatness even when they argue for their smallness, it changes lives. On the contrary, when you listen to someone's smallness and can't hear them, you kill them off. Just imagine being in a room where nobody gets you and nobody can really hear you. Notice what happens to your Self-expression, aliveness, and effectiveness. We have tremendous power in how we consciously choose to listen to others.

Domination, complaints, & accountability

WHEN PEOPLE DON'T WANT to be responsible for something, one of the ways they avoid being responsible is by creating a complaint and using it to dominate others. Of course, this isn't some kind of conscious action, but becoming aware of it gives people access to do something about it. For example—people who have a weak relationship to their word and are "fine" being out of integrity all the time will often create complaints about those who have a commitment to their own integrity and hold them accountable to their word. They will create complaints such as this person is annoying, pushy, pressuring me, manipulative, obnoxious, etc.

This stories or interpretations we create about another actually impact how the other individual occurs for us, how we literally experience those people. Then they will use that complaint as a way to dominate the other person. Some common ways of domination are:

1. Calling them those names up front
2. Telling the people around them that they are a certain way
3. Avoiding communication as a way to stay in control
4. Manipulating communication as a way to stay in control
5. Invalidating the person holding you to account

Getting what's behind the communication
BULLSHIT REASONS

WHEN I FIRST GOT INTO the personal development world, I would share my experiences with everyone and a lot of people would tell me they had no interest in checking out any of the stuff I would share with them. However, their *no* just seemed off. Like the same kind of off—you know when someone is lying to you, and you intuitively know it, that kind of off. The kind of off that a fat kid in middle school experiences when a girl tells him *s*he just wants to be friends, when deep down, he knows she just wasn't interested, and that she was being nice about in order to not hurt his feelings. What he is left with is **not** what she was pretending on the surface, but what she **wasn't** saying. When there are inauthenticities in the space—even if people pretend otherwise—people can almost always feel it intuitively if they allow themselves to get present to the horseshit.

I've noticed this with anything. When I share about ways I can make an impact and add value to organizations, I will get plenty of people sharing with me all kinds of ways it isn't possible or how *they already know it* and *are already doing it* within their organization even when it's clear they aren't. When I share about incredible opportunities that I know at the deepest part of my soul would add value to someone else, I get similar rebuttals quite often from those who don't have the ears to hear.

The common pitfall to a situation like this is to start interacting with their reasons. People will have reasons for everything and people who are smart will make them sound very compelling.

So when people say things that you *know* will add value and they immediately react by saying things such as

1. *This isn't for me.*
2. *It's not a priority right now.*
3. *It's too expensive.*
4. *I don't have time.*

Those would all be common examples of bullshit made up reasons that are hiding something. Sales people all know this. However, much of sales training is using manipulative sales techniques to overcome rebuttals which actually doesn't build long-term relationships with clients and creates inauthentic and transactional manipulative types of relationships.

Some possible things their immediate knee-jerk responses could be hiding are:

1. *The fear of looking bad.*
2. *The fear of changing old habits.*
3. *The fear of trusting.*
4. *The fear of upsetting someone else.*
5. *The fear of rocking the boat.*

While, yes, it's vital to continually focus on adding as much value as possible and continuing to expand that vs. blaming someone's bullshit excuses—it's important to listen to *what's behind* what they're saying and really getting the commitment behind their communication. Getting it and then taking responsibility that you get that they get it goes a long way. Listening and partnering with people at Stage 4 is quite distinct from using persuasion techniques at Stage 3.

Being all in

FULLY COMMITTING in life takes courage. It puts you at risk for something. People who always have an escape route for their commitments are not very powerful in life. Therefore they have to start manipulating and controlling to compensate for their lack of integrity in life. They get results in spite of this, not because of it. And of course, if you're playing a game called "one part committed, and then one part looking for the way out"—you'll start creating an environment conducive to that which is also very unworkable.

And when you start backing out without honor, people notice. People notice the childishness in your behavior. There are three kinds of ways for people to participate in life:

1. Auditing
2. Doing the best I can
3. All In

People who audit are merely observing.

People who are doing the best they can know they are busy and up to a lot in life so they often have excuses of why they can't do something, but they'll be *very sincere* that they are *doing the best they* can and they truly believe their sincerity, and *they're really nice about it.*

123

People who are *all in* get all the busyness and constraints of people who *do the best they can,* but they don't let that get in the way and figure out how to make it work.

If you're up to big things in life being all in is the responsible position to play that game. Doing the best you can doesn't cut it long term and people figure it out very quickly even if you think you're good at hiding it and pretending you're all in and just auditing won't ever cut it.

Often we pretend and get smart with ourselves (literally we get manipulative with ourselves to justify the "*alright-ness*" in our actions) of subtly backing off like we think others won't notice. It's slimy and genuinely disgusting behavior. If we just stop being useful to others both from a space of action and from a space of emotion, then, all of a sudden, it's okay. Yeah, not really.

I talk a lot about how in the sports world, all great athletes have a coach. Well, all great athletes are *all in,* and all great athletes just don't quit in the middle of the game. Could you imagine if Tom Brady started noticing that some of his wide receivers just decided they would run slower and start allowing themselves to get covered more by the defense in the hopes that he would just stop throwing to them? That would be the dumbest fucking thing on the planet, but that's literally how some people operate in life and then what's even more disgusting is they actually think they're getting away with it.

And just like every responsible athlete knows, there comes a time when it's time to retire. When your body is too worn, and your body can't perform the way you want it to, and when you've been used up, and you have given your all, and now there's nothing else left to give—you are complete. You end your career cleanly. You leave responsibly. People may be sad in your leaving, but they are not angry nor see you as untrustworthy. They still want to participate in life with you but instead of having you on the field maybe now you they want you as a coach. Perhaps you go into broadcasting. Perhaps you start a company.

Throughout it all, you still have your power.

Being responsible for your listening of others

You can listen to what someone says. You can also listen *for* something like a commitment or intention behind what someone is saying. You can also listen and react to your automatic judgments, assessments, and opinions *about* what someone is saying and that has the impact of leaving someone with the experience of not being gotten and heard.

Imagine what life would be like if you took 100% responsibility for your own listening vs. all the lazy bullshit of just living life listening from all the automatic stuff.

It's lazy thinking and it lacks responsibility.

Putting people down

DURING THANKSGIVING 2016, a family friend asked me why I share in the way that I do. Why I feel compelled to do so. I shared with her that I only share with those who have ears to hear and where I have space to make a contribution to the environment and the people in my communities. For me, it's an obsession. It's something that makes me feel alive and gives me deep purpose in life.

Sometimes all it takes is taking a stand for someone's greatness and seeing something in them that they don't see in themselves. That can create a space to give them access to certain new ways of being, thinking, and acting based off a new shift in perspective of the world. Taking that kind of stand for others can change people's lives.

ON THE CONTRARY:

Putting someone down for being where they're at only brings you down to their level and perpetuates whatever you're actually trying to empower them to transform for themselves. Create space, nudge them forward. Be in that dance and see what dance moves need to be taken to produce that breakthrough and then guide them. Forcing them to the other end of the room will just have someone fall over and run back.

Be the water to the flower

DON'T WAIT FOR THE RAIN

THERE'S something to be said about making time for people and our relationships in life. Not as something that just happens, but something that is done with the intention of fostering and deepening the relation-ships with those around us.

When people are dying—one of the things they most care about is the people that truly matter to them the most and to be able to have meaningful quality time with them. So many people walk around not making time for the people around them. That's a whole *scarcity-time* conversation. There are busy CEOs who make time for people, so there really aren't any excuses. When you structure your calendar and operate from a space of being able to create time for people vs. needing to sort things out first and wait for the right circumstances (looking for time and scarcity mindset), you'll end up having less time for the people that matter to you the most. It's kind of like when you haven't found time to write your essay in college that's due, and then the night before you pump out eight pages. Amazing, you created the time when it mattered. If you find yourself already resisting this or having some reaction to this, then there's something about your identity attached to some kind of scarcity conversation around time. Some people literally organize their whole lives to make sure they don't have enough time as it would validate their identity. If those people had an abundance of time, they wouldn't know who they were as it would literally kill off a part of their identity. The justifications as to why you don't have enough time only cost you your aliveness. Actually, if you find yourself needing to justify anything— you're identity is running the show, not you as Self. And, as long as you're in a space of justifying or defending, you'll be blind to new available actions for you to take to create an abundance of time or whatever you don't have enough of in your life.

Don't be on your deathbed and wishing you did. Show up intentionally and create time and space in your calendar deliberately. You either create time, or you're at the effect of time. In a sense, when you're at the effect of time, you're a slave to your *scarcity-time* conversation of not having enough of it.

People are amazing. Don't take them or your relationships for granted. Be responsible for sourcing those relationships, fostering them, and growing them. If the relationships are an ever blooming flower, be the water. Don't wait for the rain.

Authenticity in the game of politics

SOMETHING I'M crystal clear about is that many people avoid or leave an involvement in the political realm because they experience themselves as not being able to be effective at making the difference they want to make.

I'm also clear that manipulating, not being straight with people, being inauthentic, putting up false fronts, and not taking actions from a place of Self will always impede on our ability to make a difference.

For whatever reason, many of us are trapped in these 5-year-old conversations within the realm of politics:

- undermining others
- creating zero-sum game relationships
- being anti- or against something (which just props up whatever we're against)
- a constant struggle, fight, and taking actions rooted in survival

Now we may look at some people in politics who have gotten very far and have clearly done it by lying, stealing, and manipulating. Well sure, and some people have made money gambling, and I wouldn't call them good investors.

There are also people that have done quite well for themselves in the world of politics standing for something, being really clear about their vision and mission, and being very clear and upfront.

It's pathetic how many of us look for the lowest common denominator in our context for many of our trainings, books, ways of being, and we learn to get better at a bankrupt game that inevitably leaves us feeling drained, exhausted, and hardened inside.

Not only that—it's a much harder game to play. Much harder.

Create games that inspire and empower you and if you don't know how to do that – seek out those tools that teach that. Getting better at manipulating is a very inefficient, ineffective, and bankrupt game that will only hinder what we're up to in the political world. You can't be creating possibility while operating in the world of survival. It doesn't work.

I know that's not an easy thing for some to get who don't know anything else. However, I'm clear people gain access to that and thrive with it in their own ways. Now yes there are elections where someone wins and someone loses. Of course, but that's not what I'm talking about, and I will leave it at that.

25 principles

1. Where there's smoke, there's fire.
2. When an interaction seems "off," there's usually some kind of inauthenticity in the space or lack of integrity. Interacting with it only digs you into a deeper hole.
3. When the space is authentic, even on the surface—shitty things like losing a job, breakups, or something not going the way you wanted doesn't cause much of a prolonged reaction.
4. Calling people out on their shit seldom works when it's done from a space of making them wrong vs. shining light on unworkability and sharing what you're committed to. Just being straight and letting people get confronted with their own shit is more powerful. For an excellent book that delves into being effective at this, I highly recommend "Never Split the Difference" by Chris Voss.
5. Your environment is just as important than your own individual development. Choose your friends/surroundings wisely. They will rub off on you no matter how arrogant you are that it won't.
6. Your gut is almost always right. Listening to it when the societal agreement isn't there is useful. The more you follow it, the more connected you will get to that intuitive part of

you. The more you rationalize it away, the more disconnected you will get from it.

7. Physical looks matter and they matter a lot; therefore, it's healthy to be obsessed with being as physically attractive as you can be. It's politically incorrect to say this due to our anti-fat shaming culture.

8. If you have a mental illness and you're defensive about it, it's most likely rooted in having your *identity* or *ego* survive, and there's nothing actually wrong with you. *Experiencing it out* will increase the chance that you disappear what you've spent years of energy putting towards "getting better," "fixing it," and "working on it."

9. Texting diminishes the quality of conversations and gets in the way of communication.

10. Anything can be worked out through communication. Some things can be worked out through texting, and it's less effective and riskier.

11. Rape is second most destructive to murder due to the amount of work it takes for someone to fully mentally heal themselves from that kind of trauma—most won't, and part of their aliveness gets killed off forever.

12. Anger like passion is healthy. Suppressing a side of you because it looks bad or untransformed leads to suffering.

13. When love degrades into morality, the experience of love degrades.

14. The moment you "know" someone you kill them off and they become "static." The flip side is constant discovery which leads to never-ending butterflies.

15. You can commit to *ever-deepening love,* or, you can commit to comfort above everything else. You can't have both. The terrifying feelings that come pre-breakthrough are exactly what's supposed to happen from that place of ever-deepening love. This is the sole reason why most people don't have that. If it were easy, everyone would. Our culture isn't a pull for that kind of dynamic, so it becomes rationalized away as "not realistic."

16. The moment you stop your mission for a shiny object—you

start failing at the mission, and you lose the object. *Attachment* to the results only gets in the way of producing the results you're committed to. If you squeeze a cute puppy too hard, you'll kill it.

17. People know when you're lying even if they don't know what you're lying about. Inauthenticity in the space reeks!

18. Positive thinking on top of suffering leads to further entrenched suffering. You become what you resist.

19. When stuck, sleep on it and commit to something. Let your brain do the work and give yourself time and space. Forcing things and rushing things when you're not authentically there stalls progress.

20. We all have nasty sides. Nobody can transcend their humanity. Owning our inner asshole allows out humanness to shine through.

21. It's not our jobs to micromanage other people's behavior. It's draining and serves nobody.

22. Committed victims are poisonous to the mind and will actually seek to ruin your life if you refuse to be victims with them or victimize them. They are energetic black holes and vortexes of negative energy. Don't give it one second of your energy. They are the largest population of victimizers that aren't distinguished by our culture except in very extreme examples such as in the movie "Gone Girl."

23. You are the average of the people you spend the most time with therefore seek out people who already have what you want. That's more valuable than any program, book, or coach.

24. When you discover a truth—attempting to do something with it turns it into a manipulative belief system. You destroy the truth by doing something with it.

25. Writing or speaking in order to appease the masses diminishes you Self-expression and leads to mediocrity. The greatest voices speak up knowing most won't hear them and earn trust and respect over time or they don't.

Being the "what's missing" in life

YOU CAN'T EXPECT to have love if you're not willing to give it yourself.
Looking for love while being closed off is a great way to keep finding
closed off lovers which will then further your reaction to closing off in
reaction.

Don't expect honesty when you don't allow yourself to be open and
honest with others.

When something is constantly missing from your life, you are the
common denominator in all of that.

Whatever is missing is often what you're just not giving and putting
out there into the world to begin with.

Reacting to smallness

WHEN YOU STAND for someone's greatness, they will often spend energy trying to justify how small they are and destroy all possibility. Keep standing for people's greatness and their lives even when they give you every reason not to. I love unconditionally and I don't apologize for that. It's not worth my life defending myself or trying to *survive*.

Unless you have a commitment to live from that space survival, it's probably not worth your time either. Don't waste your life surviving and reacting to other people's smallness and survival mechanisms.

Resisting inauthenticity

⁂

WHEN YOU HAVE a commitment to authenticity and a commitment for people not to get in their own way, what shows up is seeing all the inauthenticity in the world and people arguing for their own limitations. If you want to make a difference with these people, resisting it is actually one of the worst things you can do as a function of your commitment. When you resist other's inauthentic behavior, you end up often leaving the other person to experience being judged and invalidated which will not do anything to forward a space of authentic sharing. If you want to make a difference with these people—keep speaking your truth, keep listening for what's important to others, and invite them out with others who have a commitment to authenticity and who practice what they preach. One of the quickest and most impactful ways to make a difference in someone's life is to get them into a new environment.

Throw a party—invite great people!

Give up resisting any inauthentic ways of being and focus on creating structures that forward authentic ways of being. That's an incredible access to transforming other people's lives.

Waiting to let your guard down

IF YOU ARE WAITING for something in order to fully live, fully give your gifts, fully love—and do all of that without holding back, you then suffer. That's a choice you make moment by moment.

There is no better time to let your guard down and give your all. Contribute whatever you have to contribute in each situation. Give your love fully.

Express yourself fully.

And, wow, some people may not like that.

Some people will think you're weird.

Some people will react (and it's up to you whether you start altering yourself and reacting to their reactions).

So yes you may have to give up playing it safe, looking good, and have to give up what's predictable and comfortable.

Me, personally—I'm incredibly uncomfortable playing it safe because I get that that's actually a truly unsafe way to live life. I don't know the proper way or the best way to live life or even have the truth about that. However, I am pretty clear that holding back only creates suffering, and decreases how effective you are at whatever you're committed to creating in life in your heart of hearts.

The more time you spend not living like that—the more you suffer and the more uncomfortable it will be to let go of whatever isn't serving you which is getting in the way of you playing life full out. It may be spending less time giving to people who take. Now imagine you've been doing that for 30 years with the same person. Maybe it's really starting to share with your spouse authentically for the first time in decades. Maybe you end up losing them because of that, or maybe you end up becoming closer.

One thing I can promise you is that you will have no way of predicting what happens circumstantially because of you making this choice and you will have more power, freedom, Self-expression, peace of mind, vitality and most likely greater results for whatever you're truly committed to deep down in your heart of hearts. If you find yourself needing to justify or rationalize what you're committed to in life, then that's not it.

If it doesn't make you feel alive—that's not it.

Do not wait to hold back. Do not wait for the stars to align. Do not wait for the perfect circumstances. Let your guard down. It can be hard at first. However, the more you do it, the easier it gets.

One pitfall, however, is "waiting for the moment not to be safe" and then recoiling into your old patterns and justifying the behavior as *"see I tried it, and it didn't work."* The *not working* part would be rooted in an inauthentic space of trying to force an outcome or manipulate what happens. In that case, you would be taking actions in order to produce some kind of reaction or outcome as opposed to taking actions because it's authentic for you as an expression of your highest Self. Coming from a space of "waiting for the moment not to be safe" is a disaster waiting to happen.

Perhaps you share authentically, and you lose a friend or a lover. Let them go or keep sharing and keep sharing, and keep loving, and see what happens.

Whatever makes you feel alive—regardless of the outcome.

Notice I didn't say what makes you feel good. Having unprotected sex with a stranger through a glory hole at a sex shop while shooting up heroin might feel good. However, for probably any of you reading this that would be a violation of your own integrity as you'd be compromising your own values which would leave you diminished. Feeling good and undermining being true to your authentic Self-expression is still ego driven. It's still in the realm of your automatic machinery—not your true

Self-expression. Of course, I use that extreme example to make a point. So go out and be courageous in the face of your fear. Be bigger than your circumstances.

One practice I'll suggest is that anytime you start to feel tense or need to hold back, use that as a sign to allow yourself to feel that way and then share what's coming up for you or simply create a new way of being for yourself. Don't devolve into fake positive thinking. For some who are very guarded, this could take months to years to have natural mastery in.

If you're willing to do the work you won't be sorry. Reading this is not a replacement for doing the work. If having more knowledge was all that it took to make a difference then all anyone would have to say is "let your guard down, and love," and everyone would do it. Of course, that doesn't ever work, and the act of simply knowing it intellectually as something you should do makes no fucking difference in life. So, yes, you all already know this. Just knowing this won't work.

Surround yourself with people who will support you and who also are committed to this. This makes it that much easier to quicken the time between when you're being closed and letting go of whatever you need to let go of to be open. It quickens the time to shift your way of being when you're disempowering yourself because your environment won't tolerate that way of being and will only listen to you as bigger than that. An environment that gives into your closed off-ness will only make this game harder for you. Do the work. Create awesome shit.

Beliefs & the occuring

PEOPLE WHO HATE themselves or have a belief around how there's something wrong with them or they need to be fixed tend to snap at you when you try to bring them up and love them. People who are always stressed out will find you stressful. Righteous people will always find you wrong. People who lack integrity will find people who value integrity as pushy or uptight or some kind of version of annoying to deal with the threat of having to confront their own integrity. Fortunately, it goes the opposite way too. Be around people who will always listen to you knowing you are great and want to forward your life as much as you want to forward theirs.

Listening for smallness

ONE OF MY commitments on the planet is to listen for people's greatness regardless of circumstances. It's for selfish reasons as I love seeing people thrive around me and I love the kind of person I get to be for myself and for others being like that in the world.

If you're like me in that way one of the things that absolutely undermines that commitment is to start feeding into how poor, helpless, and how much of a victim to circumstances someone is and in turn start listening to them as though they were small. When you have the above commitment, listening to anyone as a small person would be completely out of integrity with what you're committed to in the world. And like the saying goes, "without integrity, nothing works."

Yes, be with where someone's at.

Yes, get someone's experience.

And no, do not buy into the fact that someone else is small, helpless, or a victim to their circumstances.

I am deeply committed that people never have to suffer no matter their circumstances.

Taking a stand for what's possible

✦✦✦

YOUR SELF-EXPRESSION IS a function of how people listen to you. Often, the difference between being on the cutting-edge and being crazy is how people listen to what you have to say. When you put out ideas into the world that create possibilities for others and they don't see it for themselves, they will often do anything it takes to destroy what you're creating because it doesn't fit into their worldview. To all the cutting edge human beings who are on the forefront of transforming what's possible for individuals, communities, and whole countries—stay strong and *be* what you're creating in the face of *no agreement*. I love you all for your generosity and your stand in life.

The biggest inauthenticity I have seen—is people attempting to live like this without a community that supports them by continuously listening for new possibility. To attempt to live like this on your own or around people who will be undermining to new possibility will make the game that much harder. It would be like trying to heal race relations while being a member of the Ku Klux Klan. It probably wouldn't be the best community to be surrounded by and supported by. Or imagine trying to create an awe-inspiring romantic relationship where the two of you together make a huge impact in the world, and you're being surrounded by a community that thinks that *relationships are hard* and *difficult* and *a struggle*—and all of these scarcity mindsets around love and relationships. The chances that one of you rationalizes away the possibilities created within that relationship drastically increase.

If you are committed to transforming what's possible for human beings, make sure you have a community that supports that.

Creating space for others

✦

WHEN YOU SHARE from your deepest core, completely in integrity with who you truly are – the space you are for others will increase the probability that you will inspire and have others be present to their own core and greatness. You will increase the chances of bringing out the best in others. Sometimes you will also bring out the worst. When others see something about themselves that they may not have even been present to in their whole life, it's the default position to simply justify away their own greatness. This keeps their identity alive. We as human beings, when acting unconsciously, will destroy everything to keep our identities alive. People who are not ready or willing to see light will recoil in the darkness when they are in the presence of light. People who are ready will rise to the occasion.

Either way, be an authentic space for all. Love when you don't have a reason to and love even when you have reasons not to. I'm not saying that so you can fulfill the identity of some monk. I couldn't give a shit about that unless you wanted to be a monk, then I'm all for it! I say that because allowing someone to diminish who you're being in the world makes *you* small. Remember, Gandhi was kind to Hitler, and it wasn't because he condoned Hitler's actions. Acknowledge others—even if that sometimes means they can't *be* with it—and they'll fight their own wars in their minds around it.

Throughout those storms, just keep loving, keep loving, keep loving. Someone once said, on the other side of fear is freedom. I don't know if that's a universal truth but I think it's pretty damn close to it. You don't have to be everyone's friend, lover, etc. – because that isn't always workable.

However, we all have the power to be that kind of space for others regardless of their reactions. It's being the change that we want to see in the world that moves mountains. Not convincing others or persuading others. In that space – things move. At the end of the day, we are all human beings doing what we know how to do. When you get that at your core, not just intellectually, you'll naturally bring compassion wherever you go. If you're already there authentically then you know what I mean and you're already more evolved than 99% of humanity in that area of the human experience.

You wouldn't get angry at a rock for being a rock. Human beings will be human beings.

"Choice implies consciousness—a high degree of consciousness. Without it, you have no choice. Choice begins the moment you dis-identify from the mind and its conditioned patterns, the moment you become present. Until you reach that point, you are unconscious, spiritually speaking. This means you are compelled to think, feel, and act in certain ways according to the conditioning of your mind. Nobody chooses dysfunction, conflict, pain. Nobody chooses insanity. They happen because there is not enough presence in you to dissolve the past, not enough light to dispel the darkness. You are not fully here. You have not quite woken up yet. In the meantime, the conditioned mind is running your life. Similarly, if you are one of the many people who have an issue with their parents, if you still harbor resentments about something they did or did not do, then you still believe that they had a choice—that they could have acted differently (and I would add "anybody" for that matter). It always looks as if people had a choice, but that is an illusion. As long as your mind with its conditioned patterns runs your life, as long as you are your mind, what choice do you have? None. You are not even there. The mind-identified state is severely dysfunctional. It is a form of insanity."

— ECKHART TOLLE

Not smelling our own stench

THE NEED TO CONTROL AND MANIPULATE

EVERY TIME we lie to ourselves, break our word, and blame circumstances or reasons, we die a little more inside and become less connected
to who we are. Our aliveness continuously gets destroyed.

The longer we keep our messes around, the more we forget they are
even there. We are essentially living with our own stench until we can't
even smell it anymore. Then instead of cleaning it up we have to control
more, manipulate more, deal with stress more, and lack peace of mind,
and spend more energy on being in survival.

Possible ways to avoid life

HERE ARE four *possible* ways to avoid life:

1. **Fight:** Critical, Demanding, Insensitive, Intolerant, Uncaring, Blunt, Judgmental, Anger, Rude, Control, Dominate.
2. **Run Away:** Impulsive, Talkative, Hurried/Harried, Insincere, Overwhelming, Unreliable, Frantic, Distracted, Not Present.
3. **Do Nothing:** Unresponsive, Stubborn, Withdraw, Serious, Picky, Under-plan, Closed-minded, Lazy, Over-Analyze.
4. **Hide:** Approval seeking, Excuses, People-pleasing, Codependent, Justification, Rationalization, Wishy-washy, Under-commit, Never fully commit and always have a way out, Incongruence.

We attract our mirrors

THERE'S A NEARLY universal principle that we attract our mirrors.

If we are waiting for people to earn our trust, our love—we shouldn't expect people to be unconditionally loving around us nor expect people to be listening to us from a place of trust yet from a place of skepticism.

If you want to be surrounded by authenticity, trust, love, pure oneness—then be that way with others. That will create the space for others to be that way with you and they either will rise to the occasion and match you, or they won't. Either way, be great with them.

The ways of being of the people around you are related to who you are being with them. We can all agree that in some moments, people can be assholes, people can be warm and loving, and that you can have the experience of oneness and full presence. So just right there, everybody is capable of all those ways of being.

Without integrity, nothing works

WITHOUT INTEGRITY, nothing works. You can run your life out of your reasons, your wants, and your circumstances, or you can run your life out of your commitments. Both valid. Both give you a particular set of results. What are you committed to? What is your life about? Where are you out of integrity with those commitments?

Wherever you are stuck, confined, constrained, or simply have a loss of freedom, power, or Self-expression there is always something inauthentic there that you are lying to yourself about.

Being authentic about our inauthenticities gives us an enormous amount of freedom and new openings for action.

Sharing yourself authentically

PURPOSE AND ALIVENESS

In June 2008, I had my first taste of real personal development work. Yes, I had read books by Dale Carnegie, had done public speaking stuff, and had done lots of rah-rah-rah stuff but nothing that was experiential and totally transformational in nature.

After I discovered so much cool stuff, had all these new insights and epiphanies, one of the first things I got was how much my environment did not support what I was truly up to. I was surrounded by people who you could say were not very conscious or aware, had a commitment to going through the motions in life, and had no commitment to non-stop expansion and growth. When I broke free of all of that, I was met with resignation, cynicism, close-minded skepticism, general defense mechanism triggering. I literally became a trigger warning for people in survival. At first, I thought it was something over there with me. I would ask myself,

Am I sharing wrong?

Being too pushy?

Am I being too aggressive?

Am I being too something?!??!

It was some form of putting myself in the wrong and blaming myself. So in reaction to this story, I made up about myself of how there was something wrong with how I was sharing – I started "toning it down." I began suppressing myself, my insights, and my new ways of being. This led to me being totally out of integrity with my core. I literally felt dead inside. What was more fucked up about the whole thing was that the people around me still had the same views, judgments, and defense mechanisms.

The moment I observed all of this, I discovered something really liberating. I got that to suppress your light because some people will get defensive around that is by far one of the dumbest possible things you can do if you're committed to living life in integrity with your core and making a difference. So now I share without apology and without any need to hide myself or diminish my words in order to appease others. I still piss off and annoy *just* as many people. People still have their judgments and views about me. But the impact to all of this is that I get the opportunity to make an *exponentially* greater difference in the world, all while having a heightened experience of sustained vitality and aliveness.

And that's the point. I share authentically and unapologetically no matter my circumstances and no matter who I am with. So for anyone feeling afraid, I hope this post gives you some courage to share yourself freely. No matter the environment. No matter the people. You have a story to tell. You have insights to share. You have a gift to give. Give it. Share it. And if you don't know what it is. Follow your intuition. Do what makes you feel alive. Then follow it. Keep sharing and sharing and what you'll discover is that through your authentic sharing (as distinct from tactfully thinking about what to say and how to say it)—you'll start to discover and continue to hone and grow your gifts and you'll naturally pulled to be in action around what there is to contribute from that place of Self.

Positive thinking to cover up bullshit

POSITIVE THINKING in order to cover up what's authentically missing in one's life merely perpetuates whatever one is trying to compensate for in the first place.

Being responsible for your internal machinery

IN THE SUMMER OF 2014, I remember someone sharing something with me and then they quickly added, "I hope I didn't offend you and I really hope that didn't come off the wrong way." I responded by saying, "I have no commitment on ever blaming my own internal experiences and reactions on you."

Once I got that I'm 100% responsible for my own emotions, thoughts, reactions, defense mechanisms, and all the automatic stuff in my body internally—there was an experience of freedom and peace for me. And over time, my brain chemistry altered and those reactions became minimized, and most of them disappeared completely.

Some results:

1. Arguments with my best friends: *0*
2. The success rate of having separation with another and communicating it out to completion until everything was worked out: *100%*
3. The only exceptions to this have been when the other individual wasn't interested in giving me the space to talk things out with them and preferred to leave things left unsaid. However, you'll notice if you've been someone who has not been committed to communicating everything out in the past,

and then you elevated your game and you took on that new behavior, you'll notice how many more people will be willing to engage with you when you come from a place of openness and a commitment to completion vs. a commitment to invalidating the other and being right about something

4. The number of times I've had to disconnect from someone because I blamed them for being too "pushy, annoying, aggressive, offensive, etc.": *0*

5. The amount of drama in my life and conversations I have daily that diminish what's possible and forward separation: *a few times a year*

Let people throw their judgments, defense mechanisms, and all their petty garbage that's not them (yet they think it's them). Give space to it all. Really listen for what they're committed to (behind every complaint there is some kind of commitment or they wouldn't have the energy to keep complaining). Then return all of that through being a space for full acceptance and love. Will everyone get you? Nope. Does it matter? Nope.

Expand yourself into partnership

❧❀❧

THE PRESENCE OF AUTHENTICITY, spiritual power, and awareness often terrifies those who lack a commitment to that kind of way of living. Your light will make space for others to see their light, and will also scare people away into darkness and have them recoil. Those are not your partners. Never diminish your light for anyone. Yes, you can bring patience. Yes, you can bring compassion. Yes, you can bring gentleness. Yes, you can bring something to the table that enables another to hear you through their lens of reality.

However—not at the expense of diminishing your own light in the process. That serves nobody. Focus on those who fan your flames, who inspire your mission, who will want to expand with you—*not* self-project their own internal experiences onto you and run at the first sign of discomfort.

Create partnerships that serve the world better than you could on your own.

Power in politics

POWER within the context of politics is a conversation I find both inter-esting and also vital to understand. What many people don't get is that manipulation and being inauthentic will only get in the way of producing the results we want to produce in our lives. Now you might say, *"Well Eric, that sounds nice except look at all these politicians who lie, manipulate, and put on inauthentic fronts for people—surely many of them do okay and go off to become Congressmen, Senators, and Presidents."*

While it is true that we often get political leaders in the United States who have gained political capital through being inauthentic, we should first examine just how effective these behaviors are. Consider that there have been lots of belief systems created in political activist circles around the need to be inauthentic to gain political capital. When we see someone who is constantly manipulating and cheating their way to the top—it can validate this belief and add to the "data points."

It's my view that this is simply the lowest common denominator and a game with so many playing that there will always be some people that are bound to win. It's no different than if "day trading" was considered the ultimate way to be a good investor and out of a million day-traders, we pointed to the ones that made money, and then, started to build whole systems and educational trainings around those kinds of behaviors. In that case, the "data" and the patterns would be based off ineffective behavior and false premises. Essentially, we'd be picking the most effective people out of an ineffective group.

Now going back to politics.

It would be easy to dismiss what I shared above (especially if you're a political consultant or activist reading this) and continue to look for evidence to fit that belief that in politics what works is to keep manipulating, surviving, and being run by fear. It could also be an opportunity to really start looking beyond that.

You can ask ourselves the question:

"How can I produce the results I want in my life with ease, fun, and without having to manipulate or being something I'm not in life, and what resources are at my disposal to help me accomplish that?"

When people feel the need to manipulate (if you're very honest with yourself), it comes from this need to survive. I can promise you that with equal resources, experience, knowledge, etc.—the person that feels the need to manipulate will always be less effective in producing the results they're committed to for themselves and their life than the human being who lives from a place of possibility and that place of their authentic Self. And that's a moment-by-moment choice. So if you want power, letting go and giving up what gets in the way (and then giving it up again) will give you access to whole new levels of effectiveness in the results you're committed to producing in the realm of politics or in life.

As someone with a political background, I truly believe it's time our generation stops diminishing ourselves to the lowest common denominator in politics and start learning and being equipped with more powerful and effective technologies that come from an authentic place, which is simply more powerful than even the most effective manipulative tools such as the *Alinksy Model.*

That will make some people threatened, and they'll begin to cling to their old ways of thinking, and that will have some people try to bring you right back into survival mode, and that's okay. They're just doing what they know to do given their own experience, knowledge, background, and circumstances—and I ask you to bring compassion to those people and in those situations. The tools are out there. The teachers are out there. The student must make the conscious choice to go all in and be open to contributions from others and doing the work. I have no interest in listening to people's reasons for why they can't. And that's just in life.

Hiding yourself comes at great expense

❦

SOME PEOPLE GO where it's comfortable. Sometimes the highest peak performance states arise out of being comfortable in the face of feeling discomfort. That's what leads to growth beyond the automatic patterns of behavior.

Are you a commitment-phobe? Stop it. There's some underlying fear, story, context, or thought you tell yourself in the face of creating a commitment (often bigger than oneself but not necessarily).

It's all ego and fear based in nature anyway.

Be what's missing in your environment.

Be the light in the darkness.

Be the light where there's fear.

Love the people who get reactive and judgmental towards you.

The more you notice all the automatic shit, the more clear you get about your natural purpose, your natural mission, and the gifts you have to share and contribute that give you the experience of aliveness.

Some people just will never get that concept.

That's ok, love them anyway.

So when there's energy or patterns in the space you don't like, be the one that breaks it up. Be 100% responsible for the space.

Don't react to the defense mechanisms and reactions, just get it, and continue to create.

Every generation goes through creating new patterns that then allow for new ways of thinking, being, and acting to come into existence into the world. Just like we are born into a world where we inherit much of that—we can also create patterns for others after us to inherit.

And you want to talk about patterns?

There's even a part of me doesn't feel quite safe sharing this publicly.

Why?

Because I'm clear some people will judge it as "woo-woo" thinking, and simply justify away what they don't understand.

When I was first getting present to all of this stuff, I would have never shared any of this because internally there would have been a part of me feeling sick to my stomach and angry how people didn't get what I got (and many others of my generation and some in the generations above me have tapped into).

It would feel lonely and isolating. Now I'm clear to withhold my gifts, to not share, to let others dim me out of fear of judgment is absurdly stupid.

If anything, I'm committed that the space I hold for others makes it safe for others also to get present to their inner gifts and the things they've tapped into that perhaps have been rationalized or justified away long ago.

Consider that the more you hide yourself in life out of some fear only comes at your own expense to your own aliveness and the impact you make in the world.

The people on the planet who have made the biggest impact have not suppressed these gifts. And yes, they were resisted at times.

That's just part of the game called being a human being.

Triggering defense mechanisms

❦

WHEN YOU SHARE your authentic Self—that space you create will some-times trigger defense mechanisms to those without a commitment to also be that light. In those moments—it's easy to ask yourself out of a *fear of wanting to avoid looking bad*:

Should I tone it down?
Should I suppress myself?

And yes—there are sides of you that may not be appropriate to share in certain situations. However, sharing from a place of Self will always lead to you having as much power, freedom, and vitality no matter your circumstances; *and* there will be people threatened by your light.

Never diminish your light to please another. Those who stay in judg-ment and feel threatened and run will do what they do—love them anyway and in the process, you'll touch the most people. You'll inspire the hearts and minds of the most people. You'll increase the probability of making the most difference and fulfilling the most on your mission. Even sharing will very likely leave someone who is reading this feeling defensive, threatened, cyclical, pessimistic, or suffocated. That's ok. Shine your light so brightly. Penetrate even the darkest of fears and hold space for others no matter where they're at. Simply, *be* great. Shine bright.

Be ruthless and relentless in fulfilling your mission at your core. And be unwavering in your dedication to whatever you're up to in life. Be the *"what's missing"* in your environments as opposed to trying to fix and change everything. Never diminish your light and being able to *be* and *produce* all of these things for the sheer purpose of not *rocking the boat* and making someone with no commitment to authenticity and a commitment to fear comfortable. You diminish both your gifts to the world and your ability to be of service to others thereby diminishing your probability of making the difference you're committed to making in the world. Now go out and play and trigger some defense mechanisms along the way. Onward!

An awesome daily practice

THIS HAS BEEN a daily practice of mine for many years. It's awesome and maybe you'll find it awesome too. Try it for a week or a month. Just commit to something, be willing to commit fully, and see what opens up for you.

Take a look right now and notice what is in the way that has you not be giving your gifts fully. Use the *noticing model*.

Noticing
1. Notice that you are opinionating.
2. Notice that you have an opinion of your opinionating.
3. Notice that you try to control your opinionating.
4. Notice that your opinions don't care, and keep flowing anyway.
5. Notice that you are not running the show, your opinions are.
6. Notice that you are not your opinions, rather, you have opinions.
7. Or, Notice that your opinions have you.
8. Notice that this is going on 24/7 in the background.
9. Do not attempt to correct or fix the condition – simply Notice.

Then once that is all out of the way, spend at least a half hour fully committing to giving your gift fully. It doesn't matter what it is, just contribute fully from a place of Self. Know when you go to sleep tonight that you had nothing else to give.

Killing off possibility

YOU CAN BE the most loving person in the world, and people will still call you unloving.

You can be the most generous person in the world, and people will still call you selfish.

You can be the most committed person in the world to people, and people will still say you're a narcissist.

So have the courage to take action, share, and stay committed even in the face of people calling you even the nastiest of things. When you know in your core what you're committed to, the bigger you play, the more people will feel threatened by you.

Gandhi was shot.

Lincoln was shot.

MLK was shot.

Often, people will shoot down conversations that they don't see possible or shoot down the person or people generating those conversations.

Create what you know at your deepest core is possible anyway and don't you dare fucking stop. You'll only regret it on your deathbed.

If this weren't the case, everyone would play big because it's our natural expression to consistently contribute our gifts on larger and larger levels.

Beyond comfort

THE ONE REQUIREMENT

YOU CAN BE COMMITTED to comfort or committed to ever-deepening love, breaking through all boundaries and barriers, breaking open people's hearts which is often a terrifying experience. On the other side of that is freedom and more comfort than you've ever experienced in your life. Don't believe a word I say.

Try it on for yourself.

The next person you date – love them with every grain in your body. Don't play it safe. Don't hold back. Give your all and then some. Be willing to be a fool. Be willing to have people run away in fear (and they'll have a reason or justification and the most likely will not be authentic and tell you they're terrified of you or too confronted).

However, what you'll do is weed out people who aren't willing to operate from that deep of a level and the people who do show up, the people who do match you, you'll experience a level of relatedness, a level of love, a level of constant exploration where instead of butterflies decreasing over time, they'll increase, where every kiss is like kissing your lover for the first time.

It's all possible.

And it's not theoretical.

It's also not hard. The hardest part is having the patience and the self-discipline to never waver when someone fails time and time again to match you.

There's one requirement to all of this, however...

The one requirement to all of this is you must already be at a place where you experience yourself being whole and complete already. If you're still relying on others for your own completeness, you'll crumble. So if you're at a place where you still need someone for your own completeness – do whatever work you need to do to get to a place of being whole and complete.

Once you're there and you've established healthy boundaries for yourself, give up all boundaries, give up all resistance, and completely let it all go. Be willing for everyone to reject you, to run away from you, to be terrified by your way of being. Only then – can you authentically experience this. And I promise you (very few things I can actually guarantee and promise you when sharing wisdom-based principles) – once you experience these kinds of relationships, you'll never want to ever settle for an ounce less, ever.

Misery hates possibility

PEOPLE WHO CONFUSE your confidence and unwillingness to tolerate bullshit with arrogance are usually just hurting inside and simply have no access to acting any other way. Bring compassion to that. Love them anyway. Be great with them anyway. Never let anybody stop you from creating and from living your deepest integrity at your core. There will always be people who look to bring you down when all you're interested in is standing for their greatness. There will always be people who, no matter what you do, will find some reason to justify some negative judgment of you. Create and live from your deepest truth anyway. The larger you play, the less energy it takes. You'll weed out those who only play the game from intimidation and force and attract those who come from a place of empowerment, and authentic collaborative partnership and teamwork.

A commitment to non-stop expansion

CONSIDER that whenever we're terrified, whenever we're feeling uncomfortable (except for a real physical threat)—most people's automatic mechanisms/machinery/whatever you want to call it will naturally want to shut down, want to close off, or want to run away or resist in some way.

Consider that if we're committed to our own expansion, growth, and development as a human being—those actions rooted in survival are completely out of integrity with our commitment to ourselves.

This leads me to a cool story.

In the Summer of 2005, I attended a summer program at Brown University for high school students. There was a moment in that program where I made a conscious choice that every day I would go out of my way to feel uncomfortable and that I would see anytime I was feeling uncomfortable as an opportunity for me to grow.

So anytime I had uncomfortable thoughts, feelings, emotions, bodily sensations, or just for whatever reason something absolutely terrified me (with the exception being a real physical threat) – I would simply allow myself to feel that way, not resist any of it, and use it as an opportunity to expand myself and to take my comfort zone to the next level.

It's been amazing how doing this almost every day since that promise I made to myself has helped my comfort zone expand to the point where the kinds of things that may terrify most people just don't for me anymore.

There's nothing for me to overcome anymore around those things. If there's any single conscious choice I've ever made in my life that's had the highest yielding results (as measured by the amount of energy it took to produce X result)—that would be it.

An incredibly small micro-action. Something that takes almost no time at all.

Practice it at least 1x daily.

The results will stun you. Enjoy the journey if you choose to go down that rabbit hole. Don't take my word for it, experience it for yourself. And I promise you, it's worth it.

An environment that listens for our greatness

THE BEAUTIFUL HUMAN beings that radiate an open heart and have a certain level of presence tend to experience that in others naturally. The ones without that commitment become petrified, terrified, and use that as a reason to run. I find that sad and it breaks my heart. The more we allow ourselves to be with the greatness of others, the more our own natural goodness and greatness shine through. The more we resist it, turn away from it, and don't give ourselves permission to be with it – even when it's terrifying – we recoil back into our own darkness. It becomes significantly easier or harder depending on whether our environments support our own greatness or not. Our extrinsic environment is not everything *and* it makes a huge difference.

Creating authentic spaces

WE CAN ALL TAKE 100% responsibility for creating authentic spaces around us. That doesn't mean it's in our control, but we can see it as a place to think from. It's a mental model, not the truth.

I would rather someone express their anger at me in all their fury than to ever become the object of someone's disgust, hatred, or resentment. I would rather someone express their passion than to ever be in the presence of false apathy. I would rather someone express their sadness around me than to be around fake positive thinking. I like when people are honest to their core with where they're at. I don't like inauthentic sincerity. I like grace. I like goodness. I believe in the good of all people.

However, if that isn't expressed in the space or that person or group of people doesn't have the awareness about where you're at—they'll hide themselves and withhold communication based off experiences in the past where it wasn't safe to share freely (which is actually the default space for human beings).

Withholding communication is a form of lying

WITHHOLDING communication is a form of lying. It creates distance from another. When people come clean and speak the truth—it creates a space of completeness. It diffuses any of that stuffiness and tenseness that comes from not saying what's really there for you to share. It's like a sigh of relief and more often than not almost funny that it wasn't being said before. Usually, everyone already knows and the thought of it is almost always scarier than it actually is. And the longer time goes on— the more and more distance gets created. Then, people start reacting to that distance and stuffiness which is a byproduct of withholding communication. They pretend to speak the truth to *"fix"* what's going on. That leads to more of the same and often leads the other person you're engaged with to feel disrespected or dishonored, while on the surface it's called *the truth*. It's just more reaction and not really getting to the source of it. It makes no difference.

Attachment to people

DON'T ATTACH yourself to people. Commit yourself to expanding people's lives.

Talk isn't cheap, Part 1

TALK ISN'T CHEAP; people are just cheap with their talk.

The reason many people think talk is cheap is due to the fact that most people really do have a knack for saying things when they feel it in the moment and then decide to back out the moment their thoughts or emotions change.

That's not what commitment is about. While many people think commitment somehow makes you constrained, it actually allows you to experience more freedom, flow, and workability in life.

Talk isn't cheap, Part 2
THE FOUR CANONS OF SPEECH

TALK ISN'T CHEAP; people are just cheap with their talk.

People always love to talk about how actions speak louder than words. And yes, obviously, if you're saying one thing and doing another, people will stop taking you seriously.

However, talk is actually incredibly important. Without language, we would have very little to almost no access to experience. Reality in and of itself is created in language. And, no, I'm not talking about the fucking bullshit positive thinking where you just say happy shit and positive affirmations and your world shifts. In fact, that's a very on-the-surface access of what goes much deeper.

I'm not even saying there's anything wrong with thinking positively or using affirmations. If it makes a difference for you, use it when appropriate. However, that can become a new inauthentic technique to fix things, and it tends to be rather ineffective when it becomes the new coping mechanism to cover something up.

Language can be used to create and destroy. For instance, if you tell some 5-year-old that he's stupid and surround him with people who also tell him that, he may eventually believe it and live his life under a context of being stupid or that there's something wrong with him.

Context, which is created in language, is for human beings as water is for fish. For the most part, human beings are blind to it. However, it's the context we have for our lives that shapes our actions.

There's a TED talk given by the world-renowned coach Tony Robbins who talks about how when he was 11-years-old, his life was transformed. I want to share with you a quote from that talk that speaks to the power of context and how language impacts that:

"My life was touched because when I was 11-years-old, Thanksgiving, no money, no food, we were not going to starve, but my father was totally messed up, my mom was letting him know how bad he messed up, and somebody came to the door and delivered food. My father made three decisions, I know what they were, briefly. His focus was 'This is charity. What does it mean? I'm worthless. What do I have to do? Leave my family,' which he did. It was one of the most painful experiences of life. My three decisions gave me a different path. I set focus on 'There's food.' What a concept! But this is what changed my life, shaped me as a human being. Somebody's gift, I don't even know who it is. My father always said, 'No one gives a shit.' And now somebody I don't know, they're not asking for anything, just giving us food, looking out for us. It made me believe this: that strangers care. And that made me decide if strangers care about me and my family, I care about them. I'm going to do something to make a difference. So when I was 17, I went out on Thanksgiving, it was my target for years to have enough money to feed two families. The most fun and moving thing I ever did in my life. Next year, I did four, then eight. I didn't tell anybody what I was doing, I wasn't doing it for brownie points. But after eight, I thought I could use some help. So I went out, got my friends involved, then I grew companies, got 11, and I built the foundation. 18 years later, I'm proud to tell you last year we fed 2 million people in 35 countries through our foundation. All during the holidays, Thanksgiving, Christmas, in different countries around the world."

So what Tony shares here is brilliant. When he shares about his father—you could say his father had a context for himself in that situation that he was a failure. At some point in Tony's father's life, he made a decision that he was a failure or there was something wrong with him, or he could never do it right or something in that realm. I could guarantee you that wasn't the first time he had a version of that in his life. On the contrary, Tony created a completely different context for the situation and used that context to be in the background for the actions in his life up to this day—one of being a contribution and being of service.

While we can't always control our circumstances, we can in each moment choose the context for our lives. For ourselves, for others, for every situation, and for our life on a macro-level. While that can occur as bullshit positive thinking, it's actually quite real.

Here's a quick exercise if this isn't real for you yet—for one week take on an empowering context for your life. This being theoretical makes no difference hence why I stress doing the work. It's easy for this to be another nice sounding bumper sticker that doesn't alter what's possible for yourself in life.

HERE ARE some possible contexts to choose:

- *Fun & Play*
- *Contribution*
- *Ease*
- *Making a difference*
- *Discipline & Focus*

I could easily list 100 possible contexts. The point is just pick something that aligns with you. If what shows up right now for you is resignation or cynicism take a look at what the context is for your life. If it's something like I don't make a difference and there's something wrong with me and I need to fix myself—well, no empowering context would validate or fit into that worldview. When you can distinguish the stories you've created about yourself, others, your life, and the world around you (which are created in language!!!) they cease to occur as reality and then occur as something you made up. When you get that (and there's never a "now I get it," it's a constant game of distinguishing shit we makeup and becoming free when we experience ourselves being disempowered in life which happens to anyone up to something big in life)— you become free of it. That's a moment by moment phenomenon. The moment you start to tell yourself that everything is distinguished and you have no disempowering stories—then that can easily turn into the new inauthenticity.

So I hope this starts to open up for you that while language occurs for many of us like something to describe the world it's actually creating our world. If you don't have much experience with this principle this can come off as a bit woo-woo or in the realm of a nice sounding bumper-sticker or theory. If that's where you're at, I strongly encourage you to get the most out of this, to really spend some time doing the work below and being totally okay where you're at. For those of you who are experienced in this kind of thinking—then I hope this serves you as a reminder and a way to stay in this conversation. (It's just a conversation created in language!)

So when we communicate using language, you could say there are three basic guidelines for effective communication. This is something that one of my friends and mentors, John King, co-author of the New York Times bestseller, "Tribal Leadership," shared with me.

1. Communication begins with listening and ends with speaking
2. It's not what you get out; it's what you get in.
3. You are responsible for what people are left with after you're gone.

That third point doesn't mean it's your fault. But if you take the position that you're responsible for what people are left with after you're gone, then when you see someone not getting what your intention is or being left in a way that doesn't leave them with what you intended, then it's up to you to for them to get it. It's not something I can tell you how to do. However, if you're reading this and into personal growth and development, then you're already in the minority of people who are interested in engaging in these kinds of conversations. These ideas aren't for most people (at least not yet). So if you set your intention and make the commitment that you are responsible for what people are left with after you're gone and create it as a matter of your own integrity (created in language vs. it being more cheap talk) then what will show up for you are possible actions you can take.

However, as John King would say, "there's no such thing as failure, just correctable results." When you find yourself out of integrity with point 3, remember, there's nothing wrong and nothing to fix but simply just new actions to take. One common way that is appropriate is to simply acknowledge that it wasn't your intention to leave them in any kind of disempowering space and apologize without invalidating yourself.

An example of this would be something like: "hey I'm sorry that what I said left you feeling like X, it wasn't my intention. My intention was to share with you Y out my commitment to Z."

This compares to invalidating yourself which could sound something like this: *"Oh my god...I'm so so so sorry...please don't hate me...I feel so bad right now...am I ok? I'm such an idiot for saying that...I don't know what I was thinking...please forgive me for saying the wrong thing."*

While language inherently creates, being able to distinguish that it creates gives you some power over what you're creating as many people think they're describing a situation when really they're creating it.

There are 4 ways language is used to create. These are what are called the 4 canons of speech which is one of many principles and models John King created:

Canon 1: Declaration

Declarations are the most powerful kind of statement we as human beings can make. Declarations can be shared standing in the presence of no evidence, support, or agreement. Think about Gandhi standing for peace in an environment that called for violence. Or Martin Luther King, Jr. sharing his dream which created a whole new future for African Americans in the United States or JFK declaring we were going to put a man on the moon.

If these men had used "best practices," "case studies," or were looking to the past to best predict what would have happened in the future they would have found that Gandhi should have used arms, that Martin Luther King's dream was not an accurate assessment of reality, and that JFK was delusional as he was saying something that was currently not in the realm of possibility for most people.

Essentially, declaration statements that actually create futures for both yourself and/or others to step into, they take no proof or evidence, and it's simply about creating a new possibility. Sharing declarations takes no empirical evidence as empirical evidence lives in the realm of probability, not possibility.

However, the world of probability is incredibly important as most people cannot hear declarations without some kind of probability or evidence.

That leads to Canon 2.

Canon 2: Assertion

Assertions are standing in the presence of looking to the past to predict a probable and almost certain future. Examples of assertion-based speaking show up in case studies, best practices, white papers, and tactics such as "underpromise-overdeliver."

Before I continue to the third and fourth canon I want to make a few points:

Point 1. Declarations are not any better than assertions or vice versa. Both can be used at appropriate times.

Point 2. If you want to take the love out of love—ask why. Think about that for a second. Love is a declaration. Something moves in a relationship between two people when you declare love for someone else and they experience love in that very moment. The moment you go into the trap called "why do you love me?" leads one to justify and come up with *reasons* for the experience you created, and before you know it, that experience degrades into the realm of belief and intellectual knowing and kills off the experience. Essentially, when we look for reasons or ask why, we undermine a declaration. Don't take my word for it though.

Point 3. We live in an assertive or agreement reality; therefore, one needs to be responsible for the *listening of the room* (listen for the listening) in order to gauge what is appropriate to share that forwards the conversation and create something. When I say *listening for the listening of the room,* what I mean is *to gauge intuitively what can be heard and can't be heard in any given environment.*

Point 4. Create enough evidence to warm up the listening in the room to be able to hear a declaration so it lands with people and they really get it (see above for three guidelines of effective speaking).

Canon 3: Requests

1. Generated by a complaint
2. *The effectiveness of mastery is turning complaints into requests*
3. "I get your complaint—what is your request?"
4. Turn a problem into an opportunity. Make a request of someone else vs. complaining about the situation
5. *Find Complaints*
6. Complaints have very little value. Examples would be: "The American People are fed up with Hillary Clinton" or "The American People are fed up with Donald Trump." In those examples, there's no point of action. Compare this to "The American People are fed up with Hillary Clinton/Donald Trump and his/her point of view"...(and then identify an opportunity)
7. Accept, Reject, Counter-Offer
8. Making a request of someone is *not* the same as making a demand of someone. When you make a request of someone, they have full freedom and space to say yes, no, or make a counteroffer to you. The more you come from this way of thinking, the more environments and situations you'll create around you that leave others feeling freed up with their own Self-expression, and, you'll end up being more effective in the process.

How requests fit into demands and invitations:
Requests create.
Here's an example:
"I request you have this done by July 13th at 9 am."
The pitfalls with requests are when they are disguised as demands.

I'm sure we all know that boss that makes requests but you really have no choice to say no or make a counteroffer. That's a demand disguised as a request and it's nasty and inauthentic.

Demands are not necessary in life. I know for some people that may cause some internal resistance. If you're someone who makes a lot of demands of others and feels the need to constantly control—then I would especially encourage you to spend two weeks giving up all demands. I think you'll be pleasantly surprised if you're willing to take that on.

Then there are invitations.

Invitations are a bit lighter in how they feel. They aren't necessary either. However, they have helped me a lot in my own training and development.

By default, I'm a push in life. I have a habit of forcing outcomes. I push to make things happen. It gets in the way and people can be left feeling suffocated or feel a lack of freedom around me. My requests can sometimes occur as demands to others even when they're not. It's something I need to constantly be responsible for and also clean up when someone feels disempowered or experiences a lack of freedom around me as that's never the intent.

If you're someone who has a naturally dominant personality and is successful in life and up to big things perhaps you're a natural push too. If you're a natural pull then making requests may actually take some muscle and you'll have the opposite problem!

For you pushers out there like me, your requests can often land with others as demands.

An exercise that worked for me was to spend a few weeks only making invitations. This felt incredibly counter-intuitive. However, it made a huge difference in experientially learning how to let things happen and be naturally pulled my way. It allowed me to tame down my forceful personality without feeling like I was diminishing my own Self-expression or hiding myself in any way. After just a few weeks, my requests became much more effective.

That's all I have to say about that. Take from it what works for you.

Canon 4: Promises

If you asked most people the question: "who is responsible for the fulfillment of a promise?" they would usually say the other person. However, a much more effective point of view (not the truth) is to come from a place that you are the one accountable for the fulfillment of another person's promise to you.

If you're the CEO of an organization, then an even more powerful place to come from is to actually take the view that you are responsible for the fulfillment of promises from employee to employee and creating and fostering a culture of integrity. Here is one simple thing that I will commonly share with another when they promise me something or become accountable to me. I will ask them a question along the lines of:

"Do you need anything from me to support you in keeping that promise/accountability?"

This creates space for them to see what they can put in place with my support to help fulfill on their word. It also enhances the experience of partnership. It's not that people don't want to ask for help even though that is sometimes the case. Instead, that question can often get someone thinking about actions they could take around building support structures that they wouldn't even have thought to take in the first place.

So remember a few things:

- *Talk isn't cheap. People are cheap with their talk*
- *The three principles of effective communication*
- *The 4 canons of speech*
- *Don't let your speaking devolve into inauthentic positive thinking*

Have life be of your design and you're the artist! Language is your paintbrush. You're either creating or destroying. You either have language or language has you. That's your choice in each moment.

Standing for something bigger than your individual concerns

THE BEAUTIFUL THING about standing for something bigger than yourself is that your Self-interests become about something larger than *just* your own individual stuff. For instance, I'm part of the *liberty movement* out of my commitment to expanding freedom for all people on the planet. Now it's no surprise that not everybody within the movement approves or likes my lifestyle. Not everybody resonates with all my values and the ways I choose to live my life. But that's okay. Because we share a common bond called *freedom and liberty* that brings us all together. I don't connect with everyone based on the basis of personality. I do with some people but with others—our personalities are not why we're in each other's lives.

So the point to all of this: Figure out what moves you, what drives you, and what has you wake up in the morning. Then, partner up with people who you could partner up with to forward that greater intention, whatever it is. The more people, the better (more fun, more vitality, more you forward your mission).

And at the end of the day—we all die anyway.

Don't fake your zen

The moment a transformation, enlightenment, or whatever you want to call it becomes your new identity—it becomes inauthentic in of itself.

As the life coach, Cora Poage puts it:

"Don't fake your Zen," unless of course, you're committed to sounding like a fake robot not in touch with your heart and your intuition, who dribbles and vomits jargon and isn't willing to do the actual work – then be my guest."

The psychological trap of success
through being inauthentic

RELATIONSHIPS, including the one to your authentic Self, trump technique every time.

I first learned the psychological importance of being successful and producing results while being yourself through observing the jail people get into when they go on for years *not* doing that and how hard it becomes for them to let go at that point in life. A lot of people walk around life thinking if they play some part or some role for long enough then once they arrive, they can be themselves. Just look at many politicians if you want to get a taste of that.

That kind of asinine thinking is literally setting yourself up for living in a jail. It's much harder to unwind and let go and let things fall to the ground and crumble into pieces than to never allow yourself to be in that position in the first place. So next time when you tell someone to be themselves (which typically makes no difference just telling someone that), just remember that they may have a lot to lose by letting go. That's very difficult for many people, and, I'm sure would be very psychologically difficult for me if I were in that position.

So instead of just giving advice, provide value. Make it safe for people to share with you. Think from the question, *"If I were in their position, who would I need to be with them to help them feel free around me?"*

When you can truly get into someone's world and really listen for who they are at their core vs. all the automatic stuff, you can truly make a huge impact on someone's life and you will most certainly elevate the quality of relationships around you. This in turn inevitably increases your own results in life in ways that aren't linear or black and white.

Standing for something from pull

᯾

SOME PEOPLE ARE afraid of being pushy. However, going around with that fear and then taking action to avoid coming off like that will actually lead to a diminished Self-expression. At the same time, going around feeling someone will never take action will often lead to others feeling pushed by you and micromanaged by you.

Speaking your truth out of a commitment to taking an authentic stand for something vs. manipulating, coercing, or some kind of survival will always allow you to keep your peace of mind and personal power. If someone does get upset or takes what you say the wrong way, then you can acknowledge it and share it wasn't your intention to leave them feeling that way and simply correct course along the way.

Authentic Push & Pull

Human beings live inside a series of conversations that shape the way we see ourselves and the world around us. One dominating conversation in American culture is around being "pushy." People live inside conversations around:

- *Not being too pushy*
- *I hope this person doesn't find me pushy*

- *I'm not pushy enough*
- *I just let things go with the flow*
- *Things will happen the way they are meant to*
- *I don't want to force something*

Cultural Concerns

There are many more concerns in the world of being too pushy in American culture and they often impede our performance around what we are committed to in our lives.

Consider that attempting to avoid being too pushy and pushing to dominate an agenda can both be two sides of the same coin. Often, our conversations around how pushy or not pushy we need to be are around our own survival at the expense of our own Self-expression and vitality.

Consider when we are completely on mission, aligned with our purpose, operating from our higher-selves, and completely in flow, the prevailing concern isn't about being too pushy or not pushy enough but simply honoring our mission at the deepest part of our core. In those moments, if you look, you will see that some people perceive you as "negative" associations of you, such as a version of the following:

- *Being too much*
- *Being pushy*
- *Being overwhelming*
- *Being too intense*
- *Persistent (in a bad way)*

Then, if you take a look, there will often be people where the very same behaviors occurs as:

- *Confident*
- *Persistent (in a good way)*
- *Having grit*
- *Tenacious*
- *Grounded*
- *Integrous*
- *Easy To Work With*

The Experience Of Operating From Self

When you are operating around your deepest purpose and on mission at the highest level of Self, there's a natural not caring how your actions occur to others and there is the experience of the freedom to be, express, and create. You will notice in those moments you will experience being more productive, in flow, grounded, and naturally not caring how you come across and seeing the "impersonal" aspect of it (both positive and negative associations).

What Gets In The Way: Push/Pull

What gets in the way of this is the concern of how pushy you are. First, don't resist your natural instincts. Some people are natural pushes and some are natural pulls. Natural pulls will often be awkward at not moving things forward and it comes off as "weird" in the space or they will feel disempowered around it. Natural pushes often push too hard and feel like shit doing it and feel the experience of Self diminish in those moments.

My Experience With Coaching Clients

When I work with clients, I have them get to acknowledge their natural proclivity. For anyone who knows me, they will know I am a natural push. It's no secret and pretending like I am not one only fucks me up and has me resort to being a domineering asshole. Not acknowledging your lack of pushiness, one often becomes a frustrating do-nothing to others who want to work with you. Two sides of the same coin.

Requests & Invitations

An exercise I often do with clients is I share with them the "IDR Continuum" which stands for Invitations, Requests, and Demands. Clients who are natural pushes discover for themselves that their requests are often demands disguised as requests. Even when they are not they can often land as demands. People who are natural pulls and who are afraid to push or have some negative association around it (as an expression not manipulation), will often be making invitations when they should really be making requests. I give a homework assignment that for an entire week they can only make requests (the ones who have a hard time making them) or can only make invitations (when they want to just make requests or demands).

Not A Technique

What the pushes find is that their productivity goes up by making only invitations and the pulls productivity goes up by making only requests. Of course, this can degrade into an inauthentic manipulative tactic rather quickly so I make it clear it is just an exercise and not a formula.

Permission-Based Dynamics: *Entrepreneurs & Dating*

Two areas where I see this significantly make a huge positive impact on people's lives is in the area of entrepreneurship and the area of dating.

Now why these two areas specifically?

Because there's no contract. It's all permission-based. If I want you to come on my podcast, I can't fire you if you don't show up. If you break up with me, you don't get a deduction in a paycheck (...unless of course, I'm your sugar daddy *#jokes*).

Entrepreneurial Work

When it comes to entrepreneurial work, the more you start to get in your head about how you are feeling overwhelmed by some new opportunity, not ready for something, not sure about something, the more it will impede your performance. However, it's not uncommon for someone to say they want to come on a podcast, then you invite them on and they "aren't ready" and don't come on until 6 months later. In 6 months, I could have done 3 more episodes with them. It's easy to see where others limit their own performance and harder to see it in ourselves.

Like clockwork, anyone who experiences living fully from their mission and being successful at it will observe others limiting and diminishing themselves when brought with new opportunities. The truth is, people will only operate within their own box. If everyone could see new possibilities and take on new opportunities by the horns without getting in their head, there would be many more business owners and fewer people taking on jobs they hate and felt stuck at. At a job, there's routine, there are basic expectations, and there's the threat of being fired if you don't perform. With looser partnerships, there's no immediate noticeable negative impact derived from getting in your head and stopping yourself. Of course, there's a huge impact it's just blind. It's the unseen. There's no boss to encourage you or demand you do your job. Your mental garbage takes over and it clouds your decision making against your own interests. However, when we share and share and share and are proficient at making requests and invitations, people experience a sense of freedom and support around us. In essence, they get the space to be and rise up to the occasion. A demand destroys that. A request that lands as a demand, or is a demand in disguise, does the same.

Dating & Romantic Relationships

Dating is the same way.

Have you ever noticed a woman who on the surface seems really smart, driven, and all-around has her shit together but then you see the kinds of men she tends to go for and they are fratty meatheads who don't have a personal development bone in their body? You can bet your fucking ass that this girl has a thing around push and Self-expression. Why else would you only date men with a diminished sense of Self-expression? See, men who are fully Self-expressed will land as overbearing, pushy, overwhelming, and other negative experiences in that world. I've also observed women who tend to attract men who are pushovers and they are never happy in their relationships. Nearly all of them are constant demands for attention so they attract men who will feed that flame. Men who practice weird pickup shit tend to attract women who are into that and they tend to be immature and manipulative. In essence, when you start making invitations and requests authentically, you end up attracting men or women who value the freedom and space and are in a certain headspace that will thrive off that communication.

The Dynamics/Games You're Committed To

At the end of the day, if you find yourself in certain dynamics, it's easy to keep going harder at what you are already doing. If you are afraid to make requests, then often being more passive becomes the new technique. Like women who expect men to put in way more than they do. It's a game that pushes away mature men that really value partnership and don't want to feel like they are doing all the work. They will push away givers with strong boundaries and end up attracting manipulative men, wealthy sugar daddy wannabees, or pushover nice guys who will feed into that. And like men who expect a woman should always do all the work, who won't go down on them, etc, and end up attracting really giving women who give to takers and have low self-esteem.

When you are unsatisfied with the dynamics in your life, it's always on **_you_** to notice the dynamics/games you're committed to engaging in.

Set the conditions, see who shows up to the party.

12 reasons to always give your all

1. No matter how honest you are—there will always be someone who thinks you're manipulative.
2. No matter how kind you are—there will always be someone who thinks you're a jerk.
3. No matter how generous you are—there will always be those people who say it's really all about you.
4. No matter how loving you are—there will be some people who say you're not very loving.
5. Some people will see your confidence as arrogance.
6. No matter how much you share and how vulnerable you are—there will be those who think you lack vulnerability and are "hard to approach."
7. No matter how accepting you are of others—there will be those who think you're judgmental.
8. When you're authentic, people who are holding onto something, withholding something, or lying about something big may feel threatened by you.
9. When you're holding others to their word and they're not committed to their own integrity—they will call you pushy, overwhelming, or intense (in a negative way).
10. Give your all in each moment and never diminish yourself in

order to please someone else's insecurities in the world. You make the world a darker place when you do that. Do not meet people down to their bullshit, but allow them the opportunity to rise above it. Some will. Some won't. Love them anyway.

11. Give your all anyway as none of the other reactions have anything to do with you. You can spend years and years and years trying to adjust your tone, your words, and everything in between—and you'll just have a diminished sense of yourself, a diminished sense of power and expression, and those people will still almost inevitably have the same judgments about you anyway.

12. Remember #11

Honoring your word and trusting oneself

⁂

THE MORE YOU don't honor your word, the more you lose the experience of being able to trust yourself.

When you lose the experience of trusting yourself, the default modus operandi devolves into a downward spiral of integrity and then using manipulation and control as a way to fix it. The way to fix those kinds of control and manipulation issues isn't exerting willpower. As long as the space of dishonoring your word stays the same, you'll revert back to being a manipulative jerk.

Essentially, trying to stop manipulating over a space of lacking integrity will lead to you eventually manipulating again. It would be like trying to tell someone who is addicted to sugar to get into intermittent fasting. They'll always break their fast as their addiction to sugar would inherently cause them to feel like they're about to pass out. The urge to break their word would be too strong and psychologically not sustainable over the long run.

It's no different than people who never fully commit to things and then have lots of anxiety and stress. Coping with that will only do so much. Being fully committed will create that natural state of freedom and peace of mind without having to think about it or doing yoga in order to get there.

Get to the source. Find the weed and pull it the fuck out vs. learning how to deal with the weeds and planting some pretty flowers over it. The weeds will always kill the flowers over time.

Clarity about workability

ALWAYS BE clear about what works and doesn't work for you. Of course, some people don't out of a fear of offending people or pissing people off. But it's like the saying goes, "you get what you tolerate."

I think some people know this but have a hard time practicing it in reality.

The truth is, some people simply won't respect what you have to say. Some people will try to turn it on you, accuse you of things, start gaslighting you, etc.

And if they do that then you have your answer right there and you have peace regardless of whether the conversation is peaceful or not. But when you're willing to lose everything to have what you truly want in your life—the right people will stay in your life and you'll *weed out the crap*, so to speak.

And this doesn't have to be for big things either. When you get in the habit of doing this, even for little things, those little things add up and it makes a huge difference.

Unreliability

UNRELIABLE PEOPLE who are slime-balls with their word are a great example of what not to do in life. If you know someone like this, get the impact and then get what the impact is on yourself and on others when you do this with others. Occasionally you might meet someone who is very successful who exhibits these traits. If a person like that is your first example of a role model, it can in some ways be detrimental. What people who model those people don't get is that they have all of that success despite those undesirable traits not because of them.

"If you're lazy and unreliable, it doesn't matter what you're good at. 'What do you want to avoid?' Such an easy answer: sloth and unreliability. If you're unreliable it doesn't matter what your virtues are. You're going to crater immediately. Doing what you have faithfully engaged to do should be an automatic part of your conduct. You want to avoid sloth and unreliability."

— CHARLIE MUNGER

99% Integrity & 50/50 Dynamics

THERE ARE two prevailing mindsets that most people never question. There're also lots of justifying around these two prevailing mindsets. The results of these mindsets lead to dissatisfaction and lying.

Mindset 1. *"I can't be perfect so I'll strive to do the best I can."* While saying something like this can often come from a good place, it often leaves one with a kind of psychological permission to break their integrity and this has a detrimental impact over time.

Say someone is late for a meeting or a party.

"I'm sooooooo sorry I'm late...I really didn't mean to...I feel so bad...I really did the best I can to get there on time."

A "sincere" statement like that lacks power and you can almost bet that person will do it again. The statement lacks responsibility.

Now let's try this on:

"I told you I would be here at 10 AM and it's now 10:10 AM. The impact on me not keeping my word and me not keeping my word even with these little things over time is that it builds up and over time you'll start listening to me as someone who isn't reliable and the impact it has on me is that I have less trust in myself. I could blame the traffic but from now on I'm committed to being on time and that means what I'll put in place is giving myself an alarm on my calendar to leave well ahead of time to account for the possibility of traffic. I will never be late

again. Please forgive me for my tardiness. Is there any other impact that me being late has on you?"

Now that may sound excessive, and in some cases, it may be. But having that kind of rigor with yourself will give you your power back both with yourself and others when you don't keep your word. There's no invalidation of yourself. Just simply creating workability and restoring it when it's out. Even the slightest lack of integrity diminishes workability just a tad. Fast forward that for a decade and that tad now becomes a massive fucking hole of shit. You've seen it before.

Mindset 2. *"I'm responsible for my part and you're responsible for your part. I give 50% and you give 50%."*

While not always said, this mindset is often implied, and it leads to disaster. 50/50 degrades very quickly. 50/50 in a relationship is *"doing significantly under 50% waiting to happen."* Essentially, the moment someone does anything that even looks like, reminds you of, or from your point of view *clearly* is doing under 50% of their expectation (regardless if that's how their experience of it is), now you build up resentment, create a story about how they aren't doing their part, and now you use that as an excuse to do less and match their efforts. Then they react to your reactions and before you know it, the relationship becomes unworkable.

Instead, try on 100/0 instead of 50/50. Meaning you're 100% responsible for a relationship or an environment working. That doesn't mean doing all the work unless you want to be responsible for doing all the work. That also doesn't mean it's your fault when something doesn't work. It's a place to think from that gives you some power and allows you to see actions you can take that would be blind from you if you were only looking at doing "your part."

When people are in a relationship and experience "their love being dead"—it's not usually something that happens overnight. Instead, it's more often than not the slow buildup of many small acts of non-love.

Hiding parts of Self

AN ACCESS TO PSYCHOLOGICAL SHACKLES

MANY PEOPLE LEARN the following lesson through experience. It's much better to learn this following lesson from the mistakes of others. The lesson is *the importance of being successful and producing results while being yourself*. Taking on that commitment for your life will make life more enjoyable or will just enforce what you're already doing.

However, a more powerful psychological incentive than just choosing to be committed to this vision is to look for the pain that it would cause you if you didn't take this on. Avoiding pain is a greater psychological motivator for human beings than seeking out pleasure or reward. So how do we make it more painful to *not* stray from the path?

Observe the jail people get into when they go on for years *not* doing that and get present to how hard it would be for them to let go at that point in life.

Make it such a big fear in your life to simply be doing life while hiding yourself *thinking one day once I "get there," I can be me*. Think about the jail that would put you in. Furthermore, think about the ever-strengthening psychological chains this creates on behavior as time goes on and on and on.

"Chains of habit are too light to be felt until they are too heavy to be broken."

— WARREN BUFFETT

It's *much* harder psychologically to unwind and let go and let things fall to the ground and crumble into pieces as opposed to never allowing yourself to be in that position in the first place. Essentially, as strong-willed as you may think you are, do whatever you can like your life depends on it to never allow yourself to be psychologically shackled in the first place. So next time when you see someone who is going through life hiding parts of themselves, have some compassion. Just remember—they may have a lot to lose—and more to lose than you could possibly ever know by letting go—and that's very difficult for most people.

If you want to make an impact with those people, here are some things you can do to move the needle:

1. Keep bringing compassion to those people and being where they're at.
2. Surround them and connect them with people who are already showing that example.
3. Have them be around you and have them see where you're being you and that your environment reacts to it in a way that has you be acknowledged positively and gives you positive social proof. Over time this increases the probability it is safer for someone else to do the same.
4. Never try to change them. The more awareness others get to where they're being inauthentic, the more they will get present to the impact. The idea is to have them discover how painful this is to keep living like this and how much it is getting in the way of what they're truly committed to in life. Only they can discover that for themselves. Just knowing intellectually is not enough.

Integrity issues

PEOPLE WHO LACK integrity don't have integrity issues.

The only people with integrity issues are those who take an interest in their own integrity. People who don't take an interest in their integrity which is 100% derived from them not getting the impact of them not honoring their word actually don't have integrity issues in the areas of life where someone else who gets that impact would.

Integrity is not about keeping your word but about honoring your word. If you're up to huge things in life, you will not always be able to keep your word. However, you can always honor your word. The moment you are not able to keep your word, let the other person know about it and get the impact of it. Then, make any new commitments going forward.

Caveat Emptor: Knowing you may not always be able to keep your word is not an excuse to look for a way out. If you do this, the power of this principle is lost.

It's when you truly can't keep your word, not when it isn't reasonable to keep your word. In fact, getting this inevitably leads to being much more unreasonable with the actions you take in life compared to most people. The mindset I use for myself around keeping my word is to pretend like world peace is on the line or that if I don't keep my agreement my mother will get shot. Psychologically, avoiding pain is more motivating than achieving pleasure. However, visualize what works for you if visualizing some horrible consequence works for you in order to help you come up with ways to be unreasonable to keep your agreements either to yourself or to others. Nobody HAS integrity like it's some trait either. Someone who goes around trying to tell people all the integrity they have is most likely coming from a moral space or a space of looking good. Integrity has nothing to do with morality and making integrity about morality takes away all the power from integrity in the first place. The morality conversation around integrity is purely cultural and not related to the impact of integrity in any way.

Integrity has four impacts:

Impact 1. It creates an environment of elevated performance. When integrity is lacking in the space, it's like trying to play football with a huge giant hole in the middle of the field. It doesn't mean you won't be effective—it will just take more effort to produce the same result. You will have results in life in spite of your lack of integrity, not because of it. High performers who have shit integrity often get this confused. It's also exhausting because you have to keep giving extra effort to score a touch-down with a huge giant hole in the middle of the field. In reality, this shows up as control, manipulation, attachment, excuses, and pushing forcefully through life. The impact is more stress, less health, less alive-ness, and worse results in reality even if those results are already great.

Impact 2. It creates an impaired experience of being whole and complete.

Impact 3. It diminishes your level of being able to trust oneself.

Impact 4. It diminishes the power of your word.

Here is another distinction I'd like to make: *Integrity has nothing to do with morality*.

When integrity degrades into a morality conversation like it is good to have integrity—it loses its power and it degrades into some belief system or concept about integrity. Integrity can also lose its power when it degrades into a technique to look good, like, it looks good to have integrity so therefore I will show people how much integrity I have.

I'm going to use a very simple example and be extreme to make a point:

Scenario: You tell someone you will arrive at your meeting at 4 pm. You get into a car accident and can't make it.

Someone who doesn't get the impact of being out of integrity would do something like:

a. Not show up to the meeting

b. Maybe a few days later say something like: *"hey, I got into a car accident."*

Now nobody would even question this and this would be a very reasonable thing to happen in the case of the accident.

Someone who gets the impact of being out of integrity and interested in getting their own power back would restore it as quickly as possible:

An example of a dialogue related to this is as follows:

Person A: "Hey, I am calling you from the road. Waiting for the police to come. Got into an accident. I promised I would be at your meeting at 4 pm. I will not be there at 4. The impact of me not keeping my word is now what we have to talk about gets delayed, there is an impact on your schedule for the day, and things now get put off. Is there any other impact on you with me not being there?"

Person B: "When would you like to reschedule for?"

Person A: "I don't know when I can reschedule for, but I will get back to you with three times that work for me within 48 hours from now."

Over time, the difference between these two ways of operating in life is staggering. When people suffer, they are stuck in a lie.

In life, things happen. Person A says X. Person A does Y. Within an instant, our minds create meaning towards those actions. Our mind creates opinions. It creates opinions about those opinions. All of it is automatic in nature. Through all of that, the mind then starts creating conclusions and starts generating actions to take based on those conclusions. Again—completely automatic in nature and rooted in survival.

This collapsing of what happens vs. the interpretation of what happens is often blind to people due to it happening so quickly. To make it even harder to distinguish between what happens vs. the meaning around it—they reinforce each other and end up creating this feedback loop in the process.

Example: *Someone lies to you. You make it mean you can't trust people. Now you start looking for evidence of how you can't trust people. The more evidence you collect, the further your belief around trust gets reinforced. Do that for 30 years...*

and people now are untrustworthy...and the world can't be trusted...therefore you've made the conclusion in life to not share too much with others.

People have literally hundreds to thousands of these things going on at any given time. And they are completely blind to you. If you were aware of them they wouldn't run you When an interpretation is distinguished as just that—it INSTANTLY ceases to control you.

However, when these interpretations go undistinguished, it's insanely disempowering as we are trapped to the realities or personal truths and beliefs that these have over us. Our behavior and literally all the future actions we will ever take in our lives get dictated by these automatic survival mechanisms. All of this is going while we going around thinking we have free will vs. only being free within a limited box of possibility. The field of neuroscience has shown us that our actions are only limited to the way our reality occurs to us. Literally, 100% of the actions that you will ever take in your life will be correlated to your body sensations, mental attitudes, feelings, and thoughts.

For instance, if you were angry at your boss and decided to write your boss an angry reactive email but then at the last minute you decided against pressing send and slept on it instead you may say that your actions were not aligned with how the situation occurred for you as you felt angry at your boss but decided against it anyway. However, if you really looked at it, you'd be able to see what allowed you to take an action called "not sending an angry email to your boss out of reaction" was correlated to a thought called probably something like, "if I write this angry email out of reaction, it won't serve any purpose and could possibly damage the relationship with my boss. Instead, sleeping on it and then writing something more grounded and constructive as opposed to just being reactive in the moment would serve the situation better."

If you didn't have that thought in your awareness and if none of your bodily sensations, thoughts, feelings, or attitudes about the situation correlated to not sending the email, you would have sent the email. Therefore, learning principles that allow us to change the way reality occurs for us will always be more powerful than simply trying to alter behavior without shifting the experience of life in which those behaviors exist within. That in itself is a principle.

So back to interpretations.

We can try to do things different, better, more, and even meditate on something for hours but regardless of how smart we think we are, what new technique you learned in a self-help book and regardless of what new circumstances come our way—as long as these interpretations go undistinguished, you will just get a more/better/different version of what you've seen before, and the disempowering patterns will continue.

So, yes, truly being able to distinguish these interpretations (regardless of whether they accurately measure reality or not) set you free. When people get stuck in life and start suffering, it's *never* the circumstances but the interpretation around them. And that doesn't mean terrible things don't happen to people or people don't get victimized or deal with extreme poverty and hunger and no access to water.

This leads to getting you made all the shit up, gets you to be 100% responsible for them, and gets you to see this is not who you are stuck to as some kind of fixed way of being.

This then leads to opening up the domain of possibility. Not like positive thinking bullshit but truly new openings for thinking, being, and acting that weren't even available to you before. This is where the shifts and transformations happen. You literally expand what's possible for both you and your life *regardless* of where you're currently at from a homeless person on the street to a successful CEO who is generally happy with life and has a great relationship with the people around them.

Attracting powerful people

I VIEW all people as powerful. Coming from this space, I can also observe how people are diminishing their own power in life. The impact of this is that I will often get the opportunity to become a mirror for others. It's what I've been trained to do over many years and a huge part of what my life is about.

The vast majority of people enjoy this. And, there are some people who hate having people be a mirror for them and would rather be around people who are committed to their smallness which then, in turn, validates their identity. These are people who are literally committed to their own smallness and mediocrity. While the latter aren't people in my circles, I come across them when I venture out.

There's that saying, "Set the conditions and see who shows up to the party." My way of being and that kind of space I create wherever I go weeds people out who are clinging to their own bullshit. In addition, that way of being attracts people who are committed to their own greatness and love that they can grow in my space and me in theirs.

I'm in a position with lots of responsibility as I often see what's possible when other people are blind to it. It's what I've been trained to do and something that's a natural Self-expression for me and a gift that I have.

One of the byproducts of this space as people in my tribe tend to be empowered to then, in turn, be this way for others. The more possibility you see in an environment, the more grounded you can be in environments that don't see possibility and are more grounded in survival.

The impact of being this way in the world is as follows:

Impact 1. The people in your life become more powerful which then impacts you directly. A football quarterback with an amazing offense will inherently be a better quarterback than one with a terrible offense. It is in your own personal interest to have people see their own power around you.

Impact 2. The people in your life who are not committed to their own power and more committed to their own righteousness about their own mediocrity and their own identity will leave your life. Yes, they will almost always leave. Your way of being will be too much of a threat.

Impact 3. The new people you will attract will add to your community even more so than the current people in your life who start to see their own power.

Holding grudges and resentments

HOLDING GRUDGES, resentments, or listening and speaking to people for anything other than their greatness comes from a place of fear. It creates separation and creates a feeling of emptiness, tightness, and the experience of not being whole and complete. It's the easy way out to look "out there." However, getting complete has only to do with us. Giving up some judgment, giving up some grudge or resentment, giving up trying to change/fix someone or something and choosing to accept the things and people around you just the way they are and the way they're not. That creates the space to give your all. That creates the space to share your gifts with others. That creates the space to contribute without any heaviness or weirdness in the space. I can't explain it but you'll know it when you experience it.

Being ourselves the minute we meet someone

IN THE PAST TEN YEARS, I have not once had to "not be myself" in a relationship and use some weird little creepy trick or tactic to keep things alive. It's much easier this way. What people don't get is that many of these relationship "tricks" only work because they just end up attracting others who are also committed to engaging in that kind of dynamic. So you think it worked, but really all it did was attract someone who was into that. Not sustainable, and cuts corners. If your goal is to be loved unconditionally, you should be extremely interested in being your-self the minute you meet someone. It's an amazing way of being for self-selection. You don't have to find the people meant for you, they will find you. Yes, you will turn off a lot of people. However, if you're attempting to lure someone through being something you're not, then sure, you can do that. However, then you'll be trapped in an inauthentic way of being and breaking free from it will that be much psychologically more diffi-cult later on. Don't be attached to any relationship. Just be clear what you're committed to, who you're committed to being, and what you're committed to as the vision for your relationship dynamics and ONLY play that game.

Fearful people

FEARFUL PEOPLE ATTRACT other fearful people. Then, they complain they have a scarcity of great people in their life. Want to know what someone's character is like?

1. Observe who their friends are.
2. Observe the kind of people they're in a relationship with: romantically and platonically.
3. Observe the people they choose to avoid.
4. Observe their consistent complaints in life.
5. Observe how often they blame others for their own external experiences.
6. Observe how often they don't keep their word and make excuses.

No single observation is "the truth." However, the more of these observations you make, the more you can see very clear patterns. This has avoided me plenty of trouble over the years. Not listening to this has caused me lots of trouble over the years.

When acceptance degrades into an inauthentic front

WE ALL KNOW people who say things like "Yeah I'm an [insert 'disempowering/negative' trait here] but you need to deal with it, and I won't date anyone who won't just deal with me and accept me for who I am" (and they'll say it in a defensive tone, of course!).

It plays into the common phrase of "If you can't accept me at my worst, then you don't deserve me at my best" which is now common to see on the profiles of online dating profiles.

But here's the thing—It's not acceptable to be selfish, manipulative, to lash out at others and not take responsibility, and to simply be out of control and not take responsibility for your emotions. It's not acceptable to find anything you don't like offensive and lash out either.

It's on us to take responsibility for when we are jerks and not to tell people to just *deal with it* or *handle it*. For people to think that others should be grateful for giving them the opportunity to be shat on is, quite frankly, disgusting.

Integrity & successful force

INTEGRITY GIVES you access to higher levels of performance and results in life. There's a reason that when integrity is restored in businesses, relationships improve and profitability, on average, skyrockets. There's a reason that family members who weren't speaking to each other, often forge relationships and experience deep profound love (sometimes for the very first time).

The moment integrity becomes a morality conversation (regardless of your moral view on being someone who is a man or woman of their word), it loses its power like so many principles that lose their power when they degrade into a belief or dogma. Those who take no interest in consistently restoring their integrity will find themselves constantly having to dominate, control, persuade, convince, and will never really feel free. When you get used to this kind of living condition, it becomes the norm, and often you don't even notice it.

On the contrary, when you're constantly focusing on where you can restore integrity (it's a daily practice for me)—it's not what you can control or dominate but where you can start giving things up. I always say that people who have become successful through dominating or controlling others have really psychologically burdened themselves as they now associate pleasure and positive outcomes with control, force, and behavior that lacks integrity.

The blind spot is not seeing they have produced those outcomes in spite of that, not because of it. Imagine an All-Star quarterback winning many games on a football field with a huge hole in it not realizing that if the hole was restored, that quarterback would have thrown even more touchdowns. Integrity is one of the most powerful principles I have ever learned in my whole life. It's right up there with the *cultural map*, the *flow model*, and the *triad*.

Hiding yourself

AN ACCESS TO DESTROYING YOUR LIFE

SO MANY PEOPLE walk around completely dead in life and dead in their "relationships."

People literally destroy what's possible for themselves and their lives by hiding themselves.

Two common examples:

Example 1. Being run by fear and being too scared to say too much or say the wrong thing.

Example 2. Not sharing what some person means to us out of a fear of not having those feelings reciprocated or coming off the wrong way or being judged.

I'm sure many of you have heard something like, "I hope you don't think I'm crazy for sharing this with you..." or "My problem is that I care too much."

There are so many bullshit disempowering phrases that have crept their way into our culture and were created by resigned and cynical people of prior generations. I think it's actually crazy not to share and just get by in life and our relationships while having parts of us feel a little bit dead. Sharing with someone how much you care or who someone is for you is not crazy, and if they think that's crazy, then that speaks to the kinds of relationships that they are committed to creating in their life. Tell someone how much they inspire you. Share with someone how much you value or respect something about them. Tell your mom or dad what an amazing parent they are in front of others.

Choose to be open, even amidst the experience of feeling hurt or sadness. By choosing this way of being you never allow yourself to be hardened by others. To love and give and share your gifts with the world takes truly honoring yourself, and that takes courage, especially in a world that doesn't always value that. When we hold back, we destroy our lives. We destroy the opportunity to live a life of purpose and truly live out who we were born to be. We as human beings are not meant to hide ourselves and be numb. That's not being human. That's hiding our humanity and being dead. Being alive without really living.

Skepticism of authentic intentions

THE PEOPLE that are most skeptical of your generosity are people that are typically takers in life or think they need to deserve someone's generosity or love. It's no different than people who contextualize you giving them an authentic compliment as manipulative flattery.

It says more about them than anything. Don't ever let people like that make you small.

Disempowering conversations
around love

WHEN PEOPLE SAY things like "love hurts," "love is painful," or "love is dangerous," it's always based off something in their past. Love is one of the most incredible, healing, and soul-nourishing forces on the planet. Yes, people being cruel can be sad. People who you love doing awful things towards you can be sad and feel downright painful sometimes. But what's sad is to justify those things that happened to you in the past as a way to justify some disempowering story about love. To me, that's really fucking sad. To withhold love, to be disempowered around love all because of something in the past only gives people in your past power over you. It only creates blocks within yourself leaving you with less power, freedom, Self-expression, peace of mind, vitality, purpose, and aliveness in life. That, in turn, makes you stingier with others making the world darker a place. Not using your gifts to your highest possible good.

Now all of that is sad to me. All of that has an impact on both you and the people around you. And to use all that disempowering behavior and blaming it on love is just simply absurd.

The source of control freaks

THE SOURCE of being a control freak stems from a lack of integrity. When you're honest with others and just as importantly with yourself, there's nothing to control. You can simply take empowered action from a natural and authentic Self-expression, give your all, and let things go where they go. This leads to greater results in life than trying to get results with control.

The game of control is a trap much like a Chinese Finger Trap. With a Chinese Finger Trap, the harder you pull, the harder you need to pull to get out. The trap becomes ever tightening with the more force you exert. When you let go, you're free.

When you give up control, you actually end up having a lot more control over your own life. The need to exert control always stems from a context that without you exerting control you would have very little control. That's a very weak position to live life from. However, to be a liar whether it's huge lies or small broken agreements that build up over time will *always* have you going back to controlling and manipulating in some way. To get rid of control and manipulation you need to get to the source which is the lack of integrity which is creating the unworkability that you're trying to manage aka control and manipulate. Just look at a guy like Warren Buffett and how he runs Berkshire Hathaway.

That's the ultimate example of literally letting go of control.

However, if he had lied and manipulated his way to the top, he would not be in the position he's in today.

Control and manipulation never actually produce the result you want. It's never like—"okay *now* I can let go." No, it's the opposite. The more results you produce through manipulation and control, the more you have to control and manipulate.

3 KEY POINTS around control and manipulation:

1. **It always seems like you're fooling everyone.** Usually, everyone already knows.
2. **You end up exerting more energy and in turn produce fewer results.** The illusion is that you're producing results because of manipulation and control, not despite it. That's especially psychologically difficult for some people to get if their results are already good in life and it's become part of their formula for success.
3. **It always seems like it's just about to work.** There's a mindset that goes something like this: "with just a little more control for a little more time, then I'll really feel whole and complete and get what I want." However, life doesn't work like that. It's a game that never ends with the carrot right always dangling right in front of you. It's a game one is destined to lose.

The impact of withholding communication

WE LIVE in a culture that's highly disconnected to our higher Selves. Lying is a fundamental root cause of this. One access to lying is communication withholds. When people withhold communication, you become just that much more disconnected to your Self and thereby to the world around you.

That famous saying, "The truth will set you free" has more of an impact than many people know.

When people have a fear of saying "too much" or "the wrong thing" and then have all of these disempowering stories they create around that, they literally destroy their own aliveness and the amount of love in their life. It's truly fucking sad. Our culture tolerates this too, hence why when people do this it usually just goes unnoticed. This way of dishonoring the human spirit is considered "normal."

When people stop withholding communication vs. letting their fears of vulnerability, shame, or any other ways they make themselves wrong for wanting to say what they want to say, there are several impacts:

Impact 1. The easier and easier giving up withholding communication and allowing yourself to be vulnerable naturally becomes

Impact 2. The more you're connected to new experiences you may never have been present to before. For example—you naturally feel yourself being inspired or being moved by someone's heart. You'll be able to let your natural poet come out. Great poets and songwriters simply flow and are connected to something.

Impact 3. You'll be more productive, you'll physically feel better, you'll emotionally feel better, and you'll be present to whole new realms of aliveness and vitality.

Speaking for your parts vs. from your parts

ALL OF US as human beings have many "parts" to us. In each moment, the choice is whether we are choosing to speak *for those parts* or *from those parts*. Speaking *for your parts* allows you to live life *at cause (with the opposite of that being at the effect of something—being run by our internal state, our circumstances, or the the whims, desires, and emotional states of others)*, with intention, and from a very powerful place of Self where there's a natural intuitiveness to what you do. Speaking *from your parts* is based in the past, from reactions, personality, and all the other things that "shape" you and it ends up running you vs. you running it. That one simple choice ends up causing two entirely different futures for the lives of human beings.

Fear is a liar

Unless there's an actual threat, *fear* is a liar and rooted in survival which is a function of your mind making up stories which then you believe and let shape your experience. This is great for most of the history of mankind but doesn't work so great for us anymore as we aren't dealing with being chased by a lion anymore yet our brains/machinery have not changed much since.

One of the ways you can really make a difference in someone's life is by simply not tolerating nor listening to their lying aka acting from a place of fear.

Taking a stand for someone else and holding space for someone while not feeding into their lying and fear, while not guaranteed, has the possibility to make a huge and lasting difference in someone's life.

Becoming conscious

THE MORE CONSCIOUS YOU BECOME, the more you'll trigger and threaten those who need to control and who are running more on automatic. That's not a sign that you're doing anything wrong. In fact, when acting from deep intuition and triggering the people around you, it's an opportunity *not* to give something up but rather to move on and expand your reach and find people inspired by your light and onboard with your mission, who are not threatened by it. Those will be your true partners in life. The ones that will honor and cherish what you're up to. That's the space for collaboration and partnership. There's a huge amount of freedom in creating that kind of environment for yourself.

Slavery of the mind

IF YOU CLOSE yourself off to something without ever experiencing it, then you're not doing the choosing—your automatic judgments, assessments, reasons, and evaluations are. There is no freedom in that. You're merely a slave to the automatic machinery of the mind.

Just imagine for a second

"Imagine that the world had no middlemen, no publishers, no bosses, no HR folks, no one telling you what you couldn't do. If you lived in that world, what would you do? Go. Do that. In China, there's a factory that can make the same widgets your company makes—for a tenth of the price. Down the street, there's a restaurant busy stealing your menu and your wine list, but charging 20 percent less than you can charge.

The last travel agent has left the room. Magazine publishers gave up all their growth to bloggers. Wikipedia didn't have to grab the reins of authority from the Encyclopedia Britannica; contributors just showed up and did the work. Britannica staffers sat and watched. The intermediaries and agenda setters and investors are less important than they have ever been before.

Last year, sixty-seven Web startups in San Francisco and New York were funded for what it costs Silicon Valley to fund a third of that number. So, if money and access and organizational might aren't the foundation of the connected economy, what is? Initiative."

— SETH GODIN

Transform or die

PEOPLE WHO RESIST transformation are at an ever increasing competitive disadvantage in society.

People who don't operate in the world of possibility and have no capacity or willingness to will always work to kill off those who do. It's a survival mechanism, a threat to identity. People will kill people off to justify a point of view and be right about their point of view or worldview. The lower down the consciousness chain you go, the more people are asleep and blind to their own *machinery*, and the more likely they will despise and have negative opinions about the people out there at the forefront of the next generation of transformation and evolution of thought for the human race. Those who don't evolve will have at some point—I think not too far off in the future—a huge disadvantage in getting a job, getting seed capital for a business, or making friendships. The people attached to the old models of leadership and operating from fear-based modes of being human will either have the social pressure to evolve or get weeded out.

Being honest about where you're at

BE with where you're at. There is power in that. When you're not— underneath it all, even if you justify to yourself that you're whole and complete and blah blah blah (insert woo-woo transformational jargon here)—you will still not have the experience of being whole and complete. And, on top of that, people will often be left with you being fake in some way. I trust the fearful, insecure, asshole who owns their shit more than the confident person who pretends to know everything and tells everyone how they're basically Gandhi (but only the good shit about him). When you are being totally where you're at—it has power. You're totally honoring yourself just where you're at. And when you don't —you're just lying. Nobody likes a liar.

On being upset

WHEN YOU TALK about others as the source of your being upset, you're screwed!

An inauthenticity around time

IN JULY OF 2011, I distinguished an inauthenticity around my relationship to time. I realized how sometimes I'm always busy because I created a story that making myself available for people would lower my social value.

"Hurt-people" hurt people

THERE'S THAT SAYING, *"hurt-people hurt people."* I wouldn't use terminology like there's something *wrong* with them as I don't relate to people like that (I relate to people through an ontological lens around who they're *being*) and usually they're just acting out some unresolved crap from their past. I know this is politically incorrect to say but even people committing terrible atrocities on the planet were not born that way. They're simply in survival and just doing what they know to do. That doesn't make it right, workable, or justified. It's merely to get that it has *nothing* to do with you and is *not* personal at all.

There is so much freedom in simply getting that. Reacting to their reactions or trying to *fix them* or resist them only perpetuates the crap.

How to deal with flakes

I'VE BEEN ASKED enough times questions regarding *how to be effective with flaky people* that I deemed it worthy to write about.

Here are 4 pieces of coaching I give people on dealing with flakiness since we have *all* dealt with it from time to time. It's actually really simple.

1. Getting angry at someone for being a flake is about as asinine as getting angry at a rock for not talking to you. If someone has a weak relationship to their own integrity then why the fuck would you be shocked when they use bullshit excuses to go back on their word with you. If you get upset at that, then it's your own fucking ego, your own attachment to how someone *should* be, and it's the ultimate *make-wrong* and invalidation of where someone else is at. It's also just a huge waste of time and energy.

2. People don't change (unless they do). You using logic will just create resistance most of the time since people would rather justify their reasons than get logical. In fact, it's illogical to try to use your own logic to have that conversation. It doesn't work. That's now how human beings are wired.

3. The worst thing you can do is to start trying to figure out why they are flaking on you and attempt to have a logical conversation about it. This is the ultimate way for someone to keep justifying their reasons and to justify their behavior with you. Any urges you get to figure out why someone keeps being flakey with you should just be used as an opportunity to spend time with people who have a strong relationship to their own integrity and just let it be. When you let the situation be, you then have the space to share what doesn't work for you and the impact the actions have on your schedule. Stick to the facts and don't add any excess interpretation about it like: *"you were an asshole."* It's more powerful to say something like: *"hey you didn't show up, and it has an impact on how I plan my day. This doesn't work for me. I request if you need to cancel on me/are running late, that you do X, Y, Z."*

4. If you have some awesome plans with someone or a group of people and they flake—you can choose to let it ruin your day or evening, choose a way of being such as anger, resentment, make-wrong, or upset—or, you can create an amazing rest of your day or evening and call up other people, go do things you love, and take 100% responsibility for having an amazing time. Set the conditions and see who shows up to the party.

Don't take anything personally

AGREEMENT #2 from the book, "The Four Agreements" says: "Don't Take Anything Personally. Nothing others do is because of you. What others say and do is a projection of their own reality, their own dream. When you are immune to the opinions and actions of others, you won't be the victim of needless suffering."

In July 2016, I got angry at a friend of mine on the phone. What she said to me doesn't matter. However what mattered was that I started resisting what she said to me and that resisted her going back on her word with me. Even though I didn't outright express it, she could pick it up my being upset with her.

[Side note: human beings can pick up on your way of being regardless of what you're saying. Just notice how many fake politicians there are who are saying all the right things and using all the right body language and then people who have a very authentic way of being are not saying all the right things but you feel comfortable and trusting around them. That's the difference.]

Our phone call ended with her hanging up on me. The next day she called me to apologize for hanging up on me and going back on her word. She asked me if I was angry. I said I was and I gave up resisting what she had said to me. I wasn't just saying it to be nice, I meant it. I had done the work. I also then explained to her the second agreement that me being angry at her wasn't personal, but it was me resisting some-

240

thing she was saying and breaking her agreement with me and having anger show up for me.

Then, I explained to her that how people react to her has nothing to do with her, both the angry reactions and the positive reactions. With that being said, the pitfall is not be responsible for how you occur for others. I know this can almost come across as contradictory. Yes, if you say something and it lands with someone else in a way you didn't intend it to, then you can apologize for how it landed, say it wasn't your intention, and then share your intention.

If they still don't get it then they still don't get it. Yes, some people will have a commitment to not getting it or to invalidating you. It's not personal.

Some people will have a commitment to praising you no matter what. That's less common, but it happens.

Both are just as automatic and have nothing to do with you. The moment you start to undermine your own Self-expression in order to "get" someone to think a certain way about you and start making it all personal—well, then, you've already lost the game. It's never personal. Ever. Even when it is. Get it?

Disappearing vs. overcoming

WHEN YOU ATTEMPT to overcome something through yoga, meditation, psychology, positive thinking, or any other practice (nothing wrong with any of them and all can be quite useful), you're already screwed. When you disappear what you're overcoming, you're free.

That's just who I am

NEVER USE *"well that's just who I am"* as a way to avoid being responsible for your flaws.

ARE YOU A PERPETUALLY LATE PERSON?
   Cool, then stop it.

ARE YOU A FLAKE?
   Cool, then stop it.

DOES YOUR INTEGRITY SUCK?
   Cool, then go make phone calls to *every* single person you've broken your word with and restore your integrity so you can have your own power and freedom back.

ARE you putting negative disempowering judgments onto someone vs. dealing with reality about the facts?
   Cool, well much of that is a blind spot so if it's a blind spot than

nothing you can do. However if you become aware of it, then cut it out and stop it and go call that person and own that you've created a story about them and let them know you are giving that up and then share with them how you're choosing to listen to them going forward (or something like that...not a tactic or a trick just more of an intention of a place to come from).

The moment you find yourself avoiding responsibility for something by saying...."well that's just who I am" or "I'm just a _____" or I don't have time for that because I need to focus on X vs. I need to focus on X ....*and* I will create a structure to *also* create putting this into place (vs. a reaction to circumstances) Let that part go of your identity and choose something more empowering OR be responsible you're choosing that *way of being* and get responsible for the impact that has on others.

How to stop overanalyzing

YOU DON'T OVERANALYZE. You just have lots of thoughts. Who you are is that thing that notices those thoughts. It's not you. When you notice those thoughts, you're free of them, and then a space for true Self-expression arises vs. acting out some automatic piece of machinery called your mind. You have a mind, or your mind has you. It's a choice in each moment.

Getting rid of 100% of drama in your life

✥

YOU ARE 100% responsible for the amount of drama in your life. Have you observed that there are people that seem to not have any drama in their lives and then people who seem to be in a new soap opera every week? It's rather interesting, I think.

For people who are readily engaged in drama, it always seems like it has something to do with their circumstances. And yes, people can be in pretty tough circumstances such as say going through the middle of a divorce, a bad breakup, town politics, etc.

There isn't some *"how to"* around this because every situation is different. However, I am clear that whenever you experience dealing with drama in your life, it's something over there with you. It's in your control and to some people, that's not their experience. It's an experience of being powerless and being sucked in by their circumstances.

While you may not have 100% control over your circumstances, you have total control of how you react to them. Choosing to **be** dramatic about them is a choice. Choosing to engage in conversations that are argument-based is also your choice.

Here's an example of an interview I did with a reporter at a political event. The reporter was trying to suck me into a soap opera and let's just say my interview didn't last too long.

Reporter: Hey is it okay if I interview you?

Me: Sure, how's it going?

Reporter: So are you endorsing Donald Trump?

Me: Nope, I've already publicly endorsed Rand.

Reporter: Oh well what brings you here?

Me: Thought it would be fun.

Reporter: Really? That's it? You think it's fun?

Me: Yeah I enjoy going to these things.

Reporter: So what do you think of Trump?

Me: What about him?

Reporter: Why do you like Rand over Trump.

Me: He's more aligned with Constitutional principles than Trump is, and I'm aligned with a lot of what Trump has to say as well, just have more alignment with Rand.

Reporter: Ok well thanks for your time.

Me: Sure.

Clearly, this ended up being a totally mindless and pointless interview —and no surprise, that interview never made the paper.

"All the drama in our lives that we experience as created by others is always created by ourselves. Without exception. Even if that statement is not true, which it is, it is the only way in which to view life where one can never be a victim and always be a part of creating what works."

— EMANUELE ANCORINI

Gossiping & dramatic conversations

IF YOU FIND yourself gossiping and engaging in a dramatic conversation with your friends, then that's a cue you need to talk to the person you're having an issue with and get that worked out. If you can't get it worked out with them, then disengage.

The moment you catch yourself engaging in drama with someone else. You can encourage them to talk to the person about it, or you can simply let them know you get it and not start engaging back to feed their soap opera.

Drama is an addiction. There's some kind of payoff whether you get to justify something or be right about something. The costs are that it sucks your aliveness right down the drain.

Leading from your current position

If you think serving others and adding value to others is about a title or position you're a doo-doo head. It's always possible to *lead from your current position.*

I was once on a road trip and while at a Casey's General Store in the Midwest I saw the manager was having some issues and coached her and her employees through it within just a few minutes and then gave them my information if they ever wanted additional support.

I was once was at someone's house and a little girl was crying. She was four at the time. I coached her on being powerful in the face of some of her emotional reactions she was having related to a little boy having had just teased her. She literally stopped crying immediately.

Now these are my gifts and everyone has their own gifts. You don't have to wait to use them. If you focus on sharing and adding value regardless of where you are—you'll naturally over time increase your chances of having higher and higher titles and reputation in the world vs. taking a bunch of actions in order to get to some kind of title or position.

Literally everywhere you go you can use your gifts to make a difference and serve others whatever they may be. I've been blessed with the gift of being able to cause massive results for people in very short periods of time. There are people that have trained for decades longer than me who are not nearly as effective as me. And I've played baseball for many more years than people who are better than me after just 6 months. Everyone has different gifts. Find them. Then use them to serve. I believe that's why we are here on this earth to use our gifts to serve and offer something to the world. When we hold them in out of fear of looking bad we deprive both ourselves and humanity as a whole.

Dealing with bullshit

IF YOU'RE DEALING with someone who is "being fake" and clearly has a lot of shit going on in the background—you cannot control that.

However, you can control who you're being in the face of that. The more you give into people's bullshit and start speaking into that frame, then you are 100% responsible for perpetuating that.

It's never out there.

When you stop giving into that kind of disempowering energy draining behavior that makes no difference—what shows up is breathing room and *space*.

A space to create.

A space to authentically express yourself where connection, aliveness, and just a natural vitality naturally show up.

When you stop giving energy to all that crap and just *give it space* instead of *trying to fix it,* or resist it, or pretend it doesn't exist and avoid it (which is another form of resistance)—the impact is that you get to keep your power, you get to create an empowering frame for the conversation and for someone else to rise into—you literally give others the opportunity to rise into their own greatness—and they may or may not take you up on that. Sometimes, if you don't perpetuate someone else's identity, they'll just stop putting energy towards you and seek people who *will* give into their identity and their interpretations about reality. Either way, you keep your power and your peace,

Expanding on Allen Brouwer's list

ON MARCH 17, 2016—Allen Brouwer who is a co-founder of Best Self Co. published a list of 11 Things Productive People Do Differently. This was something that I could very much relate to so I decided to write out all 11 points he shares and then my own personal experience around each one of the 11 points hoping to go a bit more in-depth and provide as much value as possible sharing from my own life.

1. **"The One Touch Rule."** This is the principle of doing what's in front of you vs. putting it off for later. This has made a huge impact on my life. Allen says you can "Act, delegate, or delete." As someone who is always connecting people, I used to tell people that I would make a connection and then put it off. Now, when I say that I will do it right away as long as I have everyone's consent. One little networking hack I invented for myself was for people who I am making connections to quite frequently, I have quite a few people who I have gotten their agreement to be an automatic yes to anyone I put them in touch with knowing that for the most part I have a pretty good track record of making fruitful connections. Occasionally I fuck it up but not usually. This saves me a lot of time of having to constantly ask "Hey can I connect you to this person?" I just do it. If I don't have the other parties

consent the solution is that my instant action is to email them first or text them.

2. **"Worst Goes First."** Get the least desirable tasks out of the way first. Pretty self-explanatory. Every night before I go to bed, I make a list of a few key action items that will move the needle during the day. Having mundane tasks hanging in the background can often get in the way and that includes mentally.

3. **"Don't Let Email Take Control."** I personally check my email twice a day. Once in the afternoon when I am awake. I usually sleep in so it's not usually morning. And then I check email in the evening as well. I also make a habit that for longer texts or emails, I make sure to do this by a computer. This may not be a good tip for everyone but it works for me psychologically. For whatever reason, being grounded on a laptop helps me write more clear and focused messages than something quick by text. But I have no data to show this works for everyone, so experiment and see what works for you. There's also a great tool that I know works for a lot of people called "Inbox Pause." Personally, this was just an extra step for me but I could imagine for some people this tool will actually make things more efficient. In fact, I know people who use it and swear by it.

4. **"Stay on Target and on Schedule."** Every meeting or conference call, I come with an agenda and stick to it. This helps all of us stay focused. Especially since most of the people I work with are also my friends, it's very easy for me to get into some long 2-hour conversation when we could have accomplished everything we needed in 15 minutes.

5. **"Don't Let Little Fires Burn Momentum."** There are always little things that come up throughout the day that can easily distract you from the task at hand. Also, sometimes friends and loved ones will call with what they *swear* are emergencies. When you start to make habit of actually stopping what you're doing for others on a whim, you're literally training other people to view your time as not valuable and that you can

make time for others at a moments notice. This does *not* benefit you and actually doesn't help the people around you either. The impact is that you have less time for the things that matter, your productivity goes down, and you actually are less effective at your capacity to give and add value to people around you. So the next time someone or something *demands* your attention, just be mindful that it can wait. The one place where this gets tough is if you have an environment that you've trained to be dependent on this. In that case, just create new expectations. People who respect you will honor those boundaries. If they don't—then you may want to re-consider your relationship with them.

6. **"Just say NO (like drugs)."** If you don't have time for a new project, then be upfront with you not willing to carve out the time right now. Don't be flakey and loose about this. Be straightforward. Again, people who will respect you will respect that boundary. Also be responsible that it's safe for people to continue to make requests of you in the future as we live in a society where sometimes a no means it's less safe to ask you in the future. You don't ever want to create that kind of space.

7. **"Ultra-Focus, Not Multitasking."** According to research conducted by Stanford University, multitasking destroys productivity. It has a negative impact on:

1. Paying attention
2. Memory recall
3. Switching tasks efficiently

You'll always find those people who actually *"know"* they are good multi-taskers. Even when those people are tested, they show to perform worse on tasks than those who stay hyper-focused.

(If you're interested, you can find the study here: http://news.stanford.e-du/2009/08/24/multitask-research-study-082409)

8. **"Go Off Grid."** A strategy that works to stay focused on high priority items.

9. **"Delegate and Trust."** When you can find someone to do almost as well as you, delegate it out. Allen says 90% as well, I think you can go down as low as 70 or 80% depending on the importance of a task. There are great tools such as TaskRabbit and Fiver where you can get things done for you very cheaply. There are also online virtual assistants now too. A quick google search will find you most of the resources you need. Of course, people in your organization always work too.

10. **"Put Technology To Work."** Tech is a tool like anything else. The research is pretty clear how horrible texting is for actual conversations, yet people still use it in their lives to replace communications that would be much more efficient face to face or on a phone call. Make sure the tools you are using are forwarding productivity and not getting in the way. Literally downloading a bunch of apps that just add extra steps to your workflow can become an addiction or trendy. Focus on what works.

11. **"Prepare For Tomorrow Today."** Every night I plan out action items for the next day. I focus first on a few high priority actions that if completed would *really* move the needle. These are what I call *vital* actions. To get the impact of how important this is. When the *Tribal Leadership* work is delivered at organizations, average performance increases on average by a factor of 3-5x. This takes places usually within the first 24 months. After everyone goes through the initial leadership training and given tools and models for performance, the trainer will check-in twice a quarter for a half-day training. During the first check-in, almost nobody will have been taking *vital* actions and mostly doing *somewhat important* actions to *mundane going through the motion* tasks. So when I say focus on *vital* actions—for most people, there's *very* little muscle on this and something you need to pay extra attention to. Using the *strategy model* that's outlined in the book, *Tribal Leadership*, the the performance tool I use to keep me in action. I have found it to be an excellent tool to help build habitual muscle for staying grounded with *vital* tasks.

The professional athlete dilemma

OCCASIONALLY I GET ASKED for coaching around how to speak to people more effectively where they're at. Usually (basically almost always) these are from high performing and highly emotionally conscious people who struggle with sometimes speaking at a place above where another is at and they experience not being heard and being effective.

There is certainly an art form of speaking to where people are at and nudging them forward. However—I will say this: When it comes to the people you spend the most time around and the people you partner in life with—consider this: If you are the owner of a professional sports team and you're drafting players for that team—you don't pick amateurs and coach them where they're at. You pick professionals and get them coached at a professional level. Yes, it's important to be able to speak to where people are at and nudge them forward, and you also get what you tolerate.

Being busy

BEING *busy* is a disgusting disease that's crept into our society. I don't have any clue the source even though I could speculate. However, I am clear that *being busy* is more of a mindset than anything.

You can observe a high-level executive or someone with *lots* of responsibility, who loves what they do, and is somehow able to carve out time for things that matter.

You can then compare that with someone who works just as many hours or fewer hours, isn't working on something that they're experiencing creating value for others at the highest level of their Self-expression, and they are *always* busy, and *no matter the circumstances* they never seem to have time. And they aren't empowered around it too. They're actually disempowered around their relationship to time, and it shows up as a complaint (like I never have enough time) and something that is an energy drain.

It's not the circumstances. It's a mindset which leads to an outward expression of circumstances. Put simply—being busy as a way of being is a form of lazy fucking thinking.

There's a model I teach called *The Strategy Model* which is outlined in the book, "Tribal Leadership" and a model that John King brought up at the beginning of *this* book.

What's interesting is that this model has a success rate of 80% at produce the result vs. roughly a 30% success rate for leading strategy models taught at business schools.

Now one of the interesting things is that the model gets people present to taking *vital* actions. That means actions that will move the needle. Take a look at how when very significant things have been altered in your life, how the actions you took were often large, rapid, and insanely effective at producing the result needed to fulfill on the circumstances around you changing very rapidly.

People who are *busy* in the disempowered sense tend to spend the majority of their time taking actions that aren't *vital* but merely *important* or *useful.* However, most of the time, the actions they are taking are actions that don't move the needle very much and are akin to treading water and keeping the status quo.

To get how non-circumstantial *busyness* is—take a look at someone constantly doesn't take action around something because they have a reason called: "it's not the right time." Then, when the circumstances change and their excuse is no longer valid, now there's something new that shows up which keeps *not the right time* in existence or they create a whole new disempowering constraint in the form of a reason or excuse of why they can't take action. What stays the same is their lack of action and an excuse justifying their lack of action. The illusion is that they have an excuse for their actions. The truth is that almost always their action comes first and then they have to justify why they are doing or not doing something.

Like I said before when going through Allen Brouwer's list of "11 things productive people do differently", what I can never get over and find totally amazing is that when you teach the *Strategy Model* to people, the coach is supposed to check up on the group after 6 weeks. Usually during the first 6 weeks in a class of 30 people, pretty much *nobody* has taken *vital* actions on their strategy. What this speaks to is how hardwired we are to *not* take *vital* actions in our lives, but to merely take actions based off of what we are used to in the past.

However, notice how productive you can be when you know a paper is due the next day and you *have* to finish it even if it doesn't turn out very good—and all of a sudden you pump out 8 pages in a night when you had been "thinking about it" and waiting for your fucking inspiration for a month.

Seth Godin calls it coming out of hibernation:

"Waking up a sleeping bear is difficult. People hibernate too. But it turns out that once activated, people do far more in a short time than you might expect. And so, the week before Christmas sees an insane amount of shopping. The weeks before a big election see a significant amount of attention paid. The final days of a Kickstarter lead people to action. If you wait until a marketer tells you it's time to get out of your comfort zone, you've just handed over your freedom and agency to someone who might not care about the things you care about. Far more powerful to develop the power to get out of our hibernation, on our own timetable, on a regular basis. It's no one's day but yours."

So I can't *force* you to take *vital* actions and most people reading this still won't change their habits without someone keeping them accountable. However, if you want to be in that small minority of people who *will* shift something—start making a list of just two or three *vital* actions that will move the needle. Then *be unreasonable* like peace in the Middle East is dependent on your actions and start taking *massive vital actions* that truly move the needle. Furthermore, I would *highly* recommend you do this with two other partners and touch base at least once a week. These should be people you're already friends with, who share similar values to you, and who care about personal development. From there, take on that you are responsible for the success of the other two people in your group and have your two partners make the same agreement. If you recall from my interview with John King, this is the foundation of a *triad,* and you will find building strategies and accountability systems will always be more effective within a working *triad.*

When it comes to taking *vital* actions—one of the first obvious things you will notice is how even though you have the same amount of time in the day you will be *much* more efficient with your time and you'll also most likely experience the expansion of your energetic bandwidth. You'll be able to handle more on your plate and take it on with less energy. You'll also most likely experience being in a *flow state* on a much more consistent basis.

People who claim to be triggered

WHEN YOU ACCUSE people of triggering you from a place of blame or fault—what you're really saying is that you are unwilling to take responsibility for your own internal experiences and self-project your own internal experiences onto others. You simply are committed to blaming others for your own internal state. You invalidate others while not taking responsibility for being a victim to your own internal state.

The re-activist

THERE'S a lot of people doing work to forward humanity on the planet (whether it be through the lens of politics, justice, wars, hunger, violence, etc.) yet their work evolves from a reaction to something. It's *not* a Self-expression. I call these people *re-activists*. They're just in *reaction to something* vs. *creating something that forwards something*.

They're in a state of *survival* and *resistance*. One of the functions of the principle of resistance is that whatever you resist, persists. If you're not free to be, free to act without the constraints from the past—there will always be limits to whatever you're committed to creating in the world.

Causing breakthrough results and creating new futures not based off the past are often missing from these conversations and interactions which is kind of ridiculous since the greatest shifts in humanity have almost always come from approaching activism in the way. There are those kinds of people who really alter something for the world vs. just react to something based in the past. The game I'm interested in is the former. If you are someone out to make a lasting shift in the world, then that's the game you should be spending your energy on.

Acting from possibility vs. survival

THE MORE YOU act from possibility, the more people will feel threatened by you. Fear is one of the most powerful forces as people run by fear often don't even have the awareness that they are being run by such an automatic part of themselves rooted in survival.

Often they will fight to the death with their reasons and excuses and kill off everything in the process simply to keep their justifications alive.

On the contrary, the more you act from a place of possibility, the more great partners will show up into your life, and fearful people will naturally find a way to get weeded out. The more you react and resist people's reactions, the more you perpetuate it and diminish yourself in the process.

It's a spiral that can go upwards in possibility and downwards in survival.

The more time goes on, the more you'll build community around you from these spaces.

To be in survival for decades and then start creating and essentially transcending all the automatic reactions—much of your environment will not be very happy with you and try to shove you back into your old box. This can be psychologically difficult to break free of.

Not because they want to keep you small but because their minds are wired to have you conform to whatever pattern they know about you and when you start breaking it, the way their minds strive to "survive" the breaking of the pattern is to do what they can to put you back in the box. It's not hard to be compassionate when you get that's simply how they operate and it's not some personal attack on you and actually care enough about you to put energy into you even if those efforts aren't really serving you. All part of the game called being human.

You become what you resist
WHATEVER YOU RESIST, PERSISTS.

You become what you resist and *whatever you resist, persists.* These are not some bullshit sayings that sound all nice and positive. These are two beautiful principles. I think the Maharishi and Werner Erhard both share these principles eloquently and in different ways:

"If you retaliate, you lower yourself to the level of the wrong. Rather, let the wrong be just a drop in the ocean of your virtue. A common saying is, 'Do not resist evil.' If evil is resisted, first you must stoop to that level of evil, and, second, you are further responsible for the evil influence you are producing by retaliating."

— MAHARISHI MAHESH

"My notion about service is that service is actually that kind of relationship in which you have a commitment to the person. What I mean, in fact, is that for me what service is about is being committed to the other being. To who the other person is. To the degree that you are, in fact, committed to the other person, you are only as valuable as you can deal with the other person's stuff, their evidence, their manifestation, and that's what's service is about. Service is about knowing who the other person is and being able to tolerate giving space to their garbage. What most people do is to give space to people's quality and deal with their garbage. Actually, you should do it the other way around. Deal with who they are and give space to their garbage. Keep interacting with them as if they were God. And every time you get garbage from them, give space to garbage and go back and interact with them as if they were God."

— WERNER ERHARD

Who we're being in the face of our discomfort

WHILE WE CAN'T ALWAYS CONTROL our fears and our discomfort—what we can control is who we're *being* around our discomfort and our fears. That's where our freedom and our own expansion lies.

Being hooked

FIGHTING and resisting is a function of being hooked by a situation. When you do this, you've already lost the game. It's a form of *preemptive being messed with*. The moment you allow yourself to be hooked by anything,

1. *An individual*
2. *An organization*
3. *An idea*

—you've already allowed yourself to be messed with.

When someone is out to slander you or destroy your reputation—the best thing you can do is allow them to dominate, allow them to throw their crap at you and just be with it—allow things around you to fall. That doesn't mean do nothing. But there's a difference between action under the context of resistance and action under the context of creating something and standing for something.

"Supreme excellence consists in breaking the enemy's resistance without fighting."

Environments that call for making a difference

CREATING possibility and making a difference in the world is can sometimes feel like a lonely game. Make sure you surround yourself with powerhouses in life who get you, who are always there for you, who contribute to you, and who give you the space to contribute back. If you don't have to give space to your environment's justifications, defense mechanisms, and constant acting out, then that maximizes the time everyone is in creation mode and experiencing aliveness and not operating in survival.

Supportive environments

WHEN YOU START to see new possibilities in your life, you will naturally want an environment to support you taking actions around what you see. Having an environment that supports you creating new things possible for the world is key.

Sometimes, an environment that expanded your life to get you to where you are today is now the very environment that is getting in your way.

The illusion of safety

EVER SEEN a man or woman dating someone who was completely dull and you were like: "what the fuck! how could that person ever be interested in *him or her*!"

Or have you been that person who always wonders why you attract men or women into your life that tend just to be dull? Because I'm sure you know if you're someone really out there developing yourself that there are lots of people on this planet who are really deep, intelligent, and highly conscious human beings.

It almost always boils down to this illusion of safety and staying comfortable.

I have an ex-girlfriend who used to complain about all the terrible guys she would meet. She also used to tell me that I was the only guy that wouldn't give into her bullshit and how grateful she was for that.

As you can imagine, I didn't last long. Little did I know at the time, I didn't stand a chance to begin with! Shortly after, she got back together with an ex-boyfriend of hers who was verbally abusive. Several years later, she ended up later marrying a guy who was one of those "nice guys," a total pushover, and someone who would consistently give into her shit. He was someone who wasn't capable of going very deep in conversations and people who knew both of them knew she was capable of much more depth than the man she married.

While she was engaged, she would share with me how she wished deep down she could be with someone who got her the way I did and who she could share herself at the level she did with me.

Of course, for her to get what she truly wanted in her heart of hearts, she would have had to let go of the need to stay "safe" within her own comfort zones and start associating that level of comfort as being unsafe until psychologically that space of "comfort" was actually what left her uncomfortable. It's basically training yourself to feel pain and associate danger to that illusion of safety. She'd have to start getting uncomfortable with someone giving into her bullshit.

Now I'm sure we all know that guy or girl, or have been that guy or girl, so my story is nothing out of the ordinary, it's actually pretty typical.

David Deida sums it up best, and this principle around *trust in relationships* applies to both men and women,

---

"If you are with a man you don't trust, it is only because you prefer un-surrendered love to surrendering wide open in total trust. It feels safe. You are afraid to let go of control–part of you doesn't trust love's command–so you have chosen a man who doesn't demand your surrender with his depth of integrity. If you did trust the command of love, you would only settle for a deep man capable of opening you more deeply than you could instruct him."

And

"Few men are capable of entering a woman's heart and opening her body, but few women are capable of offering their heart and body to be claimed open in this way. Fear is the feeling of refusal. Fear is the feeling of mistrust. Fear is the heart's contraction that withdraws openness behind walls of protection. Fear is the act of unloved, the negation of love, the refusal to open and offer love's openness as your gift. Anything less than a life of total loving is fear. Fear—the refusal to open as love—is the only reason your relationships are less than blissful. Fear forms shells around your heart and closes your body so that love cannot move deeply into you, claiming you, opening you, allowing you to trust deeper than your sense of self. If you trusted and received more deeply, you would naturally surrender open, alive as the most powerful force in the world: the devotional offering of love..."

And

"Beneath all your shells, your deep heart is always full of love's light. So, at heart, showing open as light and flowing open as love's offering is the most ecstatic and true way to live. Yet, you are confused because your shells can be so strong. You can come to believe the lies of your shells, and therefore, you can live an entire life betraying your deepest desire: to be recognized as light, adored and worshipped as love's radiance, offering yourself as a gift of love to be claimed by true divine masculine integrity, ravished open by love's deepest claim of your heart. These shells block your emotional currents, so you feel stuck, sometimes numb, sometimes enraged, sometimes hysterical, but not very often does your deepest ocean of love-light spontaneously emerge as free, unobstructed waves of heart-open emotional flow."

And for women:

"As a young woman, you may have dreamt of masculine saviors: horses, pop stars, white knights—any animal or human, real or imaginary, that could take you somewhere new, beauty, your true light, your boundless ocean of love, and take you to the place you always wanted to be: surrendered open like the sky filled with moonlight, taken by your beloved into the bright domain of love's bliss. But at some point, you probably stopped trusting the yearning of your own feminine heart. You became suppressed in your desire to be seen and worshipped as love's light. You came to believe that guiding your life's direction is more important than trusting the fathomless love-wisdom that flows naturally from your deepest heart's radiance."

The mind is a dangerous place

DON'T GO THERE

ALWAYS TAKE a stand for yourself while keeping an open heart at the same time. The two complement each other. That combination is a source of natural courage and strength. Real power and real strength are always sourced through an open heart. It is accessed through allowing ourselves to be vulnerable, and through authentic action. Being led by our hearts, our intuition, and not our minds. Our minds are great when it comes to solving a problem, playing scrabble, doing research, or creating a strategy. However, the mind is a dangerous place when it comes to being a leader, making a difference, and creating powerful friendships, partnerships, and relationships. It will merely kill off our dreams and kill off possibility coming from a place of analyzing, justifying, and defending. The mind is automatically wired for survival. That is not fruitful for the foundation of leadership, partnership, and experiencing an authentic connection with others.

Your environment influences you
EMBRACE IT AND USE IT

WHEN YOU ARE CLEAR, people around you become clearer in your space. When you are unclear, others become more unclear in your space. You are a human being and you are powerful. Choose your friends wisely, as they are powerful too. If you want to complete your projects effectively and with velocity, spend time with those that perform at that same level. Certainly, minimize your time with lazy asses. If you want to be a great writer, spend time with those who have written extraordinary pieces of writing. Certainly, don't spend time with those who think pursuing a writing career is stupid. You get the idea.

Possible ways to create max value

1. Be courteous to others.
2. Be on time.
3. Listen when others are speaking.
4. *This is distinct from what the narrative in your head is saying about what the other person is saying. This gives you a means to be in another's space and really getting their world which is limited when you're consumed by your own internal state.*
5. Be supportive of others.
6. Integrity (without it, nothing works).
7. Be congruent.
8. Keep your agreements.
9. Be emotionally open.
10. Be honest.
11. Suspend judgment.
12. *This is distinct from not having judgmental thoughts. You will always have judgmental thoughts. What you have a say about is whether you have those judgmental thoughts or if those judgmental thoughts have you.*
13. Be accepting.
14. Give others eye contact.
15. Be here and now. Essentially, be present.

16. Change your perspective if it doesn't serve you and others.
17. Don't gossip.
18. Give 100% participation in everything you do.
19. Give a 100% commitment. ("100% commitment is a cinch, but 99.9% commitment is a bitch!").

"Working On It"

AS A WAY TO NOT TAKE RESPONSIBILITY

HAVE you ever met someone who has been working on their anxiety issues for 17 years or someone who is on their healing journey? Consider whatever we're "working on" is usually just a front for an unwillingness to be responsible for something.

The Healing Journey Is Bullshit

For a lot of my life, I thought there was something wrong with me. I was 7 years old and on the playground in school. A girl named Eva walked up to me and screamed "you have cooties!" Everyone around me laughed. My chest closed up, I emotionally shut down, and I felt completely disconnected in my own body. At that moment, I told myself there's something wrong with me, and then I spent many years collecting evidence to fit my case until it just became the way it was. However, the "I" was not really me but the little voice in my head that is constantly running in the background spewing automatic thoughts. Who I am is the one who notices the little voice. Those two I's — the one that is an expression of the Self and one that is the automatic machinery going on in the background that we have is often collapsed into the same thing. For the purpose of this article going forward: when I refer to "myself" I'm speaking of the Self or the one who notices the automatic survival machinery. When I refer to my "identity" I'm speaking to the automatic machinery, the roughly 60,000 thoughts I have per day.

The Personal Development Identity

I've been into personal development since I'm a teenager. I read all the famous self-help books, practiced meditation, knew all there was to know about gratitude and vulnerability and being in touch with how you feel, I did therapy, and was very into learning about Charlie Munger's mental models to help be rational in life. While I am passionate about personal development/the human potential movement today, my initial started with my identity pulling me into the world. Doing personal development was simply a means to fix myself under the made up belief I had for myself called "there's something wrong with me" which I had collected thousands of pieces of evidence for over many years. Over the years as I got better and better at "coping" with it, underneath it became worse and worse. Whatever we resist, persists and we become what we resist. At the neurological level, every time I was doing something in order to fix something being wrong with me, to fix some disempowering way of being, some disempowering story I had about a thought or emotion, I ended up creating more synapses for the very thing I was trying to overcome.

Experiencing Being Whole And Complete

Living life from this context left me with the experience of not being whole and complete, like there something always missing. My version of fixing this was "to get better" which was just a way to fix or in personal development jargon "heal" something from the past.

There's Something Wrong

"There's something wrong here, I need to fix it" became I need to heal myself, discover my disempowering patterns from my wounded inner child, be vulnerable, and practice gratitude, and whatever other technique based bullshit I did. All this led to my identity doing lots of work on itself to get better and now knowing lots of jargon, techniques, and practices to fix and heal myself.

Transformational Jargon

I still had massive anxiety, I still felt deep down like something was missing, and I still didn't feel completely vital and alive even though I had all the purpose-driven language. I even used the term "transformation" even though it was mostly my identity doing the driving of that wheel which just led to a more, better, different version of the past. There was still a heaviness to my life. However, I would justify where I was at and avoid responsibility by telling myself I was on a "healing journey" and that I would simply be able to be where I was at and that it would be a long process of "getting better."

It's All Meaningless And Made Up

When I saw that everything in my life was made up, when I saw that I was not my identity but had an identity, that I was not my personality, but had a personality, and that I wasn't even my body, but had a body— I was free. However, the moment my identity took on that I was free, it became the new trap, the new identity. That is the pitfall.

Disconnecting From The Machinery

However, in that moment of disconnecting from my machinery and fully connecting with my own self-expression, everything I had been "working on" for many years disappeared. I saw that it was all identity-based work. It was all about fixing, changing, and dealing with the past. When I got complete, my past stop impacting to me. There was this weight off my shoulder. There was no more healing journey. There was nothing to heal. The Self is already always perfect and whole.

Being Free From Anxiety And PTSD

After going through a traumatic experience, I went to a therapist just as a double-check on my own mental-health. The therapist says, "I don't understand how it's possible you don't have PTSD right now." I said, "because I'm not my identity." She didn't understand and I spent some time with her sharing with her what I discovered in this realm for myself and encouraged her to be able to take this on herself so she could make a difference with her clients/patients going forward.

Distinguishing Self

This distinguishing of Self is still missing in much our cultural conversations around personal development. In the realm of therapy, anxiety and depression is often still treated as an illness and something to fix or change despite many therapists with a mental health background reporting cure rates of nearly 80-90% within just a few days. In the realm of personal development in a non-therapeutic sense— "transformation" has now devolved into a buzzword where people look to heal themselves from their past and go on this journey. The psychological trap is that you will see results and that it is certainly more effective than repressing everything. However, it's just a more "woke" trap of fixing yourself than say giving yourself a lobotomy or putting yourself into a mental institution where you will be treated as you are sick and have something wrong with you which you could say is "not woke." However, they are two sides of the same coin. They are both about fixing, changing, and getting better from the past. They are both about figuring out why you are the way you are and practicing techniques such as vulnerability and gratitude or psychological re-framing. There's nothing wrong with any of that. It's simply not a very reliable access to transformation. Those who practice transformation as a place to "get to" miss the point. There is no healing journey. The healing journey is a journey of "always almost there." It's often intense and dramatic and chaotic. Transformation is access to the Self. Experiencing Self vs our beliefs about it. A focus on loving yourself, I can't love others until I love myself, positive thinking, working on it, coping, surviving — that's all in the realm of survival. That's all in the realm of fixing and changing. It's whipped cream on shit which is still shit. Eckhart Tolle gained access to this space through attempting to kill himself. Werner Erhard gained access to this randomly while driving over the Golden Gate Bridge. However, there are many people who spend a lifetime working on healing themselves, working on getting better.

Transformation Only Happens In An Instant

As Werner Erhard would say, "Transformation happens in an instant and it's never longer than an instant." It's not something to be explained, understood, interpreted, or gotten intellectually. Healing inherently is healing from the past. It's not completion. It's not transformation. It's another form of fixing, of technique, of more, better, different, than the past. It's still connected to the past.

Transformation Is A Threat To Self-Healers

The healing journey is a journey where you will die "already almost there" or "already almost healed."

This threatens people— especially those who have been "doing the work" for many years.

Human beings like to over complicate things, especially when some part of their own survival is at stake. If everyone got this, the need for therapy (in its current form) would plummet overnight. It's no different than if Warren Buffett taught every investing class in the country, many classes would only be a few weeks long and most of the modern portfolio theory would cease to be taught at all. A lot of professors have a lot of psychological skin in the game to keep the status-quo around.

The Enlightened Asshole

I'm writing this part of the book from California right now—which is the Mecca of "the enlightened asshole." The one's on their healing journey. "Doing the work" gets in the way of "getting complete."

You can spend decades "doing the work" and it only takes "an instant and never longer than an instant to be transformed."

Completion

The healing journey is a game of brokenness and of victimhood. It's a game of avoiding responsibility for all of it under the guise of already always almost there.

Fuck that shit.
    Get complete.

The transformation of human beings

AN EXPONENTIAL EXPANSION OF BEINGNESS

THE TRANSFORMATION of human beings tends to happen rather quickly, and, is exponentially driven. If you want to get really deep into that topic, I would highly recommend reading a book called "The Singularity is Near: When Humans Transcend Biology" by Ray Kurzweil who serves as the Director of Engineering at Google.

So back to the transformation of human beings happening rather quickly—

10,000 years ago the conversation of what it meant to be a human being went from nomadic to agrarian. Who you were was determined by society.

Then approximately 300 years ago, Self-determination became a possibility through it being invented in language—as before Self-determination it wasn't even considered as a thought let alone a way of being —and we had another transformation of what it meant to be a human being.

Now we are in a time where we are going from fixed body bags with personalities to becoming spaces for possibility. Where we simply create through language and not through fixing and changing what's already there. Trying to fix world issues without talking about human transformation is as asinine and moronic as talking about creating peace through war.

286

Being lit up by the little things

In 2011, I took a job delivering bake-your-own pizzas in Larchmont, NY which is a wealthy and relatively small town in Westchester, NY. I could easily make 100 dollars in a night for just a few hours of work. I would hang out at my parent's house waiting for the next delivery order to arrive. It was basically free money.

In February of that year, I was delivering pizza to a household and a little boy, probably around 4 or 5, handed me a tip when I delivered a pizza to his mom. He laughed after he gave me the money. That lit me up and was one of the highlights of my week that week and certainly of that night.

Have you ever noticed that 15-year-olds get lit up less by little things and are less present to the experience of aliveness than little kids? Have you noticed that 45-year-olds are even less connected to this experience on average?

We call it growing up. I call it growing walls, growing belief systems to protect us, and in the process, I call it creating more disconnection to the experience of being alive.

If you had asked me if I was open-minded, nonjudgmental, and a free spirit before I distinguished this for myself, I would have said absolutely. However, here's something interesting to consider. Notice how often children can't wait to wake up in the morning compared to the average adult. They're full of energy and can't wait just to be alive.

Furthermore, notice how many times *you* wake up, and *you* aren't really feeling it. If someone asked how you are doing, you might say, "I'm fine," if you were being authentic.

So what the fuck happened? How the hell do we as human beings (on average) go from being stoked to be alive and get out of bed to "being fine"?

First, what there is to notice are the areas of your life where you're *not* lit up. Now, it's very easy to start justifying to yourself the areas of life where you are. Congratulations, you win a prize!!!—*No, not really.* (in case you didn't detect what appears to be my obvious sarcasm)

But, no, seriously—that won't make a difference and will serve only to protect where you're already at. Yes, it's great to acknowledge where you're at, but don't use where you're at as a means to protect yourself and shield yourself from expanding from that place.

Remember, *there's nothing wrong* or *nothing to fix.* Just another level to expand your life.

So what the fuck happens from age 5 to age 55 to so many people at one varying degree or another?

Well, imagine you're a kid in class, and you raise your hand because you know you have the right answer. And then you say the wrong answer and everyone laughs. What did you tell yourself at that moment? Well hey!!!—Congrats, you just created a new filter or *context* (created in language) for you to live life through. This happened to me. I made it mean I needed to be smart and be liked. And believe it or not, those things are really important to my *automatic machinery* or *identity*, and if I'm not conscious of it and not present, I'll start proving how smart I am or start needing to convince someone to like me which undermines what I'm committed to in a certain situation. We all have our own version of this! In fact, we all have *many* versions of this. *"Knowing you don't"* is a way to bullshit yourself and for your *identity* to protect itself from being killed off.

Now what I shared above was just *one* filter which shaped a context for my entire life. By the time we are teenagers, every human being living on this planet has already created thousands of filters and contexts which shape our lives, thoughts, and actions, yet are completely hidden from our view. All of this gets in the way of experiencing life and being lit up by giving your all, truly being Self-expressed versus being run by our *automatic machinery, identity, ego,* or whatever jargon word you want to call it.

A big filter for me was created from a moment in my life when I was in Kindergarten. I was on the playground and this girl Eva, who was a friend of mine, in the middle of playing outdoors for recess, screamed, "YOU HAVE COOTIES, YOU'RE THE COOTIE BOY."

I let it get to me. I started feeling embarrassed, scared, sad, insecure about being me, and started having thoughts such as "there's something wrong with me," and that "people are mean." I developed an overarching contextual mental attitude or mindset that this was something I needed to overcome.

Fast forward to my senior year of high school, and I'm wearing sunglasses wherever I go, constantly feeling like I need to look good for people, and constantly feeling a need to avoid looking bad for people. I also spent years reading personal development books—but through an inauthentic place of *trying to fix myself* and getting people to like me better because I thought it was something I needed compensate for not being good enough or having something wrong with me in life. You can easily see that's an un-winnable game. And thank god I distinguished those things by the time I was 20; otherwise, I have no clue how I would have ended up, but I would have either been an egotistical jerk or someone who was sad all the time and truly thought he hated himself. I lived nearly 20 years of my life where a fucking kindergartener version of myself was running the show instead of my authentic Self-expression. The rule about *interpretations* and *stories* is that: once you distinguish the shit you made up about others, yourself, and the world, *it stops running you.* And it's not intellectual, it's a very real visceral sensation. Just knowing that doesn't make a difference. You have to do the work.

The first place to look is to start *noticing* where you're in a headspace ranging anywhere from *"just fine"* about something to *"really miserable."* You will be rewarded with what you discover.

When I distinguished this, one of the first unexpected things that happened to me was I started seeing trees on the street in a way I probably hadn't seen them since I was very little. You know the way a little kid gets excited by the dumbest shit? I was literally looking at fucking trees, trees I had seen many times before, but this time I was completely being moved to tears by how beautiful these trees were to me. I was literally experiencing the tree as opposed to just seeing the trees and having all my concepts, thoughts, and opinions about the trees in the way. I was seeing and experiencing the trees through the lens of my authentic expression vs. all the filters I had in front of me that I didn't even realize were there and didn't even know that I didn't realize were there. And because I didn't even know I didn't know they were there, there was nothing I could do about them.

I can't promise that you'll have that very exact experience. Your experience and what you discover will be unique to you. It's also not a one time deal. It's not like I saw a tree and cried and now I won or some stupid shit like that or now I get to claim I'm some fucking righteous enlightened being who can cry just by looking at a tree and do it as some way to prove to others or myself that I'm some wise guru. No. It's a game that's constantly worth playing if you're committed to aliveness and authenticity in life. It's a mountain with no top (until you die).

Simply you can just enjoy the journey and all the unexpected results that keep coming your way through this practice. And like anything I share—you have to do the work, it's not an intellectual concept getting that makes the impact. Most people already know this on some level.

You will never be able to follow your own deep intuition until you clear up the doubts in your mind.

Intuition vs. mental noise

THE MORE YOU follow your intuition, the stronger it becomes. The more you justify it away or get intellectual about it, the less connected to it you become. This isn't some technique or some trick. This is just another sense that we have that is too commonly not used, nor valued, in our society today.

Many people call their cognitive dissonance and lack of connection with their intuition to something akin to mental noise or some fear of acting irrational.

In the personal development world where it seems like the new fad is just to pretend you're a professional in neuroscience and quantum physics—it's very easy to call intuition just a brain generated phenomenon as a way to invalidate the power of it.

Should I not honor my eyesight because it's just my cones in my eyes interpreting information and sending that information to the brain and that we know what we experience seeing may not be a 100% accurate reflection of reality? Of course not, that would be stupid. It's not perfect. It simply helps us model the world, and it is useful.

So just like eyesight is something we have, intuition is also something we have, a natural knowingness about something in a situation. Yes, it's brain generated, and no it's not just mental noise. There is a signal in the noise that gets ever more powerful if you build that muscle in naturally learning to distinguish it intuitively. It's a very powerful sense in which the more you follow it, the stronger it gets. The more you ignore it, the weaker that signal becomes to the point where many people are clueless and lost when it comes to this topic because they've stopped following their deepest integrity/deepest heart for too long. To them, all of this will occur as woo-woo. And if it does for you or there's something you're resisting about this, that's an opportunity to take a look and get committed to discovering this for yourself. My tip to that is just the next time you have a gut feeling about something just start following it. It may be wrong too. In the beginning, it may not be very accurate or seem accurate if you justify something away. However, over time this gets much more finely tuned, and you'll follow that intuitive place of yours vs. what you may confuse for intuition which is all that past based machinery trying to make you survive. That runs you into trouble. So the fear about intuition often boils down to trying to avoid doing something irrational and stupid which is actually a pretty rational fear when intuition and past based machinery gets collapsed because it's very likely you will do something stupid.

What we have control over

WE CAN'T ALWAYS CONTROL our emotions, thoughts, feelings, or other aspects of our own internal machinery. However, we can always control who we're going to be in the face of them.

The domain we have control over is our ways of being and the words we choose to speak. Whether someone else can see us for how we want to be seen or really hear what we're sharing isn't something in our control.

What's in our control is the projects we create that have others come along for the ride and get the expression you're putting out into the world.

What's in our control is the communities we build around us and the partnerships we create. Set the conditions and see who shows up to the party. We have control of the conditions—not who shows up.

The need for control

WHEN SOMEONE FEELS the need to control in life, the default position is often to get better at controlling. That's beyond stupid. There are a few possible things that get in the way. And since life isn't always so black-and-white, this isn't *"the solution"* or *"the fix."*

Here are some frameworks to think from that can make a huge impact:

1. **"YOU AREN'T POWERFUL."** People who experience themselves as lacking power and living from that context will then need to control in order to BE powerful. Of course what it does is perpetuate your lack of power.

2. **"INTEGRITY."** That's a huge one. When integrity is missing in the space it's like playing on a football field with a huge hole in it. That doesn't mean you can't make touchdowns, it just becomes that much more difficult. And a great quarterback may still be winning games DESPITE the big hole. If you're sitting on a chair with 3 legs, you'll have to constantly work to balance yourself and control the chair. When the chair has integrity and has 4 legs, it is just there and now you have space

to focus on things other than surviving the chair. Restoring integrity in your life and honoring your word is an amazingly unbelievable access to the experience for the need to control to naturally disappear.

3. "CREATING STAGE 4." Often in an environment when you feel the need to control you'll often find yourself inside of a *Stage 2* or *Stage 3* environment. When you create *Stage 4* vs. trying to *fix* all the stuff and control all the stuff and *resist* all the stuff and *dominate* all the stuff at *Stage 2* and *Stage 3*—*where* you'll often just get more of the same. As the famous saying goes, "culture eats strategy for breakfast every day." The new strategy will almost always get destroyed by a culture that incentivizes that kind of controlling behavior. Having the proper *incentive structures* inside of a *Stage 4* culture are insanely impactful. However, if the culture isn't conducive to the incentive structures, they'll work no better than a strategy not conducive to the culture. A *Stage 4* strategy inside of a *Stage 2* culture just doesn't work.

4. "AN ATTACHMENT TO SOMETHING." When we are clear about what we're committed to we can then be unattached to the outcome. Are you committed to creating an amazing relationship with some amazing fucking vision or are you attached to it having to be with this person? Of course, like many truths, there are also half-truths. No attachment can lead to laziness and can be used as an excuse to not take action and not be persistent. And even wore, if it becomes part of your identity, then a lack of attachment can be a new survival mechanism, become inauthentic, and loses all its power in the process. It's a dance that one learns to intuitively maneuver over time.

Creating huge problems

YOU CAN SPEND your whole life trying to *fix yourself* and what you'll get is: *more, better, different, and some version of whatever you were trying to fix.* Then you die *trying to fix yourself*—and maybe you were always "almost there" as well.

Consider that the intention of *trying to fix yourself* is actually more effectively fulfilled by creating larger and larger problems for yourself. Gandhi created the problem of bringing peace and the principle of non-aggression to a nation where it was missing. George Washington created the problem of bringing unity to a nation that was in turmoil. Nelson Mandela, MLK, Werner Erhard, Steve Jobs, John Lennon, Thomas Jefferson, Frederick Douglass, Susan B. Anthony—they all created huge problems for themselves. When you can live your life out of some commitment to creating huge problems for yourself— out into the world, in your friendships, in your relationships, business partnerships, projects, etc—the things like *"my hair looks like crap today,"* or *"I hope this person likes me,"* become such petty concerns and you'll find yourself just not caring anymore. And authentically not caring, not indifferent which is just another inauthentic way of being to cover up caring about something.

. . .

FOCUS your energy on large problems.

Not being seen

ONE OF THE worst experiences in the world is not being seen for who you are. It's a truly soul-sucking experience for people to see you and acknowledge you for the things that don't light you up.

And then there are those people—or sometimes just one person—who come into your life—and, FYI, you can be that person for others—that doesn't care about the stories others have created about you.

They don't care about the stories you've created for yourself nor will they get enrolled in that bullshit. They won't engage nor tolerate that crap. They will only listen to and speak to your greatness, essentially interacting with your Self and not your identity.

They will be unwavering in speaking to your core. Those people are treasures. You can be that kind of treasure for others. Love fully and deeply. Give your all. If nobody in your life is able to be with the magnanimity at your core—you're doing it wrong.

Comfort zones

YOU KNOW that saying *the magic happens outside your comfort zone?* Well, it's true. I've spent more than the past decade making sure I get uncomfortable almost every single day with very few exceptions. I've made it a daily practice to the point it's just habit and I only really think about it if it's not happening.

Something I've also observed is that many people, when they get uncomfortable, instead of giving space to their feelings of discomfort and start noticing from within, instead, start pointing at others to blame them for the source of their discomfort. This limits what's possible and keeps people staying smaller than what they're capable of. It also suffocates people around you when you blame them and don't take responsibility for your own internal state.

People love talking about their dreams and what they want. Yet often when they go for it or god forbid actually have it – they kill it off in the name of comfort.

Get committed to something that in your heart rings true.

Then when things get uncomfortable, and they will, stay with it. The breakthrough is on the other side of that and you never know what you might just discover.

"Needing someone" / "loving yourself" both equate to suffering

NEEDING someone to feel whole *and* having a hyper-obsession on focusing on loving yourself both lead to suffering due to both of these mindsets being rooted in survival and creating separation with others. Before I elaborate I have a little *disclaimer:*

In American Culture what I'm about to say will trigger lots of automatic reactions in many people. Instead of listening to what I'm about to say from a place of "I agree with this" or "I don't agree with this," to get the most value, listen from a place of being curious about distinguishing something and discovering something for yourself. Please put your opinions to the side for now. I promise you can have them back after if you'd like, I won't be upset, I promise.

Furthermore, a lot of you might get offended by what I'm about to share and some of you may hear it as needy or woo-woo. That's fine, and this message may not be for you. There's nothing wrong with that and there's likely to be many things in this book that resonate with you that don't with others. This book isn't designed to be some kind of absolute divine truth.

If what I'm about to say doesn't resonate with you, perhaps keep it in the background and perhaps read it in a few years. If something doesn't resonate with you or doesn't serve you, toss it out. 99% of what I share I don't claim to be the truth, but just a powerful mental model or principle.

So with that out of the way—

To need someone for your happiness is unhealthy. However focusing on loving yourself still produces walls and is just a way to protect yourself from being hurt again—it still leads to suffering internally. It's two sides of the same coin called suffering and survival. However, if you are someone that feels the need to have someone make you feel complete, then a focus on loving yourself and creating boundaries for yourself will make an impact. You will just have to be mindful that when you get to a space of experiencing yourself and being whole and complete on your own—those very same boundaries and practices of loving yourself that you created will be the very thing that gets in your way from diving deep with someone and going deeper than you could on your own.

Only give your *Self* to those who elicit your inner core and purpose. When you find those people who want to pervade you so deeply and experience your light—or by surrendering so fully and deeply to your mission—or a dance of both...whatever empowers you more—then let go of *all* boundaries and give and love as deeply as you can—constantly going deeper—and you'll become more powerful in life through that never-ending journey than you could ever imagine. And no surprise—I bet you aren't completely moved, touched, and inspired by most people's relationships and marriages.

4 ways to get back to your core

WHEN YOU START BELIEVING your lies, resisting and not living at your edge, or pretending to have a larger comfort zone than you actually do (which is also a form of lying), you'll inevitably start losing touch with your intuition. The more time goes on, the more you lose touch with that core of who you are. If you're feeling like you don't intuitively know what to do. If you're feeling like you may not be trusting your own wisdom and your own "natural knowing." Here are some possible ways to get back to your core:

1. Start surrounding yourself with people who inspire you, who you feel energized around, who you don't have to hold back around and can fully let go and let your guard down around them.
2. Find a book that will help you remember who you are.
3. Call someone who you know you have the space to just be. Don't even need to ask for advice necessarily. Just a chit-chat can often help.
4. Meditation. I'm personally not experienced with meditation but I know it works for a lot of people who stick with it consistently.

Ways of being

PEOPLE PICK up on who we're *being*. They may not always have the language to distinguish that for themselves. Just look at someone who is insecure and their whole life is about looking good and manipulating and avoiding looking bad and even though they know all the right body postures and all the right rhetoric and may have spent years learning how to try to survive and fit in in the world—people still see right through all of that.

Then look at people with nothing in their space, totally radiant, alive, vital, confident, and fully Self-expressed and it seems like no matter what they say (and they won't always be perfect) their words will inspire freedom and action, they'll touch the lives of others, and people will really be left with the kind of extraordinary human being that they are.

And who we're *being* is a choice we can make regardless of our past, our circumstances, our upbringing, our environment, our personality, our thoughts, our emotions, our reasons, and the people we're with no matter what they say or do.

Languaging reality

BE careful with how you language the "what's so" in life.

Here's a very cliché example which speaks to this:

You drop your coffee. Your brain has some thoughts that say "I can't catch a break" and then you say to yourself, "I can't catch a break." Then there's all the underlying emotions and bodily sensations that come with that.

Then you start to look for evidence of how you can't catch a break and the more evidence you find, the more ingrained that context becomes for your life.

It'll become how you view life and then your way of *being* will be of someone who *can't catch a break* which will further perpetuate how you *can't catch a break* which then leads to more evidence of how you're someone who *can't catch a break*.

The human mind easily goes to a space of *"there's something wrong and I need to fix it."* So the more you "can't catch a break," the more you need to *try to fix* it which then further perpetuates those brain patterns within you of how you're someone who *can't catch a break* leading to finding more evidence, stronger neural patterns of behavior— and you fast forward that 30 cycle for years and now you've completely forgotten that you've made that up. So now you're blind to the context for your life and you don't even know that you're blind to the context for your life. But what's worse is that you don't even know that you don't know you're blind to this context!

Whether it's living life through the context of *"there's something wrong with me,"* or *"I need to hold back in order to get by because when I give my all it's dangerous"*—whatever stories and hidden contexts are there in the background—the more you can distinguish those things as simply contexts that you're living life through—you now have some choice about it.

The moment you can distinguish that you created stories about the "what's so" in life—those stories cease to have any kind of power over you. Stories only have power over you when they aren't distinguished.

Being peaceful through self-projections

STANDING for someone's greatness is a muscle. Have you ever noticed that the people that think you're a liar or a manipulator when you're being straight with people are the people who do the most lying and manipulating?

I'm sure we have all met someone who is miserable in a relationship because their lover keeps not trusting them or accusing them of something. I *always* tell them to leave the relationship (not like they'll listen or anything because they have to get it for themselves) and then I *always* tell them that their lover actually has that shit going on.

I once judged a local Miss America Pageant. One of the girls there was a huge control freak. It was to the point of being almost emotionally unbearable. No surprise that she had a complaint about her mother that her mom was a control freak. And no surprise that her lack of completion with her mother was literally running her life.

I once had an ex-girlfriend who I later found out was mentally ill and suicidal. She was also a pathological liar. She would accuse me of her not being able to trust me and that I was manipulating her. Of course, this was hurtful, as I had given my all to this girl and would freely share with her. In my mind, I couldn't understand how she could come to these conclusions. Being young and stupid I thought I could somehow "show her" I wasn't like that. It's one thing to know these things and another thing to get what you know intellectually at the level of your heart and not at the level of your fucking head. Essentially, experiencing wisdom versus understanding it conceptually. Understanding wisdom at the level of intellect usually makes very little difference.

Years later I had a meeting in DC. It was with the head of a non-profit who was interested in meeting with me regarding training her non-profit's staff in the *Tribal Leadership* work. During the meeting, she attacked the ideas I was sharing, I was being listened to as small, I was being told by the head of this non-profit that she already knew all of this. When I would freely share I would get cut-throat responses in return and she got pretty nasty with me. I finally asked her what was going on. She "explained" to me that the world was a cruel place and that it's a competitive and cut-throat world, and that I wasn't living in reality, and that she already knew *all* of this stuff so she could just buy "the book" and train everyone herself. I thanked her for sharing her "insights" with me and graciously told her that there was nothing else I had to contribute and walked out of the meeting. I simply let her have her point of view. When John shared at the beginning of the book how *Stage 3*'s often think they're doing *Stage 5*, that was a perfect example of it right there. John calls it *stage inflation.*

When people start reacting to what you have to authentically share, it has nothing to do with you. There's that saying that goes *"what people say about you has nothing to do with you."* Now it's one thing if people call you not responsible because you never keep your promises and you *actually* never keep your promises. That's different.

Getting caught up in people's self-projections, their victim shit, their own pettiness and smallness—that only continues to perpetuate their view. The more you try to resist it, the more grounded they become in their position. You also risk becoming the very thing you're trying to show you are not. You essentially stoop down into their reality as a means to appease their identity and sell out your Self in the process as vs. giving them the space to rise into a more empowering conversation where their Self can interact with your Self. *No identities need apply.* All you can do in those situations is get what they're sharing and give them the space to have their point of view. Then keep being great in life and *some* of those people will come along for the ride and some of them won't. Love them from afar and *only* engage in their greatness *regardless* of how much that pisses them off. It may not always be peaceful but *you* will have your peace...and your power.

Focusing on what matters

IN MY LIFE, every time I start working on something bigger, better, and my experience of the contribution I have to make to society increases—there's this heightened level of well-being that comes over me. Noticing that led me to a principle which I modeled that I want to share with you.

With that being said, there are a few models that give one access to the experience of general overall happiness.

The first one is by far the weakest. It's the model that says *you're unhappy therefore there's something wrong with you and you need to be fixed*. We need to figure it out, analyze it, and put energy into what doesn't work. This model is continuing to be less and less popular and, if anything, has created more sickness than wellness.

The second model is very powerful. It first comes from the space that *you are already whole and complete and all there is to do is get what's out of the way from you experiencing that*. That, of course, is very powerful and everyone from Tony Robbins to Landmark Worldwide has used this model in some sort of way or another very successfully. I call it *the empowerment model*.

Then there's a third model which goes along with the *empowerment model* very well. This is the *value creation model* and it's this very model that I discovered through my constant experience of well-being whenever I would start creating some new project (as an authentic Self-expression vs. a way to look good or prove something) or way to make an impact. The model essentially shows that there is a direct correlation between your level of overall well being, peace, happiness, and feeling of responsibility and control you have over life. Besides, all of this will be in correlation to how much value you have produced in the world for other people. People ask me why do you share? It's very simple. It's an honoring of the human spirit and a natural Self-expression. This shit makes no difference if I can't share it with others. It will just die in my head. Creating value for others in the realm of performance and human potential is a natural expression for me and I would feel like my soul was dying if I didn't share. I would be out of integrity with the deepest part of my core.

So if you find yourself feeling lacking in these areas, sometimes, all there is to do is to start creating value for others. If you do that as an expression of your highest Self and purpose, it helps even more. If you're feeling like there's something missing, the trap is *"to work on yourself."* This just causes you to go inward. It doesn't create value for others. That's such a psychological trap that has become not just accepted in society but encouraged and has become almost fad-like pop psychology/self-help.

It's usually much simpler than deeply analyzing and reading all these self-help books in order to find the answer. Just provide greater levels of value for others.

Want more love in life? Money? Friends? Closer connections? General overall happiness? Provide more value for others and expand and expand and expand that.

There's no *right* way or correct path for this. Only you can know that for yourself. Everyone knows that just not everyone *listens* to what they intuitively know. It's literally so damn simple.

There's a great book that was recommended to me by the co-CEO of Markel Corp, Tom Gayner. He's a great value investor who has created a ton of value at one of the most well-run insurance companies in the world. His whole deal in the world is to be kind to people. His whole being is about kindness and creating a great culture at Markel. He loves people. And, he's been able to live out his values through creating lots of value for Markel and for the people Markel impacts. That's a lot of difference-making and when you see Tom he's a generally pretty happy fella!

The book he recommended to me and all his employees was called "The Signal and the Noise: The art and science of prediction" by Nate Silver. For those of you who don't know who Nate Silver is, he's an American statistician who has built an incredible reputation based on how accurate he tends to be. His book was about being able to distinguish what matters from all the noise which doesn't make a difference. In the digital age, there's a lot more information but a lot of that information is useless for the purpose of making an impact. There's lots of information on how to find the love of your life. Doesn't mean it will help. And often the things that make a huge difference are one or two tiny little things that make *all* of the difference.

For instance, in the value investing game—the principles of "margin of safety" and "intrinsic value" will make more of a difference to high performance over decades in the investment management world than studying technical analysis for 20 years. Reading chapters 8 and chapters 20 of Benjamin Graham's Intelligent Investor will make more of an impact financially over decades than a lifetime of studying technical analysis which is the study of reading stock charts and finding patterns to make money trading.

In this *game of happiness*, the *signal* is the value that you provide from your highest Self. The *noise* is all the mantras, positive thinking, pop psychology, all the fixing and changing, and all the negative interpretations of reality and scarcity conversations that are easy to buy into in society.

Focus on what matters—more value to more people at an ever-expanding level.

Be what you want in others

NOT REACTING TO REACTIONS

EVERY TIME I see people closed off in some way in reaction to something in their past, a part of me literally cringes. These people in their heart of hearts want human connection. Want trust. Want love. Want all the basic human stuff. However, there's something in the way. Consider that what often gets in the way is some kind of fear such as the fear of people taking advantage of you if you're too trusting or too open.

Well, welcome to the fucking party called being alive. Yes, some people will take advantage of you trusting or being open. Duh. What's more asinine is you reacting to that like there's some kind of terrible threat there. Literally becoming smaller and more diminished based off a fear of people hurting you in some way. Sad.

I have gone so far as to ask someone to hold the steering wheel before while grabbing something while I am driving. When they do it, I've just trusted them with my life and they obliged. Even little things like that over time end up often creating huge shifts in how people are with you. I won't name names but I have many people in my life who are open and authentic with me who are literally totally closed off to others. Why? I provided them with a space to be like that with me.

If you share and get authentic with people and also get authentic about your inauthenticities with others, you'll have more people be that way with you. Like Werner Erhard says, "You don't have to go looking for love when it's where you come from." And that principle applies to more than just love.

When people have a reaction to you, don't react to their reaction. Act from a space of what you're committed to creating with them.

"If you are open with someone, he will be open with you. If you want love from someone, give your love to him. If you want kind and sympathetic behavior from someone, be kind and sympathetic to him. If you want comfort from him, prove yourself comforting to him. If you want admiration from others, do something to show your admiration for them. If you are sincere in giving, you receive it in return many-fold. The teacher learns by teaching; in obeying, the student commands the respect of the teacher. If your son readily is obedient to you, he captures your heart as a natural return of obedience. If you are kind to a child he will be kind to you; if you are harsh to him, he will revolt against you. This is action and reaction."

— MAHARISHI MAHESH

Apologizing for others as a function of self-projection

MUCH OF OUR society is not present to the impact that we have on others when we start invalidating others or apologizing for others because we are self-projecting our own discomfort within a social interaction. This impacts children up to adults who are made to feel small in a given environment. There's a beautiful story that a friend of mine Nisha Moodley shared once which speaks to this principle of apologizing for others as a self-projection and the impact this has. Her story specifically relates to children, but the scope of this principle goes beyond that.

ON APOLOGIZING FOR CHILDREN
by Nisha Moodley

A FEW MINUTES AGO, I was walking across a crosswalk, two small children, and their caregiver ahead of me. The caregiver was explaining sweetly that they needed to walk quickly because the countdown was on. Just then, the little girl tripped and her shoe came off. She turned her head anxiously while they kept walking. Her little face looked so worried. I quickly grabbed the shoe as I came upon it, and I smiled at her. "I'll give it to you on the other side!" I said.

When we got to the sidewalk, her caregiver said an awkward thank you, then uncomfortably told the little girl, who was now looking down, to say "I'm sorry."

Before the little girl said anything, I said "I don't mind!" and smiled at her warmly.

It felt as if the caregiver was dealing with her OWN awkwardness with social interaction and her OWN feelings around "disturbing" others, and was projecting that onto this little child. I was not troubled in the slightest to help a fellow human being. A simple thank you was enough.

As I walked away, I thought about how often adults apologize for children and implore them to apologize for themselves. Sometimes it's warranted, for sure, but in this case, it was clearly an accident and there was no harm done.

So what are we doing when we send the message to children that their existence is a disturbance to others, or that we're somehow putting them out by allowing them to help us? Children of the world: You are not a nuisance.

Putting you back into the box

YOUR SELF-EXPRESSION IS a function of the listening of others. One thing that is really cool about that principle is that how you listen to people will shape how they act around you. It doesn't mean it will be the end all be all but it will most certainly be a big influence. Now I'm going to take that idea one step further. If you can share with others in a way so other people start listening to that person in the way you see them—then that will have an even bigger impact. This comes into play when you put someone into a new environment and their way of operating completely shifts over time through being influenced by the new environment. It also ties into that saying "You're the average of the 5 people you spend the most time with."

The arrogant thing is to deny that you're influenced by your culture or environment. We all are and we can use that knowingness to actually improve our lives by being conscious of the environments and people we choose to surround ourselves with.

You can say that people listen to you through a certain lens. With some people, it's conscious (the people who know that how we listen to others is a choice) and with some people "it's just the way you are," and that's their reality.

One phenomenon I find interesting is how little people react when you have an insight or a breakthrough leading to a completely internal shift in who you are. Essentially, some people listen to you and are in reaction to you based off of years of interactions with you and seeking evidence that you "are a certain way." If you've been that way and you have trained others to listen to you that way, when you actually have a shift, many people won't notice. And the longer someone has known you, the harder it is for them to notice. Why? Because they don't experience who you are. They experience a concept of who you are and see you through that lens. Even when the thinking, being, and actions changes, it's quite common for the lens you're being viewed in *not* to.

For example—it's common for people to say they wish there were more people like Mother Teresa and Gandhi on the planet. However, if you share your own expression for the true difference you want to make in the world—most people will actually become cynical since they don't see that kind of thinking, being, and acting for most human beings so they may call you arrogant or unrealistic as opposed to listening for some huge commitment you have.

If you don't have the support of your environment, it makes the game that much more difficult.

So, that being said, some people will truly not be able to deal with you making positive shifts in your life. Your success and the new spaces you've moved into will literally take them out of their point of view about you. They'll press up against their box for you while you're shattering it. Some people will seek to be right about their view of you as opposed to viewing you in a new light.

As I said previously, you'll especially see this with people you've known for a long time as they have actually created a point of view together over time and then have found more and more evidence to be right about their point of view which then in turn shapes how they choose to listen to you (and they don't see it as a choice, just the "way you are").

So whether it's your personality, your quirks, the kinds of activities you like to partake in, the kinds of people you like to date, the perceived flaws or weaknesses you have (whether or not they're actually true or just perceived), etc. all have an influence on how you're listened to by people who have known you a very long time.

So whenever you start taking new actions out of new insights and thinking—it will literally shatter some people's view of you.

These people who aren't willing to be with it will either by choice or unconsciously will start attempting to put you back into your box so that you can fit their point of view about you so they can justify and be right about it.

The more you stay the same (way of being, thinking, emotions, actions, etc.)—the more their model of you (and therefore the world) stays intact. This is just part of the automatic mental machinery of our brains which has allowed us to be the most dominant species in the animal kingdom when being able to model the world actually helped us survive. It still does by the way just can also get in our way when we aren't conscious of it.

Being accused of arrogance

PEOPLE WHO ARE COMMITTED to non-stop expansion and growth will at times be called arrogant. Confidence is a function of trusting one's Self. It's not some front you put on or you trying to exude confidence in order to not be found out. That's just someone who isn't settled with who they are trying to convince the world they are something they are not. That's a form of arrogance.

Arrogance is a function of needing to prove something to someone. There's nothing secure or confident about arrogance. The right people will celebrate and honor your confidence as it's honoring the Self. People who think that your natural Self-expression is you trying to prove something to them, or somehow you putting them down is over there with them.

If someone feels you are putting them down when you are not, all there is for you to do is let them know that you got what you said left them feeling like that and it was not your intention. Simple. People who still can't get over that are "bad-news-bears" and they will drain your energy. So when you are accused of arrogance, don't resist it. Do an inner check. Are you trying to prove yourself? No? Then, awesome. If you are being arrogant, then own it. You could say something like, "Hey, I was being arrogant as fuck and was trying to prove this or trying to make myself better than you because I wanted to prove something and that's fucking stupid and shitty, and I apologize."

Never dim your light on your mission

To DIMINISH yourself and dim your own light for anyone or any circumstance is asinine and flat-out stupid. Many people often dim themselves when they think their greatness will be a threat to someone's "normalness." Reacting to that kind of reaction has you sell out on that other person for the sake of comfort. But it's a disempowered comfort. Deep down you feel like shit. Any kind of thinking that you will empower others through joining them in their smallness is about the dumbest tactic I've ever seen and it simply doesn't work.

Some people will want you to act a certain way to not upset others or make others feel uncomfortable. You will always upset someone and someone will always feel uncomfortable with something you do when you're truly being great and acting from an integral place of Self where your actions are 100% aligned with your core. It's in this space where you will be most powerful in life.

When you don't do this to not upset someone else, you literally disempower yourself and then no longer are able to be a light for others. Meeting someone at their smallness instead of letting others rise to your greatness is such a huge mistake.

Yes, it's important to be empathetic. Yes, it's important to feel for someone else. Yes, it's important to get where someone is at.

And...yes, it's important to still act from a space of Self and be that light and vision for others no matter how upset or uncomfortable that will make some people. When you're acting from that space, your light will *always* have some people feel threatened. People cling to what is in their box and if you share outside their box, some people will literally fight for their smallness when you are standing for their greatness.

Someone who never has time will never be a great example of abundance in life. Someone who is sick and overweight will never be a great example of health. Someone who doesn't keep their agreements will never be a great example of leadership.

When you shine your light and speak from a space of what's possible, you allow others to see something for themselves as well. You create an environment that maximizes others seeing new possibilities for themselves. This is how you alter what's possible for others on the planet.

Then it's set the conditions and see who shows up to the party. Don't make the conditions worse because someone is scared of those conditions and then fuck it up for everyone else. That's truly a disservice to others and yourself.

Killing off what isn't you

BY NISHA MOODLEY

WHEN YOU DEDICATE your life to freedom (no, I'm not just talking about working from a laptop on the beach), you see that there's a lot that has to die away. Most of us approach a 'death' and back away, so we live all of life afraid to die, barely living. But when you choose to die, and die, and die again, you get to experience being alive while you're living. Choosing to die to live.

Does your mentor admire you?

BY NISHA MOODLEY

LATELY, I've felt especially passionate about each of us choosing mentors and coaches who see others in their innate brilliance. Why? Because when they don't see you that way, it's pretty hard to see yourself that way. This is about being regarded your mentor as a leader, not their "follower." I'm not interested in building a community of followers; I'm interested in activating a community of leaders. To do this means that first, foremost, and always, we must regard others – all people, not just the "popular" ones or the ones who agree with us – as capable, whole, and innately wise. If the people you "follow," and especially your mentors, don't regard you this way; don't treat you and others with respect; don't lead with humility, curiosity, generosity and inclusivity; aren't open to differing perspectives (even if they have strong opinions); aren't actively seeking to learn from others (including you)... consider what following them might be unconsciously reinforcing within you and proliferating in the world. Sometimes we follow people who regard others as small, weak, fearful and in need of a leader, because that's how we see ourselves. And continuing to be seen through this lens further reinforces their status as a leader, and ours as a follower. This is the old game of divisive, hierarchical "leadership."

Blind spots

THE WISE AND THE FOOLS

BY CAROLINA ARAMBURO

ONLY WISE PEOPLE work on seeing and their blind spots to access new levels of being able to be a contribution for their loved ones. Only fools walk around pretending they don't need anyone to see their blind spots while they keep hurting those they love and not even realizing why.

Is everyone cut out for leadership?

THERE'S this common mantra that everyone is a leader and if you just take X course now you can be a leader too. That kind of manic delusional thinking is not healthy. If you take basketball coaching all your life, it doesn't mean you'll make the NBA. Leadership is a dangerous game as you're out at risk for something. You'll make exponentially more messes than the average human being and you'll be in exponentially more uncomfortable situations as well. If you're not willing to go through that, fuck your leadership.

You can have all the resources you need and still not be cut out for it. I know plenty of people that have gone through some of the best leadership trainings in the world and have some of the best resources available to them and are still terrible in the realm of leadership. It's not for everyone. It's not a game you even have to play. Doing it because it *looks good* will sour very quickly. However, if it's your calling: acquire lots of resources; get all the support possible; and make it a game worth failing at.

Entitlement

THERE IS nothing I can't stand quite like entitlement. Well, that's not true but it's certainly pretty low on my list. The world does not owe you anything. If you're being a victim to anything in life, get over it. If you can't get over it and it's degrading into positive thinking, go seek out a resource that will help you get complete with your past so it's not getting in the way of your life anymore. Literally o excuses. When I first started my investment management firm, someone shared with me that they thought I was *lucky* to be running a business.

What they didn't know is for every success, I've had significantly more micro-failures. Before starting my investment firm, I was looking to start a fund that did cultural activism mixed with value investing. I had never been done before. I had four people say there were interested in partnering with me on that and they all flaked out and I spent two years of my life failing and chasing loose ends. Lots of lessons learned there. Before I had a single penny given to me, I spoke about what I was up to for many months before someone was willing to let me manage anything.

Every day I woke up with that kind of anxious thoughts in the back of my head saying, "what if I'm too young for this and nobody actually trusts me and everyone is all talk?" I ignored that dumbshit voice saying nonsense to me and kept staying true to myself and my mission and vision for what I was committed to creating.

So am I lucky? Fuck no. Am I insanely tenacious and willing to do whatever it takes without cutting corners to create my vision and work my ass off? Absolutely. I was entitled to none of it. I had to work for it. Nobody owed me anything. The world owed me nothing.

Blaming with intention vs. reaction

PEOPLE ARE OFTEN lazy with how they blame others. They blame out of some kind of reaction to defend or protect against some kind of hurt. People rarely blame intentionally. If you can be grateful for the shit that comes your way vs. resent it, there's a whole level of growth and learning that comes out of it. I've had people do terrible shit to me. I've had circumstances not go my way. I've had things happen to me and thinking "why would this happen to me?" However when I've allowed myself to embrace the "what's so" and be grateful that these barriers were being put in my way, then I could grow from it. Years ago I dated someone who I discovered in a very painful way was very ill. She was suicidal and told me that she had borderline personality disorder. I met her in a leadership training which in hindsight was probably inappropriate for her to be in. While I do believe mental illness is often over-diagnosed in the United States and some people use labels as an excuse to not take responsibility for their lives—there are some people on the planet who are truly not well.

Loving her was one of the toughest things I ever did in my life. It was also one of the most rewarding experiences of my life and I grew more through loving her heart, even amongst her darkest moments, which were terrifying, to say the least. While I often experienced deep pain and sadness through that experience, I never suffered. I felt fully alive and powerful. I am beyond grateful for her life and her heart. While I went through some very emotionally painful circumstances with her, I would not be the man I am today if it weren't for her.

It expanded my capacity to love in ways I never even knew existed. It expanded how deeply I could go with someone that I never knew was possible. It created a level of spiritual strength in me where I have a deep knowing I can love anybody through anything and can keep my heart open without losing composure even amidst the wildest of storms.

Yes, I'm sure I have my limit somewhere but it's expanded way beyond the cultural norm. Her love towards me and her listening of me allowed me to experience myself and the gifts I had to share with others at a much deeper and more profound level.

I know at the deepest level of my core that the lives I have touched and made a difference with would have had no fucking chance in hell without her having come into my life in 2011. For the longest time, I always wondered why someone that destructive was put into my life and how anyone could fathom to treat another human being as disgusting as she did with me. However, now I get that without her, my life would be much smaller. She forced growth in ways I never knew were possible. I had to have that kind of heart and that capacity to love and stand for people's greatness if I was to unfold into the kind of human being I was committed to being on this planet.

So to her, thank you.

Being jaded

PEOPLE WHO GO AROUND JADED in life based off of experiences in the past think it's their past that makes them jaded. Total bullshit. The past has nothing to do with you choosing to be jaded and cynical.

In my experience, most people talk a bigger game than they actually deliver and suck at following through on big commitments. Does that mean I'll choose to stop trusting people and take a jaded view of others and when people share big that I just get uninspired and don't care?

No, that would be insane to kill off my aliveness and not let people in because of people in the past. I see everyone as big and I choose to listen for people's greatness. And that being said, some people suck at keeping their word, some people suck at following through, and some people really have zero respect for honoring their word and their life has the results of someone who has shit integrity.

The more you honor your agreements, the better your life works. It's just how it goes. The more you operate from your reasons and excuses as a way to avoid being responsible for honoring your word—the inverse is true.

When you create those agreements in language and keep those agreements, you create whole new futures and possibilities. New actions and ways of being, thinking, and acting become possible. When you don't honor your word and are out of integrity what you get is your old life back. It's actually pretty simple.

My point is that. Even if I took a group of 100 people and only 5% of those people followed through on their word, then I'd rather have 95% of people not follow through so I can give those 5% a chance as opposed to me not letting anyone in and not giving anybody a chance and killing off people through my jaded, negative, and cynical vibes so to speak.

Being jaded is a choice and it has a self-reinforcing impact. The more you go around jaded, not trusting, etc.—the more people you'll find closed off around you which then, in turn, furthers your evidence of why you need to be closed off.

The impact of playing big

THE BIGGER YOU play in life, the more people will be hostile to your efforts. The more straight you are with people, the more people will get upset with you and have complaints about you. Of course, the payoff is that you'll have much higher quality people in your life and have a much more amazing environment around you if you have that willingness to be disliked and look bad.

Some people falsely assume that if you are just doing what is right and moral that magically the chaos in life will simply stop and you'll be living out of a fucking *Leave It To Beaver* episode. It's actually the inverse. When you start taking action from your purpose, from your authentic Self-expression, the chaos actually gets bigger. It's not magical hippie-nonsense. It's simply that the Self is not destructible, only pretenses and identities are. When you are operating from Self (and starting to naturally operate from the principles in this book), you'll not waver or be thrown around by whatever chaotic circumstances come your way. Therefore, you make space for them as opposed to diminishing your own Self-expression to protect yourself from the storms that you (as identity) aren't ready to withstand.

Consciousness as Self while playing the game called *being a human being* is indestructible

Explaining yourself

TRYING to explain yourself to someone who has a commitment to not getting you and is more interested in justifying their own point of view about you or about what you're sharing is about as useful as trying to get a rock to talk or being angry at someone who can't walk for not standing up. It's actually completely asinine.

Withholding love

IF YOU'RE WITHHOLDING your love in order for people to love you, you perpetuate how unloving and unlovable you are. Self-fulfilling prophecy.

Being offended

STOP GETTING OFFENDED BY THINGS. Guess what? Nobody cares. Stop playing the victim and stop taking other people's words so seriously. Most of the time people just talk without really being present to the words that are coming out of their mouth or the intention behind it. Just ask someone to repeat themselves after saying some long reactive statement and you'll find most of the time they can't. They don't really remember what they said. They weren't present. Often when people say reactive things, they're just annoyed at something about their day, about their life, and it's almost never about you.

There's literally no reason to take everything people say so seriously. Getting offended all the time is just a function of being really insecure with yourself.

If you're out to make a difference with people, then stop getting offended and trying to change or fix others—even when you think they're saying stupid stuff. Focus on you being great. If you think someone's religion, beliefs, or actions are stupid—who cares? Stop wasting your time trying to explain it to them why they are wrong or trying to convince or persuade them to change.

"Don't change beliefs, transform the believer."

I guarantee you'll have more luck with a member of the KKK shifting their beliefs about different races by having people who they don't like be great with them vs. invalidating them for their racism or for other hateful views they may have.

3 common reactions to Self-expression

WHEN YOU'RE the kind of person who is not only in touch with your purpose at your core—but also completely aligned with it—without anything to prove or justify—there are three common and possible reactions you'll have from people. And none of these reactions have anything to do with you.

1. The people who think what you're up to is more amazing than you think it is. You're just doing what you know there is for you to do. For others, it can inspire something within them and on the surface, their reaction is along the lines of how amazing they think you are. Really, it's just a reflection of themselves and you've provided the mirror for them to see something.

2. The people who start getting resigned, cynical, and shut down in those conversations. This is caused by them pushing up against and feeling confronted when either they're so out of alignment with what they intuitively know there is to do but for whatever reason have "sold out" on themselves *or* they really have no connection to this at their core and you're simply invalidating their model for reality or threatening their identity in some way.

3. The people who start having to one-up you, justify something, or somehow make themselves a "rare" unapproachable commodity. Those people usually somewhat connected to their higher purpose, but they're taking action around it through living out some major inauthenticity. It makes their work that much more ineffective and the game that much harder. Your authenticity gets them confronted by that and leaves them feeling threatened.

Freedom of speech

BE PART OF THE SOLUTION

WHEN WE SHUT down conversations the moment we feel threatened and start becoming viscerally positional about our views—then we contribute to losing our freedom of speech as a society. The moment it becomes unsafe to share freely at the dinner table because we've "offended" someone—we're fucking done.

When it's not safe to discuss ideas—your environment is screwed!

Let us not teach our children it's not safe to share ideas with a commitment to understanding implications of a policy that impacts the lives of millions of people. Our freedom of speech is too important. It's bullshit when it's honored on paper yet not in our culture.

I want to share about something that happened in the Fall of 2013. I'm sitting at the dinner table where we're talking about Syria and this dude starts telling me that it "looks bad" for Obama regardless if he goes into Syria or not and that it's really just about making Obama look bad.

Here we are talking about fucking policy and someone gives me this reactionary response about what "looks bad"—like the destruction of human life is now being talked about as some fucking spectator sport. Well, you know what? It's not. There are real implications to policy regardless of *"how it looks."* I made it clear to this dude that I did not like Obama for the same reasons I didn't like George W. Bush, and I was appalled that he'd even compare my dislike for a Syrian invasion to a dislike for Obama.

Then I went on to list a bunch of countries where human rights violations are going on and how Obama isn't going into those countries and he doesn't "look bad" for that. Then I ask him, "so what about that?" He responded to me by telling me he wants to "stop having this conversation," and if you're in an environment where *everyone* is positional, then *you* actually end up looking like the asshole.

Now fast forward that to where society puts people like that in the category of "assholes" or "bullies" or "verbally abusing others" simply out of the fact that they can't take any kind of opinions that don't go into their emotional and visceral belief systems— and congratulations, we've lost our freedom of speech.

Do not be part of the problem. Be part of the solution.

The blessing of perfect love

MANIPULATING a girl desperate for love needs no masculine essence. Each night as you close your eyes, listen for her calling you on the adventure of a lifetime. You look at her face and see that fierce fire burning, a thrashing thunder brewing, a love that needs nothing in return, giving everything sparing no expense.

A freedom that must be worshipped and nothing less as to dampen her flame for the sake of being comfortable destroys what's possible at the very core of her being.

Continuously feel the invitation to receive and worship her heart.

Feel beckoned to continuously learn how to love her through each moment, every emotional storm, every bodily movement in pain, pleasure, fear, and love.

In spite of her flaws, in spite of her perceived imperfections, in spite of her atavisms, constantly taking her close continuously worshipping, uncovering, and discovering her beautiful essence at her core.

Taking her ever-deeper bringing flow to every inch of her body where only her radiance shines through and nothing less.

Your ever-expanding aching to bring forth the light that she already is giving space for her natural guidance of stripping away all the darkness that isn't.

It takes something to live from the edge of your comfort zone, to constantly ever-expand and to naturally, authentically, intrinsically know how to be fiercer than a warrior and more innocent than a newborn baby.

It takes something to live out your deepest truth to live out the deepest integrity at your core, continuously in every moment, pouring out every fiber of your being in each moment to protect her, yet at the same time, not be threatened by how powerful she really is. To only be in awe.

You are in awe of her power and yours.

You are in awe of her radiance, her violently thrashing thunderstorms, the ones which thrust and strike all that don't see her, that won't meet her, that won't uphold her being.

Allow yourself to be moved by her light—that ray of sunshine that shines through her body.

Allow yourself to be healed every night by her perfect love with no attachment to her expression of such.

Continue to allow her to teach through you meeting her in her fullness and you only listening to her as her deepest radiance, as her flow, as her truth, as her perfect essence at her core.

Continue to only ever receive her as a gift and nothing less no matter what—no matter the circumstances.

Allow yourself to grow through your commitment to loving her without any attachment to how she shows up for you.

Be grateful for the blessing of perfect love.

Fearing risk, fearing movement

"Those who fear risk also begin to fear movement of any kind. People act as though flux, the movement of people or ideas or anything else that's unpredictable, expose us to risk, and risk exposes us to failure. The fearful try to avoid collisions, so they avoid movement. These people have made two mistakes. First, they've assumed that risk is a bad thing, and second, they've confused risk and flux, and come to the conclusion that movement is a bad thing as well.

I'm not surprised to discover that many of these people are stuck. Stuck with the status quo, stuck defending their position in the market, stuck with the education they have, unwilling to get more. They are stuck because they are afraid to watch something new on TV, afraid to read something new on their Kindle, afraid to ask a hard question. None of this would be relevant, except: Now the whole world is in flux.

If your project doesn't have movement, then compared to the rest of the world, you're actually moving backward. Like a rock in a flowing river, you might be standing still, but given the movement around you, collisions are inevitable.

The irony for the person who prefers no movement is that

there's far less turbulence around the log floating down the same river. It's moving, it's changing, but compared to the river around it, it's relatively calm.

The economy demands flux. Flux isn't risky. Flux is what we're in for. Fortunately, flux is also what we're born for."

— SETH GODIN

There's danger in the comfort zone

IF YOU TAKE action only when you're comfortable and let your emotions choose your actions, you'll inevitably put a cap on your potential. Seeing discomfort as an opportunity for growth is where people really become unleashed. On the other side of that is freedom and a whole new level of performance. Don't take my word for it. Next time you feel tight, take action when you feel like caving.

Next time you feel you want to run away, go love and choose to keep your heart open instead. Next time you want to stop because you "don't feel like it," do it anyway. I promise it's in your best interest to make that a habit.

There's danger in the comfort zone.

Making messes

WHEN YOU DO big things in life, you will make lots of messes.

It's through cleaning up these messes that you get to experience yourself at a new level of effectiveness in life.

Your growth will never come from avoiding these situations. And yes there are some people who have it all handed to them on a silver platter but if this isn't you and you're someone who has had to carve out their path vs. it being given to them (and really there isn't such thing in purity) then this will come up and get stronger the bigger you play life.

It's not a good or bad thing for messes to happen for shit to hit the fan. It's just what comes up from time-to-time. This is how life unfolds on a path of growth and constantly wanting to contribute your gifts on a larger scale.

You will come off as intense to some people and passive to others. Your persistence and tenacity will threaten others. When you pull back, other people will be turned off by that.

Sometimes you'll be reckless with what you say and say the absolute wrong thing at the worst possible time. The more skilled you are the more capable you are of making very big messes and the more capable you are of cleaning up any messes you make and taking full responsibility for the mess which to be clear does not mean going into blame or fault mode (simply having power in the situation).

It doesn't even matter who made the mess. Clean it up! You wouldn't live in a messy house whether you put it there or not. Cleaning up messes and restoring integrity to the environments simply creates space and gives you more power. It's not about holding others accountable or justifying something. It's about restoring power when it's lacking vs. plowing through it which eventually gets draining and will impact your effectiveness over time.

Through that, not only will you deal with being uncomfortable and having incredibly uncomfortable conversations...you will move through the next space in your life and you are forever at a new level of baseline freedom, power, and Self-expression for yourself. Doesn't mean you won't ever backtrack. You will. I'm talking baseline.

You can take the position that you have plenty of spaces to move through and where you're at is wherever you're supposed to be. You will make more messes in the future. That is absolutely guaranteed. Do not play safe. Do not hold back. Go balls to the walls in creating what you're out to create in your life from your deepest truth. And yes, be responsible that sometimes that will threaten other people. You will get criticized in the future and the bigger you play the more you will get criticized.

You may have people say nasty things to you. You may get some bruises along the way. And you can be committed to correcting wrongs when they happen and making things right. There's no such thing as permanent failure, just correctable results.

So when someone is impacted along the way, yes you can clean it up. And there will be some people who are committed victims of their circumstances where all you can do is share your truth and listen and keep moving on. You can't please everyone. Trying to will only hold you back and keep you small.

So yes, take responsibility for the impact you have with others and don't apologize for who you are at your core. Yes, be ruthless about my life and no, don't compromise. Be flexible.

When someone can't deal with you—don't make yourself wrong, just take responsibility that how you will occur in a negative way to some and that's okay. There were people who can't stand Gandhi and Mother Teresa (even to this day).

There is freedom in accepting all of that.

Personally, I love the experience of being gotten just through me penetrating their being to their core. I love sharing. I love being passionate. I love being in love. I love feeling intense emotions. I love making a difference. I love to be selfish. I am a dreamer. I love to innovate and create. I work best when I'm focused and disciplined. Drinking wine and yerba mate—not mixed together FYI—helps me elicit my own creativity. I hate working out and can't stand running. However, I love to walk and occasionally sprint. I drink Kombucha a lot. I love great mind-blowing sex. I have smoked pot in my life but and smoked about 3 cigarettes ever. I have always attempted to say sorry when there is something I can apologize for. While I am committed to never intentionally upsetting people, that sometimes will happen even when it's not my intention. I would not want others upsets to taint all the good. I understand that some people won't be satisfied being my friend. With some people, I won't be satisfied being their friend either. I am clear with what I am committed to around my friendships, relationships, family, etc. I am emotional and very in touch with my emotions. I am also very much in touch with my masculinity and deeply grounded consciousness as well. I embrace both. Sometimes I can be an asshole. Sometimes I can be really warm and loving. However, no matter where I'm at and who I am with—I have a stand for this world working for the well-being of humanity. I am not perfect. I will make mistakes. I am also always willing to take responsibility for those mistakes.

Own who you are but get that your uniqueness is not special. You are who you are. Just how you're wired.

And be grateful—like really damn grateful. If you had the circumstances you truly wanted you may not have some of the gifts you have today. And in fact, often the people who have been through the most shit in life have some of the deepest and most beautiful gifts to share.

Gratitude goes a long way. I didn't get that at first. And after just a week long practice of being grateful every day—and sharing what I was grateful for with others—I started making it a habit internally for myself and it's been quite impactful for me in my life.

Here are some ideas:

Express gratitude to the people who have allowed you to share your all with them. Like, really your *all*.

Express gratitude to the people who have given you the space to share your love completely and fully with them where there is nothing held back.

Express gratitude to the ones who have challenged you, and, through knowing those individuals, that you have grown.

Express gratitude to the people who have told you that your projects and visions would fail and share what you got out of it and learned from it and how you grew from that.

Express gratitude to the ones who wanted to be part of your projects only when they took off.

Express gratitude to the people who have stuck with you the whole time.

Express gratitude to the people who have weeded themselves out around you (you don't need to express that to them, might be a bit of a dick thing to do. But that doesn't mean don't do it).

Express gratitude to the people who think you're fake.

Express gratitude to the people who get you.

Express gratitude to the people who don't.

Express gratitude to everyone who has made a difference for you in some way.

However, I really and truly experience this as a deep truth. To the people that have made promises they didn't keep, you taught me how to listen to people as their word even when I had no reason to do so. To the people who get me, I got the experience of being gotten.

To the people who have allowed me to contribute to their life—I got what it means to be a contribution.

Consistent complaints

IF YOU HAVE a consistent complaint about people not being a certain way with you, perhaps you push that away and you attract whatever you resist. I'm not saying it is. But consider looking there.

I know for me when I was in high school, I had a story of how everybody was fake with me. The truth was that I was fake with others and people who were authentic with me were either turned off by me being such an asshole or that I would find a reason to disconnect from someone being authentic with me because it threatened my identity and worldview.

These interactions wound up for me as people thinking "this person is too intense" or "this person is too pushy" or "this person makes me feel uncomfortable." I would find some reason or justification to kill these people off.

Many people are attached to their complaints. Many people have their identity wrapped inside of those complaints. Giving up complaints also means giving up the justifying of them, the reasons, the evidence. It also sometimes means giving up parts of your identity which can feel extremely uncomfortable and almost counter-intuitive at first.

However what you get in return is your aliveness and a level of ease and peace of mind that often you didn't even notice was missing in the first place.

Persuading and convincing is insanely ineffective

THERE ARE countless books on how to persuade people or convince people of something. However, this context to operate from is insanely ineffective. It's a very tough game to play and only the best of the best will be good at it some of the time. However, it almost always smells a little off.

We as human beings can sense and pick up on how others are being with us. Not doing, but being. If someone is being manipulative and being agenda-driven, it doesn't matter what you say when you're being like that—people will pick up on it and feel the ulterior motive. It's a form of lying.

Have you ever noticed that often when you get what you want you stopped getting so attached to it? Ever notice that feeling when you're sharing for the sake of sharing and you start inspiring people around you and also feel inspired by who you are? That's the world of enrollment and it's something I learned in 2008 while participating in Landmark Worldwide's Curriculum for Living.

An enrollment conversation is a conversation that leaves the other moved, touched, and inspired and present to some kind of new possibility or insight. People see something possible. Really great orators are enrolling. Really great natural salesmen are just naturally enrolling.

The fun guy at the bar that everyone wants to be around is naturally enrolling in the world of fun and play. There's a different feeling to that than trying to convince someone of something. It's almost a bit tricky because the best way to convince someone of something is to have them be enrolled in something so they see it for themselves and giving up trying to convince them lets you access that.

You could say that convincing gets in the way of enrollment which then in turn ups the probability they will feel convinced to do something. However, if you look at the times when you've really changed your mind about something — more often than not, you were the one who saw something new vs. being told it or preached it.

So just share. Share for the love of sharing which we as human beings do naturally. **Be** enrolling in whatever you're up to and you have to trust yourself that people will naturally be pulled into whatever you're up to. At the same time, being enrolled doesn't mean you have to want to do something. Someone may be enrolled in going on a trip with you, in sleeping with you, in a cool project you're working on and they still may not go on that trip, they still may not get into bed with you, and they still may not give you money towards your project or help you out in any way. And that's okay. Enrollment doesn't mean they agreed to anything. Think about your life. There are plenty of things you've felt moved by or inspired by and it didn't get you to take action.

Fear of failing

FOR EVERYONE who lets fear of failing, rejection, or disappointment stop you...just stop!

Put yourself out there so much with every ounce of your being. If you think your heroes who are really successful never fail, get rejected or feel disappointed, you're living in a fantasy world. In fact, take on becoming a master at all three. Failing doesn't make you a failure, rejection doesn't make you a reject, and not taking action to avoid all of this equates to wasting your damn life.

The fear of what could happen can feel overbearing at times. Anytime you get confronted by something uncomfortable. Allow yourself to feel that way, don't resist it and take the actions you truly know you need to take inside. It doesn't have to be the *right action*—which again comes from fear—but just something that moves the ball forward. Worst case is it doesn't and you try something else and take responsibility for any messes you make along the way.

Overtime as you push through all of this, your mental muscle around this will get stronger and your fear of failure will turn into a fear of inaction.

And this is a game with no end. If you think you're already there, then perhaps there's something bigger you could be taking on that you aren't.

Find those gaps and keep creating!

How to express your gifts fully

I BELIEVE—AS my own view, my truth—not necessarily *the truth*—that everybody has unique gifts to share on this planet.

Whether you discovered them yet or not is not the point. However, there's nothing to get, nothing to seek, and nowhere to arrive. It's all already inside you, right now. You just have to trust it, listen to that deep core knowing intuition, and then all there is to do is let it unfold.

It may not happen on your timetable. It may not happen the way you expected. However, if you keep acting from that place—beautiful things happen—and there's a beautiful and natural unfolding process. Trust it. Feel through it. Act on it. Intuition or what Napoleon Hill referred to as *universal intelligence* is the fuel and action is the car. Go out and drive. The road is endless until each one of our deaths.

TWO QUESTIONS—

1. *How do we drive?*
2. *How do we discover this intuitive nature?*

I had been struggling with how to teach the principles of intuition for a long time until I read a book called *The 5 Second Rule* by Mel Robbins.

She explains intuition and how to act on it better than anyone I've ever seen. So without going into why it works, the science behind it, and all the other stuff that you can read from her book—I'll explain the basic tool and how you can use the tool to practically apply on top of what I shared above.

Have you ever had the experience of being at a networking event and wanting to talk to someone but not going up to them, seeing someone you felt drawn to in a random location, thought about going to the gym, or thought about not eating something? Like you knew instinctively you should go talk to some person you saw at a networking event but you talked yourself out of it and had lots of reasons. You see someone at a random location and you literally feel pulled to talk to them but you stop yourself for whatever reason. You think about going to the gym and then you don't for whatever reason and you deep down feel shitty about it or guilty about it. You see that cookie or piece of cake and you instinctively know not to eat it but then you eat it anyway.

That *instinct* is what I'm saying is worth you following. That instinct is your brain's pattern recognition coming into play and figuring out actions you can take that will forward the things that truly matter to you in your heart of hearts. The cliché saying of "follow your heart" applies here. However, your brain also tries to keep you where you're at as it's trying to survive so most of the time it will choose survival over some new possibility or new action to take. It's very hard to override this as your brain will constantly find new ways to trick you into staying the same. Change is *very* difficult. It's simple but difficult.

AT SOME LEVEL, everyone *knows* what to do but then how well you actually execute is a different story. Imagine if you never stopped yourself and your default space was *not* thinking about it but execute, execute, execute. And that's possible. Not to be perfect but surely *way* better than you're doing now.

And that's where *the 5 Second Rule* comes into play.

· · ·

When you find yourself having some gut instinct and your mind starts going into thinking about it, you *immediately* say: "5, 4, 3, 2, 1," and then *right* after 1 you take action. You have 5 seconds to act. The very act of saying "5, 4, 3, 2, 1" is an action, and that in it of itself gets you out of your head. There's a lot of neuroscience behind this but basically, you've cut off all the survival wiring and you're able to act from a clear space. As you continue to do this, you will uncover new things to execute on. Many people take *years* to push themselves through things or before they *"build up enough courage"* to do it—which only actually takes *an instant* to make that choice.

Instead of trying to build up enough courage—just go "5, 4, 3, 2, 1" and take action. You will find over time many of the feelings and thoughts that keep you stuck will dissapear and your internal state will be *significantly* more aligned with the new actions you are taking. You will find yourself creating results and expressing gifts that you may not even have known were inside of you.

Even as I'm writing this I don't *feel* like writing and when I started writing this book I was not ready and had no idea how to express my gifts. I just started without thinking about it—and started writing and never looked back. Some of the greatest growth experiences I ever had are when I stopped thinking about it and just did it.

The 5 Second Rule actually gives you access to not think about things which is pretty amazing. I can see so many things in my life that would have happened sooner in life if I had this tool years ago.

When I see that cookie, "5, 4, 3, 2, 1, *health*" and I go eat something else or just don't eat the cookie or put it down.

Not feeling like writing today. "5, 4, 3, 2, 1, *write*" and I drive to a coffee shop and start writing.

I'm getting tired of writing, "5, 4, 3, 2, 1, *create a deadline for one more hour of writing*" and now I write for one more hour regardless of what comes out. Then maybe in the middle of writing, my brain starts generating actions to get out of my commitment. "5, 4, 3, 2, 1, *keep my fucking commitment*" and I keep writing

24 hours prior to writing this part of the book I was at the gym and did 3 rounds of:

- *1/2 mile jogging*
- *30 push-ups*
- *1-minute plank*

Or...1.5 miles of jogging, 90 push-ups, and 3 minutes of planks.

I often apply *the 5 Second Rule* to those planks. About 30 seconds in, my body begins to shake. Usually, with about 15-20 seconds to go, my mind starts telling me to stop and is literally generating thoughts like "I can't do this anymore." While it's easy to say that you won't listen to your thoughts—the truth is that your brain will come up with new ways to play tricks on you so that you stay put.

So with about 15 – 20 seconds to go of my planks and my body is shaking—"5, 4, 3, 2, 1, *plank*," and I stay with that plank. My body is still shaking. My sweat is dripping hard at that point. But I push through it *without* thinking about it.

Now imagine in life. You see that person you want to talk to..."5, 4, 3, 2, 1, *walk up and say hello and have a conversation."*

Who the fuck knows how that conversation goes? It doesn't matter! What matters is that you share your gifts and your actual Self-expression with the world—and in the process—you're much more likely to get results in life when you're constantly in action, disciplined, and honoring your agreements with the deepest part of your core than if you were to make excuses, talk yourself out of things, and not fully live out your potential.

There's something wrong

CONSIDER it's more effective to *be* the *what's missing* in your environments as opposed to going into *there's something wrong* mode and then spending all your efforts to resist, fix, and change.

"You never change things by fighting the existing reality. To change something, build a new model that makes the existing model obsolete."

— BUCKMINSTER FULLER

Creating an environment for innovation

CREATING an environment for innovation starts with setting an intention of having people be ready for something new. You're essentially "warming up the listening" of the environment.

When doing something new, one of the largest objections you will see is that people actually think what you're doing is worthy and that you're dead-on in your vision but the world / the organization / the group just isn't ready yet. It's the wrong time.

If you look at major innovations, it was almost always the wrong time.

So when building something new—take an interest in partnering with people who will help create acceptance in the environment to start implementing. On the inverse, if you want to be a catalyst for other people's visions you can do this for others and partner with others in this way.

Sometimes this takes conversations with key thought leaders.

Sometimes this means building structures and starting to impact people right away.

Focus on building the listening for people to accept the "something new" vs. ramming it through and people knowing what you're up to is good just "not the right time."

The former yields greater results.

4 principles for having the space to express your own genius

I SEE it again and again. Incredible people who are literally geniuses being told to fit into some box or trying to be something they are not. Yet if you ask the average person who is putting people into these boxes —they'd probably tell you how much they value greatness, how much they value innovation and genius, and how they wouldn't want the world to be mediocre. They'd also probably claim that they would want people to develop their own abilities to their full potential.

People complain about Steve Jobs being an asshole, yet Steve Jobs would never have been Steve Jobs without his borderline psychotic demands of people and his obsession with perfection in workability. I don't use that word as a bad thing but as an extreme statement. He was extreme. He was downright mean at times. It came from a commitment. People that say he should tone it down or learn to be more graceful miss the point. Nobody is ever perfect and to expect people to be perfect just ends up creating an environment of people who just suppress themselves instead so that they don't rock the boat.

HERE'S THE TAKEAWAYS—

Principle 1. If you want to express your natural genius—your higher maximized potential would be where you don't have to spend extra energy managing other people's comfort levels. This means surrounding yourself with people who will listen for your greatness and not react to any internal discomfort they may experience.

PRINCIPLE 2. Acknowledge that you will leave some people feeling internally uncomfortable and just be responsible for that vs. having it be some big deal or something you're making yourself wrong for. Apologizing for other people's experiences instantly will make you feel like shit and will keep having others judge you.

PRINCIPLE 3. Hang with people who will honor your core. This will naturally give you more confidence to be you as opposed to starting to question yourself in the wrong kind of environment.

PRINCIPLE 4. Don't resist this aspect of humanity otherwise you become the same judgmental asshole that you disliked in the first place. You become what you resist.

Living intentionally vs. by default

LIVING INTENTIONALLY and experiencing yourself as the cause of your own life. As the source of what's around you vs. life happening to you and you dealing with it is huge for people. I think most people know the difference at some level as this conversation is embedded enough in our culture. However, that awareness that exists doesn't give people access to that experience.

While this doesn't cover all of it—being able to be accountable and fulfill on one's word is a huge part of the picture. It's the opportunity to be intentional about life vs. it happening to do you, you having to deal with it, and it happening by default. You're feeling shitty so therefore your day is shitty is the kind of lazy thinking that happens when life is happening by default. There is no flow. Very little aliveness. And lots of pull for distractions.

Without truly committed speaking without making bold promises and declarations vs. only giving your word to things inside the world of ordinary and reasonableness is the difference between creating massive growth in life and having aliveness be some kind of peak moment at best. It's the difference between saying: *"I will create an amazing day and create two new partnerships today"* vs. *"I will try to do to the best I can since I feel shitty today"*

Being able to commit fully—without an escape plan and being

committed-ish—has power. When you don't commit fully, you actually diminish your own power and diminish the ability to trust yourself. This leads to less committed speaking and action in the future as someone who doesn't trust themselves can't really commit. Think about that shit for a second.

Coming from the space that *who you are is your word* has you be someone on the court in life vs. someone just observing and occasionally coming down to check out the game with all the opinions, judgments, and assessments that come with it. The latter leads to being run by your feelings, identity, and your past—which is all rooted in *survival* vs. some kind of creating that empowers you and has you feel alive.

When you operate from this space, your word actually moves shit in the world. When you give your word to something, you create an environment that upholds what you're committed to rather than your emotional state which is likely to change.

When your inner voice starts trying to talk you out of something, and you don't take action from that space, and instead, act from your commitment—you end up being larger than all of that. You then live into being who you are as your word vs. some kind of internal state or dialogue. Your commitment, your word, your promise becomes who you *actually are* vs. something that you are saying or that you said—which is how most people experience their word. In that moment—and then ever increasing over time, the relationship to how you experience both language and the world around you completely shifts.

The impact of this kind of operating is you end up producing exponentially larger results than you did before which is amazing news for people who are *already* high performers in life. It gets to the point where people will be literally baffled by how you can produce what you're producing especially if they knew you before having this kind of shift.

The other huge impact is this experience of being alive. There's a kind of courageousness, tenacity, and this kind of free-flowing energy that people start experiencing around you and you start experiencing yourself. There's this level of satisfaction that can't be faked with positive thinking or trying to convince yourself of something. It's just there as a natural Self-expression.

Fulfilling on the intention of rhetoric

WHY DO we as human beings get so obsessed with rhetoric? Well, I would argue that it's a function of looking good. We want to be liked and we want to be able to speak in a way that people hear. So there's nothing wrong with looking good and being liked. There's also nothing wrong with speaking in a way that people can hear. All great things. There's also nothing wrong with rhetoric. In fact, it's a beautiful art.

However, when it becomes used as a way to be inauthentic about something, the rhetoric stops becoming a powerful tool and ends up becoming a burden.

What moves people is not nice rhetoric. What moves people is sharing from the heart. Remember that the next time a part of you has this urge to want to get all rhetorical about something. Notice if there's something you're covering up in the process. Because if you are, people can sniff that shit out.

The game of rhetoric is one game that people play (especially politicians), but it's a very weak game to play. You are competing against everyone else also playing that game which also happens to be most people. There are probably a few people you can point out who have become insanely successful using inauthentic rhetoric. However, for every person who succeeds in spite of their inauthentic rhetoric (the illusion is that it's because of it), there are many more people who have succeeded in life because of authentic communication. I say, why not just play an easier and more effective game with much less competition?

"The fishing is best where the fewest go and the collective insecurity of the world makes it easy for people to hit home runs while everyone is aiming for base hits."

— TIM FERRISS

Blame

THE MOMENT you blame others for your own internal experiences, you've made a choice to be a slave to your own automatic human machinery all while pretending someone or something else outside of you has laid and locked your chains.

What gets in the way of Self-expression

ONE OF THE things that I would assert most people notice after going through any kind of journey towards creating purpose and empowering others to do the same is the insane amount of people who are literally afraid to let their true Selves be seen and truly known and experienced by others. Because, in my view, it comes off as downright stupid at first.

However, when you start to make distinctions for other people around how they get in the way of themselves, once they start making the connections—that shit just starts to stop running the show and they have more responsibility and choice about their life.

So here are some principles or mental models that when life is viewed through them can make a real difference in this area:

THE PRINCIPLE OF SHAME, Guilt, and Fear. When our minds go to a space of shame or fear. Not being good enough. An attachment to who we are supposed to be. All of that just creates blocks to our own aliveness and creates less clarity, more stress, and if you're someone who is religious or spiritual—more of a disconnect to your relationship to God or a higher source energy.

. . .

THE PRINCIPLE of our Strong Suits. This is a principle that is taught in *The Landmark Forum*. You could first think that our *strong suits* are a good thing. I mean it's the best parts of ourselves so that should just be totally badass! However, that's wrong. It's only half badass. Because what makes you a badass with your *strong suits* is also compensating for something else.

THE BACKSTORY to *strong suits* is that when we are born before we learn how to understand or use language, we don't yet have a personality. We have may some biological predispositions to behavior but nothing even close to what we call and define as our personality. Our experiences and social conditioning literally form our personality.

To add to all of this, there are three very distinct events that end up shaping our strong suits. And while this can be great and work to our favor, when we are slaves to this way of being—we will also get in our way when those ways of beings don't serve us or the people around us.

Understanding our *strong suits* explains to a large degree why your life looks like the way it does. When you see that it can be kind of sad when you get how little free will you had over this, it's also insanely liberating when you start to get you have some authentic choice as opposed to something you've always just assumed was part of you without even questioning it or thinking about it.

The hardest thing for some people is when these *strong suits* actually led to great results. They can for many people. However, you'll even have greater results going forward when you're running the show vs. your *strong suits* doing it for you.

There are three things to get clear about first:

You may not actually remember what happened during the timeline. When I was in the Forum, it took me the whole day to remember some of these events. Sometimes our brains really try to block this stuff out and if we aren't intentional about remembering, it often won't just come to us instantly. That's a survival mechanism hardwired into our brain.

You can have several *strong suits*. It doesn't have to be just one. For me, I have a few. Everyone is different.

Everyone has *strong suits* and you don't need to have some fucked up upbringing or have been raped or abused to experience trauma. Different events are traumatic for different people. And what gets people stuck is *never* what happened but the *meaning* they put towards those events about the event, about themselves, about the world, etc.

In order to discover a *strong suit,* you need to go back to when you're a young child. I'm talking about 4-7 years old approximately. Like that area. Again this isn't black and white so if you were 3 or 8, it doesn't really fucking matter.

I used to do Taekwondo when I was a kid. One of the most famous Taekwondo grandmasters was beaten up by a little girl when he was a kid. I would assert his strong suite was in the realm of "being tough," and he spent his entire life trying to compensate for something that happened to him when he was a kid.

For me, when I was little, I was publicly humiliated at recess and my friend who I trusted at the time called me the "cootie boy" in front of everyone, and it stuck. From that point on I became "ambitious & passionate," and, it was all under the guise of trying to compensate for there something being wrong with me and that I would be "found out." So that *strong suite* led me to always have ulterior motives, to be in control, to dominate situations, and I needed to manipulate to get my way—because down deep I really didn't feel powerful in my authentic way of being—and I didn't even know I didn't know that.

I also used my charm, intelligence, and wit to get by with people. I would never fully commit but always would have a way out just in case things got dangerous. I always was looking for danger. I was always looking for the threat of being discovered as a fraud, or that people would truly see how fucked up I was and how there was something wrong with me. So the more I did that, the more I perpetuated that story for my life which then drove me even harder and to work even harder at it. I was very successful at it so there wasn't really any incentive that I could see in trying to stop. Why would I stop something that was working already? Of course, it was destroying me inside and thank god I discovered all of this at age 20.

However, it didn't just end with being the "cootie boy." Fast forward to my teen years and now I'm overweight. I was over 200 pounds and pre-diabetic. I remember being at school and not having a lot of close friends. That, of course, validated my earlier story of how there was something wrong with me and I needed to learn new techniques and tricks to get more friends. I just remember seeing people around me and *knowing* that they were better than me, *knowing* they had more to offer the world than me, and *knowing* they were more valued in society. However, this *knowing* didn't occur for me as something in my mind that I made up—which in reality is all that it was, a disempowering story I created— it simply occurred for me as... "the way it was."

So then I "learned" that I had to be independent and "love myself." The box got tighter and I called it "growing."

I "learned" that nobody loved me and that led me to start operating with an "independent" mindset so I could get this love for myself.

I'm not sharing this as some sob story—I produced a lot of amazing results in my life because of my strong suits: "independent" and "strong-willed."

I learned to be self-taught. I learned to start thinking for myself and explore concepts that made other people afraid. I was able to get along with almost all social groups and was able to approach people and situations with less judgment and more curiosity. My curiosity is insanely high. I also spent more alone time which helped me get incredibly comfortable by myself and learned to hone my creativity and passions even more. This stuff now comes very naturally for me, and it's been a huge blessing and leg up for me in life.

Human beings develop a third *strong suit* when they're in your late teens or early 20's. This is when one starts to realize they're on their own in life.

I felt very powerless getting this. I decided I needed to go into a field where I would never have to worry about a shortage of financial resources for the rest of my life. That's what had me go hardcore into learning how to be a value investor and find amazing deals in markets. However, it got to the point where it became a part of my "personality," and I started actually distancing myself from others as a way to fit the mold and focus on "important stuff." Relationships to me at this point were a means to an end—something to be commoditized and manipulated like chess pieces on a board. They were transactional in nature. I was truly an asshole at this point while on the surface pretending to be nice.

Of course, I had a lot of success from this. I lost 70 pounds from this strong suit. I became one of the popular kids my senior year of high school and went from being picked last in gym class to being picked first or being made captain in gym class when picking people for our teams. I was still a scared and hurt little boy, but now, I had the whole pretending thing going on very well, and I learned how to be very charming. I also started building my investment track record and prepping for the day when I would run my own firm. I also started reading personal development books as a way to compensate for all this shit in the background. So I would read these books through my manipulative lens. Oh, Dale Carnegie says you should say people's names in "How to Win Friends and Influence People." Cool, now it's my new inauthentic manipulation.

However, by being an inauthentic piece of shit, I hurt a lot of people emotionally during this phase in my life and had a lot of cleaning up to do.

So what's the take away from all of this? Here are some of the things you can get as a result of seeing your strong suits for yourself:

It gives you an amazing perspective on all the meaning you've been putting onto things in your life and forgetting you were the one that created the meaning. You then stop being a slave to your meaning-making and start having some freedom in areas where some underlying shit was running the show. Whipped cream on shit is still shit, and in my case, the whipped cream was all the manipulations and tactics that I was learning on the surface. Something happens. Then you make it mean something and it almost always further validates how you see the world. Seeing your strong suits for what they are is actually kind of funny. I mean think about this for a second. Like literally a famous grandmaster of Taekwondo created his entire life because a little girl made him feel not good enough. How fucking insane is that?

Once you distinguish what created those strong suits, you now have some space to see them objectively as opposed to being run by them. Now you have them as opposed to your *strong suits*...having you!

You get freedom from them as opposed to being dominated by them. Distinguishing your *strong suits* takes you out of all the automatic garbage running the show. I cannot tell you how many people I have met who are either "stubborn" or "independent" and when they get this, they are released from it, and now are able to be contributed to by others.

Since identifying my *strong suits* in the summer of 2008, I have stopped experiencing the need to control in life. I stopped needing to lie and hide my true motives with people. I stopped needing to hide myself. My peace of mind and aliveness shot instantly through the roof to levels that only used to be "peak moments," and, a weight came off my shoulder I never even knew I had in the first place. Besides, the quality of my relationships instantly transformed—I was left with a much more profound emotional connection with the people in my life. Through giving up the need for control, I actually have more control and more power in my life, but, without all the effort and energy I used to put into it.

Strong suits got me to realize that the strongest parts of my personality were actually compensating for something else. For example, if you're good at controlling your environment, you're afraid to lose control. If you always need to be tough, you're really just scared little boy or girl afraid to getting beaten up again. If you're someone who is super nice, you're afraid that people won't like you when you're straightforward and will be offended. Identifying these things doesn't diminish your power or take them away. If anything, it makes you even more powerful and allows you to own these strengths as opposed to them owning you. When you let them go, it pushes you out of your comfort zone in a huge way and your perspective on the world and yourself becomes that much exponentially greater.

The final thing I'll talk about is our *rackets*. This is also a principle I learned in the *Landmark Forum* and for most human beings, at any given time, they're either operating from their *strong suits*, or they're operating from their *rackets*. So what the fuck is a racket?

The Life Management Alliance

The Life Management Alliance delves into this framework for thinking perfectly. A special thanks to Keith Garrick for making this available for free and giving me permission to use it in the book.

Definition: Any dishonest scheme or practice, a pretending to be one thing and being another for an undisclosed benefit to the "perpetrator," almost always at a cost to the "victim."

"The stream of excuses we use to condone our stupid actions."

374

In this case in life, we are referring to where you are fooling yourself into consistently producing some undesirable result. Unraveling that is what creates a whole new way of being.

This is actually not about right/wrong or good/bad, but about creating "what works."

Perhaps the Origination of the Concept

In a discipline/method called *Transactional Analysis*, the term was used as a core concept. The definition excerpted from Wikipedia:

"A racket is then a set of behaviours which originate from the childhood script rather than in here-and-now full Adult thinking, which (1) are employed as a way to manipulate the environment to match the script rather than to actually solve the problem, and (2) whose covert goal is not so much to solve the problem, as to experience these racket feelings and feel internally justified in experiencing them."

The one we'll use in here: An ongoing complaint justifying the behavior that is attached to it, for the purpose of getting believed payoffs that are illusionary, obtained at a great personal cost to oneself.

The Life Management's Alliance worksheet on rackets which is available for free online is extremely useful. I will now share with you what I believe to be the most vital and relevant parts of the document:

The Components of a *Racket*
1. A negative statement/belief/complaint/result or "reason why not" that persists over time, without being solved. (If one is feeling powerless or inauthentic, there is a racket.)
2. A pattern of behavior related to it.
3. Believed payoff(s) (that is an illusory one)
4. Costs of something more important

The Sure Indicators that you are doing a *Racket*
If any of these payoffs are going on. (Often more than one)

1. Making somebody else wrong
2. Making yourself wrong
3. Being "right" about anything (even if you know you are)
4. Not feeling powerful in that part of your life

<u>Probable Indicators:</u> (Note the indicator and inquire to yourself about whether it is part of a racket)
1. Being inauthentic and hiding something
2. Trying to dominate/control someone

<u>How to Be *Racket-free*</u>
Give up being right. This means giving up your point of view with another. [If your friend thinks the sky is purple and you know it's blue, let it be purple...especially if it's costing you the friendship]
This is possibly the most important lesson to learn in life to live a happy life, as it frees up an enormous amount of wasted energy and attention so that one can be clear about seeing life and what is to be done next.

<u>How to Find Out Your *Rackets*</u>
Just list any complaint or "reason why not" you've had for a while now, on a piece of paper.

Fill these in based off of what is true from the suggestions. (and then feel free to add your own)

My racket (a complaint about something, having some excuse or reason that is leaving you feeling disempowered) is: _____.

My behavior consistently attached to it: _____.
(Possible Behaviors: withdrawing, disconnecting, being resigned, feeling sad, isolated, alone, self-justification, pouting)

Payoffs: _____.
(Possible Payoffs: being right, making others wrong, looking good, believed control or protection, illusory relief of illusory fear, trying to avoid feeling like a victim or being dominated by another, believed power over another)

Costs: _____.
(Possible Costs: aliveness, connection, happiness, satisfaction, peace of mind, loss of power, reduced freedom, feeling bad, regret, shame, guilt)

I recognize this and I have weighed the costs and assessed the payoffs. I know this is not for my better good, so I hereby give up this ruse. I also hereby commit to correcting any damage and making any necessary amends.

I acknowledge that I am responsible for creating this and that I am not the victim of another or of any circumstance. I acknowledge that my perceptions and even my beliefs about what I believe are facts could be incorrect. I acknowledge that the other person is simply doing what is appropriate given his/her viewpoint, circumstances, and present awareness and that what was done or decided by the other person totally makes sense in their world, though, as with me, those could be in error.

What I Really Want Is: _____.
It is fine to want to create a specific result, but it is important to look at the feeling you want to get from or related to that result and it is important to identify what you want that would actually give you the ability to generate the results you want, such as "being powerful," "being calm and content," etc.

And to remove the barriers to getting that I will: _____.

The possibilities I create are now: _____.
(the opposite of the impossibilities plus support of who to be, what to do....)

The beliefs that are not true are: _____.

The beliefs I create that are true and empowering replacements are: _____.

What I will do to correct any damage is:_____.

(Possible Examples: forgive or ask forgiveness, make amends, make the other person whole by offsetting any damage done by me)

Communicate what needs to be said, stop withholding communication and/or hiding it. Communicate my responsibility in the matter and what I did and what doesn't work and my new promise or commitment. Listen to the other person until that person is fully heard and knows it.

Checkmark what is below and also free to add your own:
___ Communicate my responsibility in the matter and what I did and what doesn't work and my new promise or commitment.
___ Communicate what needs to be said
___ Stop withholding communication and/or hiding something.
___ Listen to the other person until that person is fully heard and knows it.

My Commitment
I hereby, now and forever, give up this racket and all stories connected with it.
I now declare this to no longer exist.
Committed to this ____ day of _____, ____.

Diminishing yourself to make a difference

You can be kind, loving, and generous and there will always be those who won't notice it or even perceive you as being the opposite. Why do you think that in the times when you're most confident, the most vital, Self-expressed, and totally being great—the people who get annoyed with you the most are the people who are often victims in their life, who are often complaining and gossiping, and who are often finding something to be annoyed or stressed about?

It's simple.

When you shine your light in the darkness, when you're clear about who you are and what your mission is in life—some people will see their own light and rise up. However, some people will also recoil as they aren't ready to see themselves. People who are most disconnected to their authentic Self-expression and know themselves the least will always be the ones that get the most triggered and defensive around you when you're being authentic Self. Those people are simply acting out a reflection of how they perceive the world and your way of being simply don't fit into it that mold.

But here's a principle I find crucially important as it relates to this subject:

Nobody ever makes huge differences in the world by diminishing themselves so they don't rock the boat. People who do that will find themselves becoming less powerful, they'll diminish their own vitality and aliveness in life, *and* they will still get judged regardless...guaranteed. Therefore, anyone who truly gets that would see that to hold back out of fear of being judged is insanely stupid and irrational.

The pitfall of speaking from concepts
and beliefs

BE A TRUTH SEEKER. Nothing irks me to my core like someone trying to have a conversation with me that's more about proving some view than getting to the bottom of things. I'm not attracted to conversations where the sole purpose of the conversation is to validate my belief about something. If you're someone in life who is committed to your expanding your own intellectual capacity and growth than neither should you!

Be interested in finding out what works and the principles behind why something works as opposed to creating some belief system about something which can easily be used to shut down a conversation.

When you jump out of an airplane without a parachute, you will fall to the ground and most likely die. That's not a belief. That's not some moral view on life. That's just simply what happens regardless of your opinions, morals, values, and beliefs about the clouds, gravity, aerodynamics, and your ability to flap your arms and fly.

So when people call you close-minded about something which will happen when you choose to engage in possibilities of inquiry and exploration as opposed to agreement conversations, when all they do is throw character attacks at you, want to change the subject, or use some other logical fallacy...there's nothing to do other than shine light on the fact that you aren't interested in those kinds of conversations and it either kind of snaps them awake or they just get more defensive in which by doing so, you then get your answer about what they're *actually* committed to. I say that because we all get into agree/disagree conversations sometimes. But when someone calls me out on it, I stop instantly because it's so out of line with what I'm committed to. You will find many others are like that as well and many others are not.

Now let's imagine if the argument to counter the airplane statement was one of the following:

1. You're an idiot; therefore you're wrong.
2. You're mean; therefore you're wrong.
3. I didn't like that tone; therefore what you say doesn't matter.
4. Gravity goes against my beliefs; therefore we shall agree to disagree.
5. My philosophy does against this; therefore let's agree to disagree.
6. I get that's your view about jumping out of airplanes so just do what works for you, and I'm *so* glad it works for you to not jump out of planes with no parachute; I just don't agree.
7. Well, most people don't think that including a lot of very smart scientists (or whatever professional title can create a sense of authority).
8. Well, the information you are getting could easily be biased.
9. Birds can fly so what you're saying isn't necessarily true. With effective ways of flapping your hands—there are definitely ways of making it happen.

Now apply all of this to your conversations in life.

Transforming a shit environment

ALWAYS SURROUND yourself with people who will match you where you're at, who will acknowledge you and listen to you for how you want to be acknowledged and listened to in your heart of hearts. Surround yourself with people who will always bring out the best in you and won't entertain your small and petty bullshit yet always work to encourage you to grow and expand. That gives life to the soul. You'll be more productive, you'll be happier, and you'll find more ease in having what you in want in life. I cannot stress enough how important our environment is to the quality of our lives. Our Self-expression is given to us by how we are listened to. Sure...we can learn to transform our environment and sometimes that's appropriate.

However, spending time transforming environments take up unnecessary space when you can choose environments that will just naturally be that way.

Complaints perpetuate bullshit

COMPLAINTS PERPETUATE BULLSHIT. They do no good and destroy your aliveness. Be what you want to see in the world and be a role model for others and give space to the crap that doesn't work.

If you are *standing* for *peace on the planet*—then look around you—do you have *peace* with the people that you have every reason *not* to have it with?

If you are standing for *love in the world*—then look around you—do you have *love* with the people who have given every reason for you *not* to love them?

If you can be brutally straight with yourself—don't expect to solve wars, extermination, genocide, political turmoil, or make a difference with people who may put up some resistance—when you throw people out of your life, cut off your relationships, go out of communication, withhold communication, or hold grudges.

If you're at war with ex-lovers, with other family members, with old friends gone astray, or haven't really been able to forgive others and create new outcomes and projects—that weren't going to happen just by going through the motions—don't expect to cause *freedom, peace, love,* or anything you're committed to causing in the world when you can only take on that *way of being* when it's convenient for you and when your environment calls for it.

384

Imagine if Gandhi was *standing for* peace in India while at the same time was talking poorly about an old friend for punching him in the face. Well, let's just say he would have been a very ineffective leader and would have had some very nice justifications and some damn good reasons.

Developing yourself vs. your vision developing you

LOTS OF PEOPLE wait until they're ready for something. They get addicted to self-help, get more degrees, read more books, or whatever distraction they use as a way to not deal with taking action now. I am all for developing yourself and your skill-sets. It's both a hobby and a passion of mine. However, it's not good when you use that as an excuse not to take action. This is distinct from reading books on programming because you want to become a programmer and you're teaching yourself that skillset or you want to become a doctor; therefore, you take action and apply to med school.

What really has people grow is when they create a vision or goal for themselves, and then despite feeling ready or not, they go out and do whatever they can to fulfill on that vision or goal. As long as you don't recoil when things get uncomfortable, and instead, you expand to include whatever comes up for you, your vision or goals will naturally move you through the spaces you need to go through to develop yourself. There's this concept in psychology called "impostor syndrome" which is a term coined in 1978 by clinical psychologists Dr. Pauline R. Clance and Suzanne A. Imes referring to high-achieving individuals marked by an inability to internalize their accomplishments and a persistent fear of being exposed as a "fraud."

It's really common. I was 26 when I first got elected as a member of the New Hampshire House of Representatives, not much later, when I started my own investment firm as opposed to going up the corporate ladder. I was 20 when I created *Energy Independence Day,* and I was a teenager when I started writing about investing and was getting paid for my articles.

I've felt imposter syndrome first hand.

When I started my firm, I did not have a network of wealthy individuals or families who would throw me money. I had to develop a way of expressing myself in a way that really shared my vision and explained what the hell I did. I also had to share in a way that shared my background and my principles and have it resonate with people with no investment background. I failed a lot at the beginning. I didn't get my first investor until many months after starting my firm. I had to re-adjust constantly and continuously learn.

I went to the Apple Store and had them teach me how to give effective presentations and we watched Steve Jobs presentations together. I had to learn to build relationships with people in new ways. I had to learn to ask for money in the 6 figures. I had to earn my way through it and I'm a different person now because of it.

When you take on larger things than you can ever dream possible, you will step out on the other end of it a different person. You will deal with things you've never dealt with, take on things you've never taken on, and you will create bigger problems for yourself than you ever experienced in your life. Dr. Martin Luther King, JR, Gandhi – they had some huge problems.

The larger you play, the larger your problems become. One thing I am clear on is that when people have dreams yet something keeps stopping them, it's never out there, even when that's what it looks like – it's within us. Once we are ready and willing to take that on, the thing that stops us disappears, we are free, and we move through the next space of our journey in our lives.

Being blind to costs

ANYBODY CAN USE a personal anecdote in order to justify an emotional argument. If the country you lived in subsidized bacon and now your neighbor who was starving has food on his table—then one could try to make the claim that the bacon subsidization program worked.

Of course what's missing from view is how many people's lives were harmed to make that happen.

The correct question to ask in that case would be *at what cost did executing this program produce the given outcome?*

To not look at the costs or possible unintended consequences as it applies to this situation is foolish.

We can apply this "being blind to costs" principle onto any area in our lives. If you live your life spending energy on manipulating and control, sometimes, you'll get what you want. On the surface, you'll see the payoff. But again: at what cost? How's your aliveness? How's your peace of mind? What relationships did you destroy in the process? What would life be like if you didn't need to manipulate and control? What is that costing you?

If the only answer you can give is an emotional argument to justify your own belief with no basis for reality, you are merely emotionally attached to a point of view, and you have thrown reason and thinking out the window.

Creating a project and then getting out
of the way

❧✿❧

I ALWAYS GET INCREDIBLY INSPIRED by the tremendous generosity of people coming together to create something for the world larger than themselves.

The first project I ever created was called *Freedom Rising*. It was an event of about 20 people aimed to cause a breakthrough with individuals who were committed to expanding freedom on the planet regardless of what their expression of that looked like.

For me, it's through delivering leadership programs so people can experience more freedom in their lives regardless of their circumstances and also through my work as a legislator by doing whatever I can to allow more people to live their lives the way they see fit as long as they aren't impeding on someone else's right to do the same.

By 4 pm on the day of the event, I would have literally been able to walk away from that event and the event would have continued to unfold and expand without me. It had taken a life of its own. I had created the space for people to contribute towards a greater commitment.

Those kinds of groups are going to be more powerful on average than taking a bunch of people with great "stats" together in a room who at their core are not aligned around something much larger than themselves.

Groups organized like that tend to resort to team building, motivational speaking, or flavor of the month consultants to work on "team strategies."

Structure never lies and a structure that doesn't lead to team and partnership will always reject the new strategy or technique.

"Culture eats strategy for breakfast every day."

— PETER DRUCKER

There is an enormous freedom to be able to create projects where people are centered around a cause larger than themselves and you can step away and give up control. Anyone who needs to constantly be in control of a project lacks very little power around concepts of team and partnership.

There's also an enormous freedom in organizations and projects where people are *naturally* collaborating like this—notice I said *naturally* —where you don't need the kinds of top-down structures and micro-management that comes with the territory of command and control organizations with no real underlying core values uniting people.

And, yes, every fucking organization has their core values list and mission statement, but it only makes a difference when it's actually in the organization vs. just being talked about or used to discipline people, which is a form of control and domination.

Resisting is less effective than creating

CONSIDER that love is more powerful than any form of resistance. *Fixing and changing* "what's so" typically leads to more of the same and it just shows up a bit differently each time. Consider where you have been trying to fix and change things. Look to see what you can create instead. There isn't usually just one answer as there are many ways to skin a cat. However, this framework for thinking does tend to be more effective when applied to whatever you're committed to in life.

3 options for less than desirable surroundings

IF YOU'RE AN ALL-STAR NFL quarterback on a high school football team then you have a few options:

Option 1. You can throw the football the way you'll normally throw it. However, doing this, your receivers might complain to you that you're throwing the ball too hard.

Option 2. You can throw the football softly thereby reinforcing mediocrity in others and in yourself.

Option 3. You can take responsibility for the receivers being great: develop them to a point where their skill level is at a place that you now have space to throw the ball hard.

Inquiry into truth vs. justifying belief

SOME PEOPLE ARE MORE interested in defending a position than they are in getting to the bottom of things. When righteousness becomes a substitute for inquiry—listening goes out the window, and it's a bankrupt conversation.

When you find someone else doing this—a *very* powerful way of making an impact in this conversation is asking some very simple questions.

POSSIBLE THINGS TO ASK:

1. If you found new evidence to change your mind about this topic, would you?
2. Are you more interested in seeking the truth and willing to consistently look to be wrong and go deeper down the rabbit hole or are you more committed to validating what you already believe to be true and not willing to have an inquiry about it?

This *often* helps a conversation become an inquiry. And if it doesn't, it simply says a lot about what someone else is committed to and it's best you let it go.

My year long social experiment

ONE OF THE most life-changing social experiments I ever took on was disabling texting on my phone for one year in 2013 going into 2014. Not only did it make me less reliant on instant gratification, it also drastically increased the richness of my relationships.

It was truly an amazing experience and an experiment I'm enormously grateful to have taken on. The outcome was more people calling me, more efficient communication (things got worked out quicker on the phone), and communication was more clear, and miscommunications which would happen occasionally by text would end up almost always being worked through on the phone where it wouldn't be rare for them not to get worked through by text and then that could sometimes lead to the nasty pattern of phone call avoidance. It also led to a diminishing expectation from others for instant gratification.

You call someone. They call you back. You talk. Simple. Before texting, busy executives had time for making phone calls. Business in both the United States and abroad worked just fine without instant gratification. It will continue to do so in the future.

In 2016 I took on a new practice which I never intend to stop which is that almost every day I make time on the phone with the people in my life.

No agenda. Just sharing.

In the age of instant gratification, so many people cut corners in their relationships. Just because someone is your friend on Facebook doesn't replace a friendship. Just because you text someone doesn't mean you're communicating. Consider our biological makeup isn't wired for communication through texting. It's also sad to me that people of my generation and younger have now developed social anxiety around real-time communication and are afraid to talk on the phone.

Often people justify this by saying "I don't like talking on the phone." However what's behind that dislike is often unexplored. If you can't just *be* with someone on the phone and share, that isn't a problem with phone calls, that's you.

While some people don't use their phones to communicate in the name of efficiency—it comes with some costs. I'm not saying texting is wrong or bad. In fact, it's a great tool. And like all tools, it can be ineffective when used inappropriately. I wouldn't pound in a nail with a fork and I wouldn't eat with a hammer. I wouldn't try to have a conversation with letter writing either, letter writing is for writing letters.

In fact, the efficiency argument often ends up just being an excuse to cut corners and ends up coming from a space of scarcity.

There have been many studies on this topic.

Researchers at Brigham Young University asked young people who were married, engaged, or in a committed relationship to complete a questionnaire regarding how they used text messages to communicate with their partner. Many of those surveyed reported texting with their partner several times a day, the type and frequency of texts sent were directly correlated to the quality of the relationship.

The results:

The more texts women sent, the more likely it was that they were happy with their relationship. The opposite was true for men.

Details of the research appeared in The Journal of Couple and Relationship Therapy.

And in 2016 in the magazine Psychology Today, Russell B. Lemie writes:

"Just how well do we read our intimate partners? As long as we're composed, we're generally pretty good at it. But whenever our threat emotions (i.e., anxiety and anger) are triggered, accuracy goes right out the window."

And of course Werner Erhard the father of the human potential movement and founder of EST even alluded to this during an interview with the New York Times in 2015:

"One of his current preoccupations is the numbing effects of digital technology on millennials. Warming to the subject, he read aloud another passage, this one from a dense Heidegger essay calling for a 'comportment toward technology which expresses yes and at the same time no.'...'The cost to this generation is enormous,' Mr. Erhard said. 'They are losing access to their humanity.'"

It's truly sad that a generation that can text with their phones can often lack the experience of being powerful and present with someone in real time. Being able to powerfully use technology to serve us while honoring our humanity is very powerful indeed.

Results:

My communication with others drastically improved.

When things get tough or uncomfortable (and they will!) I'm never in a position where I can't appropriately communicate, share, speak, and listen.

To this day, I have never lost a friendship, relationship, or ever had a conversation go poorly when it was done in person and seen through to completion. (key phrase: seen through to completion)

Creating a space for honesty

WE CAN TAKE 100% responsibility for creating an environment that allows people to share authentically with us and allows others to share authentically with others in our space.

A part of me finds it really fucking sad when people get scared to share very personal things with me because in the past they've been judged for it. I love it when people share the deepest parts of their hearts with me and share all the different sides and parts to them as I love what makes people human.

Have people get (if you want) that "You offended me" will never come out of your mouth and that if you feel offended that you don't blame someone else for YOUR experience.

Have people get (if you want) that "You're making me uncomfortable" will never come out of your mouth. That doesn't mean let people walk all over you. It means when you feel discomfort to give space to it as opposed to trying to resist it, fix it, and/or getting trapped in a mindset that they're doing something to you. It's never out there and the moment you start blaming someone else for how you feel, you're screwed!

Choosing to BE comfortable in the face of discomfort allows you to grow your comfort zones and hold space for others in an expanded capacity. That's truly a wonderful thing. That way of operating in the world is what you call "expand to include." Practice that every day for a year and you'll have expanded in ways you didn't even know were possible. *I can actually promise that.*

Have people get that things like "you're being too needy" or "too pushy" will never come out of your mouth. No communication you're not willing to be with. Practice that and the level of radical honesty that will be around you will expand. Everything becomes easier with honesty.

If you want to know why people lie in your space. It's because they don't feel safe to share. And yes, you can choose to come from the position of being 100% responsible for creating that space for people to be authentic.

Creating projects to transform how you're being heard

THERE'S a common complaint or frustration in society about people not being heard for how they feel inside. What's the difference between Gandhi standing for peace and being listened to as that commitment to peace as distinct from being listened to as a kook or some pushy individual talking irrationally and not dealing with reality?

Your access to that is first getting that your Self-expression is a function of the way your community hears you. If you've listened to as small or listened to just as your personality—you will never have the space to create great things without your environment suffocating you along the way. So how do you make space for yourself to be fully Self-expressed in your environment?

It's about taking 100% responsibility for how your community listens to you and your access is *not* through trying to convince people or persuade people you're a certain way. In fact, that just makes you look like a fucking tool and actually creates more resistance, as that's inauthentic manipulation. People can sniff out that shit from a mile away.

One very powerful access to impacting how your community listens to you is through creating a project and not waiting for the perfect circumstances. In this case, waiting for the right circumstances is a trap. It could be something as small as creating a family reunion where your intention is to creating peace in your family and during the event, everyone acknowledges everyone else authentically and you can facilitate that conversation. Or, it could be creating a pro-peace rally in Washington DC and you take on bringing influential community leaders to share. There's literally no limitations.

When you create a project regardless of whether it succeeds or fails and get your community involved, the way your community listens to you evolves.

There are plenty of great resources out there for learning how to create projects and developing those skill-sets.

My personal favorites are the *Self-expression & Leadership Program* delivered by *Landmark Worldwide*, *Leadership by Design* which is a program created by John King the author of *Tribal Leadership* and is also a course that I lead, and the book "*Tribal Leadership*", especially the "strategy model" tool which is an amazing tool that I use all the time.

Conversations that bring something new into existence

WE NEED MORE HIGHLY conscious and empowered men and women on this planet. There's currently a huge gap in areas of the world where it's particularly called for—such as in business and politics. It's not enough to simply tolerate all the make-wrong, gossip, resentments, and all the other ineffective garbage people spew that makes no difference.

There are currently many organizations popping up and amazing individuals that are creating new models into existence in the world due to many of the models of *what it means to be a human being* and *what it means to be an organization* having become outdated. These outdated models have led to ways of thinking, being, and acting that are in now many cases simply inappropriate to the kind of workability that we demand in our future even though many of those same models progressed humanity to where we are today. There's nothing inherently bad or wrong about any of them, it's that they simply don't serve the same kind of positive contribution to society that they once did.

If there's an expression, an idea, or some way of being, thinking, or acting that you can see or distinguish that doesn't seem to exist in the world today, then you can be 100% responsible for bringing it forth and helping other people uncover and distinguish this as well. We are living in an age where there's an evolution of thought that we haven't seen since the time of the Dark Ages shifting to the Renaissance. With what started in the early 1900's in the world of personal development with thinkers like Napoleon Hill to all the crazy shit during the times of the 1960s and the human potential movement to some of the incredible stuff being produced today—there is a renaissance of thinking, being, and acting currently occurring today.

When you get that, it makes it extra exciting to be alive in today's time. While most of the media and the news focuses on the new technology that's out (which is also incredibly important), you rarely see news stories (if ever) about some new distinction for transforming an environment that's been created or for a new way to stop a war from happening or creating peace in an environment of violence. Often, we may have some epiphany or insight and then justify it away because it doesn't fit some existing model for reality that we have today. If you know it in your heart to be true, start sharing it and correct course along the way.

However you choose to take action on those insights and intuitions, do not drown out that little voice of deep intuitive knowing with reasonableness or some sort of self-doubt. That deep knowing intuition is part of your gift that you have to give the world, and the world is becoming ever more ripe to engage in these kinds of conversations. What you share won't be for everyone, but with those who have ears to hear and with minds to engage, you'll start impacting others, and your thinking will evolve along the way. You will discover and uncover new things through dialogue. It won't happen through it staying inside of you and thinking about it and analyzing it.

Playing empowering games

THERE'S a complaint in society called, "I don't like people who play games." Bullshit! Everything is a *game* and not every *game* is worth playing.

People who spend their time playing the *game* called "trying to fix unworkability" will just die getting good at fixing unworkability which actually doesn't work too well. Instead, get clear about the paradigm you want for all areas of your life: business partners, friendships, sex, relationships, love, workplace culture, etc. Get clear on exactly what that looks like and what you're committed to and *only* come from that paradigm. Essentially, you're creating the rules and boundaries for the games you're committed to playing—and then, go play. The principle of game will make an impact on the kinds of dynamics you have in your life as opposed to them just being some default accident you got stuck with: both the one's that empower you and the one's that don't.

Never stop playing the *game* you're committed to playing in the name of "someday." You'll weed out people that aren't willing to play at that level or or don't see the game you're playing as realistic or possible—and those people will always have their reasons and justifications obviously—and over time your reality will reflect your creation.

The source of guilt & shame

IF YOU EVER FEEL GUILTY, shameful, or angry at yourself after taking a certain action, then I can almost guarantee you there's some unexpressed anger or resentment there from something in the past.

So instead of expressing that anger or resentment out of fear of how the other person will react, you get angry at yourself instead because it's easier and less mentally threatening. This kills off aliveness, vitality, Self-expression, and your ability to experience authentic Self-love as opposed to the kind of bullshit positive thinking giving of yourself affirmations about how amazing you are when internally you still feel *off* or *incomplete* inside.

If you want to have that experience of being whole and complete, then go express your anger or resentments, and then if it gets messy, don't cave. Keep going. Keep staying in the conversation and make sure the person you're talking to knows they have the space to say anything to you as well. This can be especially tough when it's with someone you love dearly (like a parent) who may have put you in the wrong for something you did as a little kid *or* perhaps someone that bullied you or victimized you in some way.

Reaching out to that person can be quite uncomfortable and be detrimental when it's coming from a place of survival hence why many psychologists recommend to not reach out to people who have victimized you in the past. However, what's at stake is your own freedom. The ongoing patterns will continue (and not just with you but very likely with your children as well) unless you get them complete now. Get things complete. On the other side of that is freedom. No positive thinking needed.

Lobotomy 2.0

THE MOST BEAUTIFUL people I've ever met in my life have always been the most Self-expressed, the most creative, the most passionate, the most sexual, the most warrior or goddess-like, the most radiant, the most emotionally intense, and they all had this intense drive to fulfill their commitments and make a difference by giving their all with whatever truly mattered to them in their heart of hearts.

You can almost guarantee that every one of these people would be diagnosed with some form of depression, bipolar, anxiety, or some other disorder through a psychological assessment. And then we wonder as a society people are afraid to express their sadness, express their anger, and express their pain.

We teach people to resist their humanity as opposed to empowering them to give them the tools to foster and hone their genius, greatness, and goodness. I think people who want to suppress others under the guise of fixing them is the sickness, not the cure. And I think that's a damn shame.

We've come a long way since lobotomies, but we still have a long way to go.

Creating gaps

SPEAK and act to create a gap between where you or others are at and what you're committed to. This leads to insane growth. Don't worry about speaking down and acting down to the level of others. Come from a place where both yourself and others have to grow and rise to the conditions you set. Set the conditions, see who shows up to the party. Let the pieces fall where they will.

Environments of partnership vs. control

PEOPLE WHO NEED to be in control always need to surround themselves with people who they can dominate. It's a game with a winner and a loser and has no end.

People who are about creating stable and collaborative partnerships with others, who are out to make a difference on the planet, and who refuse to engage in these win/lose power struggle games tend to:

1. Be miserable in those environments because they know deep down there's something much more powerful than the environment they are currently in (and they would be right, typically 3-5x more effective as discovered by John King when doing research for the book "Tribal Leadership").
2. Be kicked out of the environment.
3. Leave the environment and seek an environment more aligned with what they're committed to.

People who experience aliveness and comfort in an environment not rooted in actual partnership but in survival actually don't see that it's possible to go beyond that. They may get the concept of partnership intellectually but it will be about how does one control, dominate, and manipulate to create partnership with others. This, in turn, just leads to more of the same. It will be their identity getting the concept as opposed to getting it viscerally and having an actual breakthrough in the realm of being in partnership with another.

Judging character

IF YOU WANT to get a good sense of a person—maybe not the truth but pretty damn close:

1. See who their friends are, the people they spend the most time around, and the environments they spend time in.
2. See how they act when times aren't good—are they reliable, trustworthy, and accountable? Do they honor their word?

Create powerful environments through inversion

THE AMOUNT of time you know someone is meaningless. You can literally meet someone who sees you in a light that brings out a level of greatness in you that you never felt before even if you intellectually knew you had it within you. Then you can know someone for 10 years and no matter what you do, they'll always have a disempowering frame in which they view and listen to you through—which has you intuitively know that you're limited around them.

One very powerful way to have access to the constant expansion of greatness within you is to not give energy to people who don't uphold you to that kind of way of listening to you. Put another way—don't spend energy on people who won't listen for your greatness. The fewer people you currently have in your life who listen to you for your greatness, the more psychologically difficult it will be to create this. Clinging to people with a diminished listening of you *always* comes from one of two spaces:

1. They validate your identity and it's comfortable and what you know. Your identity gets to survive and you diminish what's possible for your life in the process.
2. You cling on out of an attachment to them. That attachment is almost always rooted in a scarcity mindset around this area

of life which in turn creates a downward spiral of scarcity and a perpetuation of this pattern.

Seeking out those people who will listen for your greatness and see you at the level of your authentic Self regardless if you currently have anyone in your life like that currently takes courage because some people don't have a model for this way of living in the world. However, most people have had this experience with at least someone in their lives. It's possible to have this kind of dynamic be the baseline for the relationships and the environments in your life, not just some peak moment or some fond memory. It's actually really simple to implement. Focus on those people who will serve you in this way even if it means getting back in touch with others and sharing how much they mean to you. That compounds on itself and creates an upward spiral.

Not having people like this in your life ends up creating that spiral of having more people that won't listen for your greatness. To elaborate further: the more embedded in those networks of being seen in a diminished way, the harder it is to break out of it. The inverse is true too. We can use Charlie Munger's principle of "inversion," or thinking about a problem backward or from an inverted perspective, to then go ahead and apply it to this situation. Essentially, avoid people who won't see you in a light that has you alive and fully Self-expressed.

Being in another's world

WHEN YOU'RE FEELING annoyed or resistant in any way by somebody, you're simply just not being in another's world. When you can hold space for all people and simply get exactly where they're at and where they're not and give up whatever is in the way / what you're resisting, all the frustration and annoyance disappears naturally. You can be in someone's world without having to condone their world. Gandhi had the ability to be in Hitler's world. He certainly didn't condone his actions.

Don't deal with people

WE AS HUMAN beings are masterful at letting people know the impact they have on us. However, we are not very masterful at being straight with ourselves about who we are for others and the impact we have on others.

One of the nastiest things I've observed over the years with people who have access to a certain set of principles that uplift humanity is when they use those principles and ideas as a way to dominate or bully others.

I share this because this has been one of the places in my life that for a long time was a serious blind spot for me so I can speak to this first-hand. When I'm unconscious, it's my default place I operate from when I'm in survival myself.

The truth is, people are always dealing with shit. However, we can't control that. What we do have control over is who we're being in the face of that.

If who you're being with someone isn't working, there's *always* something you can give up, let go of, transform, or impact with another how you're being with someone else. When you can focus on what you can let go of, share about a way you're being inauthentic with someone, or just acknowledge something that doesn't work and create something that works so everybody is forwarded and is left better than you found them, this removes the need to "deal" with someone else. When I say deal with, I mean to survive something. If you have a dominating boss, dealing with domination won't lead to much power, freedom, peace of mind, or vitality in dealing with your boss. It will just be some new tactic to survive the situation.

But saying something like, "Hey, I just wanted to let you know that who I have been being with you is someone who really doesn't listen because I've been judging you in my head. I've created a whole story about you that you're an asshole and a horrible person and that story has been preventing me from really hearing you. I really get you're committed to having everyone in this office be productive and effective and I was too caught up in my own head with my own concerns to really get that fully even if I've known that intellectually. I also want to say that I've been so concerned with my own shit that I realized I have spent exactly 0 energy building a relationship with you or getting to know you and that's had an impact on the productivity and the environment of this office. I'm committed to being an incredible employee to you and also committed to building a great working relationship with you as I know that will be beneficial to both of us as well as the whole office. What do you think of that?"

This kind of level of sharing will always net more effective outcomes over time vs. trying to survive and deal with something.

I developed this insight when I first got present to this principle out of doing a personal experiment in 2013, where for 6 months, I intentionally did not deal with others. That included not correcting anyone without permission, not giving people coaching or calling them out on their shit...even when they asked me to, and never giving unsolicited feedback. What happened out of that experiment was that I saw my effectiveness with others greatly increase. It also led to vastly more people asking me for my feedback and coaching. During those 6 months I always refused and nearly every time they figured it out for themselves without my help.

One thing never to compromise on

WHETHER IT'S platonic or romantic, there is one trait in another that I would absolutely never compromise on in my relationships. While I would never tell you how to live your life, I would assert when most people see the impact that their compromising on this one single trait in their relationships has on their life, they'd stop compromising on it immediately.

This trait is "the ability to see one's own flaws" and—here's the kicker—actually "be accountable for them."

Issues and problems in all forms of relationships are likely. There will be disagreements, there will be clashes sometimes, there will be some kind of emotional baggage that you hit up against at one time or another with the people you are closest to. There's nothing wrong with any of that.

However, what determines how successful you are at having meaningful relationships with others often comes down to your willingness to recognize your own flaws and weaknesses and share about them openly and honestly. This is in contrast to to hiding them due to some combination of guilt, shame, wanting to avoid looking bad, or just simply lying to yourself about what doesn't work. That has both an impact on your own power in a relationship and also has an impact on the people in your life who are closest to you. It's a form of lying and nobody likes a fucking liar.

Think about your current lover, your best friend, or an ex-lover or ex-friend.

Ask yourself these 8 questions:

1. If I shared with them something that wasn't working for me or was having an impact on me, would they get defensive and react, or, would they have an open and honest dialogue about it?
2. Would this person throw a tantrum?
3. Would this person start gaslighting me or throw it back on me?
4. Would they start walking away secretly hoping you'll chase them and then if you didn't chase them would they just stop talking to you for good or give you some kind of ultimatum or threat?
5. Would they start drama?
6. Would they make claims about your level of trust or love?
7. Would they be willing to appreciate and listen to you even if they felt a little uncomfortable, sad, angry, or upset because they care about more the relationship and you being gotten than their own comfort and justifications?
8. Would this person eventually be willing to talk about it without blaming, trying to make you feel guilty, jealous, angry, or invoking shame?

The myth of treating others the way you want to be treated

THERE'S that saying "treat others the way you want to be treated."

That's actually really stupid. People experience the world differently. And people behave in correlation with how the world occurs to them. Therefore, if you want to impact someone, share and give authentically within the context of *their* world. Get over there with them and out of your head.

Every human being is capable of doing this. When you're over there with another human being and really getting into their world, you'll know what to share intuitively.

So really, the game is really about treating others the way you'd want to be treated if the world occurred to you in the way it does to them.

"Just because someone doesn't love you the way you want, it doesn't mean they don't love you with all their being."

— GABRIEL GARCIA MARQUEZ

Using the principle of inversion to create rich relationships

IF SOMEONE FEELS angry at you, give them the space to share all the things they can't stand about you.

Give them the space to share with you the impact.

It's not about blame or fault—it's about getting someone's experience.

Give them the space to share with you the emotions they have about it.

Give them the space to share everything they want to share with you.

If someone is upset with you, give them the space for them to share with you and let them know they can give it to you hard.

There's respect in that.

What doesn't respect a relationship and actually dishonors any form of relationship quality is lying, half-truths, and wishy-washiness.

There's less fulfillment in that.

Over time, through those kinds of actions, the richness of the relationship will diminish and it will feel emptier, like an energy drain, and an increasing amount of actions that are simply going through the motions as opposed to an authentic Self-expression.

The more time goes on, the more things that get stepped over with more lies and half-truths...

The worse things become.

The more disconnected things become.

The experience of love becomes nil or *nearly* non-existent and you'll end up with more disconnectedness due to lying, half-truths, and wishy-washiness.

It's a high probability formula for producing those results.

If you don't want that then use the principle of *inversion*.

Charlie Munger, Vice-Chairman of Berkshire Hathaway commonly refers to the principle of inversion which was distinguished out by German mathematician, Carl Gustav.

Jacobi used to tell his students: "man muss immer umkehren" which translated to "invert, always invert."

What this means is that many problems in life can be solved by inverting the problem and solving it by thinking backward. If you want to be happy, avoid doing things that make you miserable vs. searching for what makes you happy.

Through the process of inversion, we can figure out that we want to have rich and meaningful relationships, then we should avoid behaviors that get in the way of that. Then what's left are actions that we should be doing such as leaving nothing left unsaid and making sure there are no elephants in the room as a function of not withholding communication and not lying or giving half-truths.

Relationship trumps technique every time

※❦※

FROM THE TIME I was very little, my mother always used to instill in me that "relationships were the most important thing in life." Like the most important thing. And you know when you think about it, it makes sense. Think about the people you feel closest to in your life. The people who get you the most.Those people in which collaboration and partnership show up naturally.

Think about the ease in which it is to be around those people. It's no surprise that productivity goes up in those kinds of environments. It's interesting because somehow along my journey I started taking in an interest in technique. And I started reading books by Dale Carnegie, Napoleon Hill, reading books on networking, and, basically trying to learn how to get ahead in life. I'd learn about Carnegie's *"How to Win Friends and Influence People"* and then I'd start calling people by their name because I thought that's what would work. And it would work for a little bit until it didn't work anymore. Then I would learn about rhetoric and tact and all these other things. I got very good at it too.

But here's the asinine thing about all of it. All of that work over about a decade didn't really have much of an impact on the quality of my relationships. It wasn't until I got this simple principle that the relationships in my life transformed. Consider that being mediocre at creating quality relationships will *always* be more effective than being great at some technique. It was after getting this that I really got clear for myself that my mother was right.

On side note—It's through authentically sharing my *Self* with the world and creating meaningful relationships in the process that I get the opportunity to honor my mother's wisdom. That's a beautiful gift to me.

Ghosting is for cowards

BEFORE TEXTING EXISTED, the flake rate was much lower and was also less tolerated. If you said you would meet someone at 4 pm, and then you don't show up, you'd look like an asshole, and that would not be tolerated. However, with texting, you can text someone an excuse at the last minute. It makes it easier to be less responsible. This has led to leaving plans loose to be more socially acceptable. This, of course, is only harmful to relationships and studies have shown that texting actually does more harm to relationships even if it feels better at the moment. There're lots of things that feel good at the moment with a shit impact. This increased flake rate coupled with flaking on others being more socially acceptable in our culture has led to increased rates of ghosting. I actually have no way to prove this other than through anecdotal stories of talking to hundreds of people about this over the years.

Ghosting—the act of disappearing from interactions with someone else with no warning or explanation. When these actions are taken for anything other than a last resort for one's personal safety, it's a cowardly act which has absolutely no or low regard for another human being. Whether it's through relationships that are business-related, friendships, romantic, or anything in between—just in the realm of the area called relating to another human being—it really doesn't matter.

As a society, we tolerate ghosting too often. Let's be clear—this is not normal behavior, and we all intuitively know it. To tolerate it is to perpetuate it and normalize it. When this happens to my friends—they are often full of anger and rage. And while some may want to say something snarky to the other person who did this to them—they knew it gets them nowhere and would just be feeding into the ghoster's own bullshit.

It would also make you look "crazy," and nobody wants to put themselves in that position.

Sometimes it works just to say something like, "It's fine that you're not interested in hanging out anymore / doing business together anymore / etc., but I wish you had been more considerate about it, instead of ghosting. I hope you'll be more communicative and straightforward with the business relationship/friend/girl/boy/etc. No hard feelings."

Some people may not think you should have said anything. However, I believe that saying nothing when you feel you've been treated like garbage is part of what allows assholes to keep acting like assholes and thinking there's nothing wrong with it.

It's super fucked up and irresponsible behavior, period. If we want our irresponsible behavior to alter as a generation—we need to stop tolerating it and speak up. Creating a culture of accountability and integrity starts with you. Normalizing destructive behavior makes society numb to it. Unfucking numb that shit!

Instant gratification

OUR SOCIETY—ESPECIALLY the millennial generation—has an addiction to instant gratification:

1. Someone not replying to your text right away doesn't give you a right to lash out at them. Nobody is obligated to respond to you on *your* schedule.
2. If you're in a relationship and you don't feel sparks, it doesn't mean there's anything wrong or that you need to fix something. If there's a disagreement, talk it out. If you're just meeting someone and you don't feel instant chemistry it doesn't mean you aren't compatible.
3. If you walk into a company and feel immediately good, it doesn't mean you're a good fit for the culture.
4. If someone says something you don't like, blaming someone for your emotions to just vomit on someone doesn't work as opposed to taking the time to sort through your own shit or talk it out. Yes, that can sometimes take time and sometimes more than just one conversation.
5. In the personal development world, younger coaches tend to be all rah-rah and super high energy when they are obviously compensating for something. Older coaches 50+ who work

with executives, large organizations, etc. tend to be a lot more grounded, present, much slower paced, and put much more care into things. They aren't teaching you 5 ways to hack your love life or here's how to get everything you want in 6 hours.

6. Long story short—life isn't black and white and things don't always immediately feel good or bad. Things can often take time. There are usually no shortcuts or tricks. The best shortcut or trick is often just simply not cutting corners with your relationships and taking your time to be present to whatever you're committed to and whatever conversations you're engaged in.

"There's a meta-trick that's far more reliable. One that works over time and doesn't depend on avoiding being out-tricked: Make great stuff. Satisfy needs. Do the hard work that leads to growth which leads to investment on its own merit. It turns out that the trick-free approach is the best trick of all."

— SETH GODIN

Partnership/social > survival. Duh

PARTNERSHIP/SOCIAL > Survival. Duh. It's truly amazing how much this mindset impacts the actions we take in life. For instance, I love helping others make meaningful connections. I'd say 95% of the time when making connections for others, people see the value. Most people get how impactful it is to connect with quality people who resonate with similar values and that leads to growth over time naturally. Most successful people who get the concept of partnership just get that instinctively. However, occasionally—maybe like 5% of the time...just a bullshit number not grounded in any statistic but "very small"—someone doesn't see the value. You can offer literally insanely valuable resources to them and they either don't get why you're even wanting to contribute to their lives, or they just don't see the value and want to stick to what they already know. And I can tell you that if you're literally going out of your way to give someone amazing resources to support what they're up to and they still don't take anything—these are the people that don't really understand partnership.

They may pretend they do. They post photos of how social they are. However, I can almost guarantee that they either need to be the main attraction and it's completely ego driven, *or* they're independent to the point they really don't let others contribute to them and they simply always do things on their terms and probably aren't really trusting either.

It's a total survival mentality. There's no grand conclusion nor grand generalization other than there's something survival in nature going on when people outright reject resources you share with them.

Each set of circumstances are different and the underlying principles rooted in protecting something, staying familiar, and survival is inherently human. There are poor people in this world whom you can offer the world to and they'll remain poor. Then, there are people who have everything handed to them and they still won't use the resources available to them. Then, there are people who don't have resources around them but know how to be resourceful and are totally willing to connect and contribute and engage and show up for life. It's less about the circumstances and more the context and perspective one listens for those interactions within. That's what shapes how those conversations occur. What shows up as an opportunity to one person shows up as a forced interaction or an ulterior motive to another. While case by case will be different, I am sure you can bet what group of people over the long-term end up being more successful. Partnership/Social > Survival. Duh.

The opportunity for contribution

ONE OF THE greatest gifts you can give another is the gift of giving someone the opportunity to contribute to you.

Here are 4 questions you can ask yourself to look for ways to increase the way others contribute to your life. If there's nothing you can up with, then you aren't authentically looking. There will always be things to see around this area, and if you do this exercise once a year, it will almost certainly be useful.

1. Where have I *not* let someone contribute to my life and what was the impact on them?
2. When in life have I been able to contribute and make a difference with someone? How did it make me feel and impact how I connected with the other?
3. When in life have I wanted to be there for someone and they weren't willing to receive my contribution or support fully? What was that experience like for me?
4. What is one area of my life, right now, where I can give someone the opportunity to contribute to my life? It could be as simple as: "Hey I'd love to learn more about what you do. You're so passionate about this. Can you recommend me a

book that will help me understand it better?" When we ask ourselves this question, there will *always* be something we can see that was not even an afterthought moments before. It's simply not common to consciously think from this space when we aren't immediately looking for guidance or help.

Seeing the best in people

PEOPLE WHO HAVE the natural ability to see the best in everybody tend to have that same gift occasionally get in their own way. Just like with many gifts, someone's strengths can also be their weaknesses, and this is no exception. There are 8 points to keep in mind:

1. Yes, love people through their shit.
2. Yes, don't let people's undermining behavior harden you.
3. No, don't start undermining yourself in order to make peace with someone else.
4. No, don't start violating your own boundaries in order to take a stand for someone as that doesn't serve anyone.
5. It's not always black and white. Standing for someone while also ensuring healthy boundaries. Loving people through their crap while also being firm, but not too firm where it destroys connection.
6. Protect yourself and the environment around you.
7. Don't protect out of reaction but out of proactiveness.
8. Don't set boundaries out of reaction and defensiveness but to be proactive.

Some of these points may sound like they contradict. The key is to be intuitive about this as boundary setting (as distinct from creating walls) is more of an art than a science. These are general places to think from, not strict rules. Every situation is different. You can use one or more of these boundary principles depending on what the moment calls for. Or you can use none of them at all. However, I do truly believe they are worth exploring so you can use them in a way that fits your lifestyle and commitments.

Making excuses for undermining behavior

MAKING excuses for another's disrespectful or undermining behavior is one of the most destructive actions you can take towards another human being other than actual physical harm. You essentially continue a dynamic where you tolerate destructive patterns to exist, you bring attachment (usually out of some fear of losing them or not liking you) to the situation, and, you end up having to lie in the process. The impact of this is that you become a liar in the process of justifying and tolerating this kind of bullshit. So you're now a liar which will leave others feeling unsafe around you or not trust you. In fact, the more you do this, the less you will trust yourself. Your power diminishes through those lies rooted in cognitive dissonance which means, over time, you'll be of less service to both yourself and others. Do you want to destroy the quality of your relationships in life? If so, then make excuses for others.

A common inauthenticity at the level of community

ONE OF THE greatest inauthenticities of anyone committed to playing life at a highly conscious level above all the survival garbage is *not* having an environment that will support you and not having an environment that will *not* let you get away with playing small and acting from a place of survival. Essentially, not having an environment that won't feed into or even tolerate your smallness for a second. When I created that commitment for myself of having a highly conscious environment around me in 2008—I did so because I noticed I did not have that kind of environment around me and found myself complaining about it. That complaint I had was the fuel to create the opportunity to build that around me. It's not that people around me were dumb. In fact, it was usually quite the opposite. Those people just didn't have the tools and resources I was so fortunate to acquire at such a young age.

Since creating that commitment, and acting on it, each year I encounter more amazing souls and incredible people. This kind of commitment produces beneficial outcomes that grow exponentially in a non-linear fashion when you continuously broaden your networks with people who are *givers* and share common values. At first, it's less noticeable, but like a compound interest graph, as the years go by, it gets significantly more noticeable and just stupidly obvious.

Through creating communities and networks of highly conscious and connected givers with shared values—the rate at which you will meet amazing individuals with similar commitments that resonate you will exponentially grow. Often, the connections you make will start to feel serendipitous in nature. If you start connecting with people in order to get something out of them and essentially commoditize your relationships, you'll attract others who will just commoditize you and you'll probably turn off those who are natural givers in life. It's a totally different *game*. The former *being social* at *Stage 4* and the latter *being in survival* at *Stage 3*.

I cannot stress enough the importance of creating very powerful communities and environments around you. If you're committed to creating huge things on the planet and you're around people committed to survival—while not impossible, you make that game exponentially harder and significantly less fun.

A *Stage 4* commitment within a *Stage 3* environment will be difficult to fulfill on...to say the least!

The impact of dysfunction in groups

CONNECT the following quote to Stage 2 and Stage 3 on the Cultural Map—

"Function (and the dysfunctional organization) Here's how you end up with a bully in a position of authority at an organization: Someone points out that the bully is a real problem. And the boss says, "I know he's a bully, but he's really productive and we can't afford to replace him." And here's how you end up with a naysayer, or a toxic co-worker: Someone points out that people are afraid to work with this person. And the boss says, 'I know, but we really need her expertise.' And, person by person, trait by trait, we build a broken organization because we believe that function trumps cooperation, inspiration and care. Until it doesn't, and then, all we've got left is a mess. The negative people who do nothing functional are an easy decision. It's the little compromises around people who seem to add value that corrupt what we seek to create. Build a team of people who work together, who care and who learn and you'll end up with the organization you deserve. Build the opposite and you also get what you deserve. Function is never an excuse for a dysfunctional organization, because we get the organization we compromise for."

Honoring relationships through communication

EXPECTING perfection from people is not very workable. However, staying silent when people are doing things that are unworkable also doesn't work in honoring relationships with the people around you including yourself.

Speaking out while invalidating others doesn't work either. Speaking out from a commitment to honoring a relationship and honoring a commitment to authenticity and connection *does* work. Withholding communication is literally a form of lying and *guarantees* that you erode and destroy a relationship over time even if the relationship still exists on the surface.

When you speak up, you risk losing someone. However, if that person is willing to talk things through, it brings you closer. So why guarantee failure by not sharing?

Of course, the answer is simple. The answer is rooted in being controlled by a fear of losing someone and that's completely based in attachment to someone. This attachment undermines one's commitment to great relationships.

When people have no interest in their own integrity—instead of being responsible and having a normal adult conversation—they will start blaming others or invalidating others as a way to dominate the situation and *survive* the conversation. All you can do is get it and love them.

I go into all relationships without judgment and with a commitment to authenticity. The only time I will end a relationship is when something is unworkable and there's no room for dialogue. If the other person continues to come from a space of blame and make wrong beyond the point of an apology being given, that's a game that sticking around for doesn't serve either yourself or the other person you're giving energy toward.

People ask me all the time how I've been able to build such incredibly close relationships over the years. It's very simple. You get what you tolerate. My commitment to authenticity means I share no matter what, no matter with whom, and regardless of the circumstances. That commitment brings me close to people and weeds out those who feel threatened. There's nothing bad or wrong about that and you can simply love them from afar. They can always come back if they choose to engage from an empowering place.

I have my flaws like every other person on the planet. However, I do have a commitment to call myself out on my bullshit and inauthenticities the moment I notice them. For people that know me intimately—I prefer to tell one on myself before someone can do it for me first. I don't like incompletion and heaviness in the space. It destroys aliveness, it destroys love, it destroys the very heart of relationships.

Forgiveness: the experience vs. the belief

I'VE BEEN an asshole to people before. I've said things I didn't mean. And I've had to ask for forgiveness from people. I've been on the other end of this too. Our culture has a lot of things collapsed when it comes to forgiveness. There's this belief about forgiveness vs. the experience of forgiveness. Quite often, people get stuck in the concept of it as opposed to actually forgiving someone. When we experience forgiving another, it's this incredibly peaceful and incredible experience. While I can't explain it per say as it would just degrade into another concept—it's one of those things that you know it when you experience it. It's a bit like love in that way. Describing love gives nobody any closer access to the experience of love. However, practicing love can be gotten without understanding the concepts about it.

One common belief or concept around forgiveness is that someone does something fucked up or wrong in some way so you will forgive them this time. Then what's left in the space regardless of whether it's said or unsaid is "but don't do it again, or I won't forgive you next time!" That's totally not forgiveness, just a concept of it, and it doesn't actually shift anything.

I once knew a man who was always late for everything. When he didn't want confrontation, he would stop talking to you for a while. When he finally felt he had enough space, he would then reach out and talk to you like nothing happened and pretend like there was nothing going on with him. His indifference was his way of not dealing with taking responsibility for something.

He was also someone that manipulated non-stop. He would never fully commit to anything. He would call it "always having an out." So when he felt trapped or when he was operating in the *world of survival*— he would attempt to manipulate his way out of the situation even if that meant just ceasing all communication. The idiotic thing is that while he was very intellectually smart and was very business savvy—in this area of his life, he really thought he was getting away with things and that this way of being in the world actually worked.

Of course, in reality, everyone already knew. The more I would resist him or try to talk to him about these things, the more he would push back and emotionally shut down. The way to handle it was to give him his space and let him do what he did. For me to think this man would not repeat any of those actions again would have been fucking idiotic. Instead, I would just make space for him to be just how he was and how he wasn't. By meeting him exactly where he was at—and doing so without violating my own boundaries—it created space for me to be with him and for me to love him as my friend.

If I were to have resisted anything about him, I would have become the very thing I was resisting. As the saying goes, "You become what you resist."

For example—there were a few times I can recall resisting his manipulations, and in the process, I would catch myself trying to manipulate him by trying to force an outcome where he stopped being manipulative.

When people get that simple principle—not as some belief system or theory, but as a way of living life—it can be pretty shocking and disgusting to us at first how we've been being with people. However, it can also be incredibly liberating when we see an access to shift something inside us by giving up some kind of resistance and making space for others. It's actually impossible for us to experience being whole and complete inside of our relationships with others when there's something we are resisting or haven't been willing to forgive someone for.

I love what Werner Erhard says on the principle of *forgiveness:*

"People often don't understand what is involved in forgiving. They think that if somebody does something wrong, and you forgive them, that is like saying that it was alright to do it that time – but don't dare do it again. But life doesn't work that way; and it's stupid or hypocritical to forgive someone on that basis. If somebody does something, you can be sure that he or she will do it again.

"That is why I prefer to talk about "making space" and "completion." To the extent that forgiveness is involved, it is more like self-forgiving and self-acceptance. When you forgive yourself for something, you have to create the space for that thing to exist. For whatever you resist, and fail to make space for, will indeed manifest itself in you.

"Self-forgiving, and self- accepting, is an essential part of being complete in relationships. If there is something about your past that you are ashamed of, or guilty about – if there is something in it that you are hanging on to – if there is something there that you are using to burden another person – that will prevent you from being complete in your relationships.

"In order to transcend having to be any particular type of person, you have to make it alright with yourself to be that type of person. The moment when you really experience that you have created yourself being whatever way you are, at the same moment you will never have to be that way again. This self-forgiving, self-acceptance, goes hand in hand with forgiving others, making space for others, completing your relationships with others. You cannot be complete in a relationship with any person whom you do not admire and respect as he or she is, and as he or she is not – rather than the way you think she is or would like her to be. Love for a person is acceptance of him or her the way he is and the way he is not. So long as you do not know who you really are, this will be difficult. You may have to give up a lot of things to which you may be attached. You may have to give up your resentments, your anger, your upset, your annoyance, your desire to punish."

— WERNER ERHARD

Creating space for powerful requests

IF YOU WANT people to feel comfortable making powerful requests around you, don't invalidate them when they ask. When I have a sense someone is diminishing themselves around me, sometimes and often I'll flat out let them know they can make any and all requests around me and *nothing* they can ask of me will make me get weird with them or have me cut off communication with them. That being said I *never* cut off communication with people and *always* work things through as I'm very clear *anything* can be worked out through communication. So what do I do? Simple. I may say something like "You can ask me to walk to California to buy you a pencil and then walk back. I will absolutely decline your request and say no, and you totally have the space to ask."

Shit like that frees people up around you. If people hold back around you and are constantly lying to you—then you probably have not made it safe for them to share. Of course, they may be conditioned to be like this based off of their past, but coming from that view that doesn't leave you with any power to make a difference in the situation.

And of course, there will just be people who will never feel safe to operate from that space and that's okay too. What will give you power in being effective is looking at yourself and seeing how you can be responsible for creating the environment vs. blaming others or your circumstances which will leave you with very little power and just have you be a victim to the situation.

Being offended degrades a culture

✥

IF SOMEONE in an organization or environment gets offended by something when that person did nothing wrong—and the person who they were reacting to gets punished for being offensive—you end up degrading the communication in that environment.

You start literally punishing people on behalf of the people who are most easily offended. In fact, an organization would be much better served doing the opposite.

Unless someone is making threats, stalking, or acting maliciously— organizations should tolerate fewer people complaining about being offended. If you aren't being threatened and you're going to gossip about how someone or something offended you—you're the threat to the environment, not them.

Over time, when you weed out *these* people and make it clear that blaming others for your own internal state won't be tolerated—you end up creating a culture of communication where people work through their issues and where people start taking responsibility for their own internal experiences.

Furthermore, when there actually *is* an issue where someone is actually making verbal threats, making racial slurs, etc.—then those complaints can get handled more efficiently. I've seen too many organizations take the opposite approach and the damage they do to the social fabric of the environment can be significant.

Givers, matchers, and takers

THERE'S A CONTINUUM OF GIVERS, Matchers, and Takers which was first modeled by a Wharton Professor named Adam Grant who wrote a book about it called *"Give and Take."*

1. Takers: they're always trying to take as much as possible from a person or situation.
2. Matchers: these are the people that will match your efforts. If you're a giver, they'll give back. If they give to you, they expect you to give back. If you're a taker, you can fuck off.
3. Givers: those who give unconditionally without needing to have the favor returned. They go out of their way to give and support. So who ends up being the worst performers in life? Givers. And who ends up being the highest performers in life? Also Givers. Givers make up both ends of the spectrum. So the game is to be a successful giver. It's relatively simple but being aware of these distinctions make it that much more powerful.

5 Tips Around Giving to "Givers, Takers, and Matchers":

1. Eliminate giving to takers. It's the givers who give to takers

who end up diminishing their lives. Lots of takers are very suave and very kind and compassionate and they'll make you feel very validated which is how they get people to give to them and how they keep taking and taking and getting away with it. Being able to spot this will save you lots of time and energy.

2. Give to givers. This is self-explanatory.

3. Give to matchers. If you're a giver you have developed lots of goodwill in the goodwill bank account so to speak. This goodwill is exponential in growth as well. Matchers will want to give back to you and to write matchers off because they won't give without condition does you a disservice and costs you.

4. Provide consistent low-effort value to others. Give in ways that take very little effort yet provide value to others. Something I love doing is giving out books and writing letters and sending gratitude with acknowledgments. Been doing that since I'm 16-years-old and over a decade later it's made a huge impact. I also share resources in general with people that I know would make a huge impact in their life.

5. Don't commoditize people. I know that can be counter-intuitive since labeling people as *givers* and *takers* and *matchers* can sound like commoditization. Think of it this way. If a man meets a girl and sees her as a piece of meat and his sole goal is to have sex with her, she'll feel it and have less of a chance of getting laid. If a man meets a girl and builds chemistry, builds a foundation, and creates an amazing connection where she can completely feel safe, surrender, and give her all around this man—there's a higher probability it leads to a relationship and a higher probability he gets laid a lot more. Having the attachment to the outcome will actually get in the way of producing the result.

I think Tony Hsieh says it best:

"I personally really dislike 'business networking' events. At almost every one of these events, it seems like the goal is to walk around and find people to trade business cards with, with the hope of meeting someone who can help you out in business and in exchange you can help that person out somehow. I generally try to avoid those types of events, and I rarely carry any business cards around with me. Instead, I really prefer to focus on just building relationships and getting to know people as just people, regardless of their position in the business world or even if they're not from the business world. I believe that there's something interesting about anyone and everyone—you just have to figure out what that something is. If anything, I've found that it's more interesting to build relationships with people that are not in the business world because they almost always can offer unique perspectives and insights, and also because those relationships tend to be more genuine. If you are able to figure out how to be truly interested in someone you meet, with the goal of building up a friendship instead of trying to get something out of that person, the funny thing is that almost always, something happens later down the line that ends up benefiting either your business or yourself personally. I don't really know why this happens or why it works, but it seems that the benefit from getting to know someone on a personal level usually happens 2-3 years after you started working on building the relationship. And it's usually something that you could not have possibly predicted would have happened at the beginning of the relationship. For example, maybe your friend's sister's neighbor was just hired as the VP of a company that you've been trying to get in touch with, or maybe someone you met 2 years ago now has a new tennis partner who would be the perfect person for that job opening you've been trying to fill for the past 6 months. Zappos.com has been around for over 10 years now. We grew from no sales in 1999 to over $1 billion in gross merchandise sales in 2008. In looking back at the major turning points in the history of the company, it seems that most of them were the result of pure luck. Things happened that we could not have possibly predicted, but they were the result of relationships that we had started building 2-3 years earlier. So my advice is to stop trying to 'network' in the traditional business sense, and instead just try to build up the number and depth of your friendships, where the friendship itself is its own reward. The more diverse your set of friendships are, the more likely you'll derive both personal and business benefits from your friendships later down the road. You won't know exactly what those benefits will be, but if your friendships are genuine, those benefits will magically appear 2-3 years later down the road."

And then I'll add—why would you be friends with someone who just takes from you?

Deep down if you're honest with yourself, that's not very satisfying. Focus on building great connections with great people and keep those boundaries around givers, takers, and matchers in mind and you will tilt things in your favor.

The role you play for others

✿❀✿

SOMETIMES WHEN YOU have an internal shift and grow, people in your environment will become threatened by it and take actions to keep you small. Put simply—it destroys their world-view and often people associate around others who will validate their own view of the world or others in the world. Whether you are aware of it or not, you're always training people how to relate to you.

Furthermore, your Self-expression will only ever be as big as the listening of you in your environment (essentially how people hear you). So when people have put a point of view together and created a model or a lens of how they experience you—when you start taking on new actions, ways of being, ways of thinking, emotional states, etc.—it destroys whatever point of view they put together about you and the natural instinct is to start trying to keep it "the way it was." That's just an automatic mechanism in the brain wired for survival, it's not personal. Whether they are aware of it or not—they'll try to put you back into their mental model of you. Why? Again—it's rooted in survival.

What a lot of people forget is that you play a role in people's lives for better or for worse. When you change the role you're in for them that's like being years into filming a movie and then halfway through changing the parts that people play. It would threaten the script. To expect that

452

script to change overnight is ludicrous. Sometimes it does, sometimes it doesn't.

Givers, Takers, and Tribal Leadership

by John King

IN A ZERO-SUM GAME, all intrinsic and extrinsic value is measured by the outcome. In the book, *"Tribal Leadership,"* five distinct stages of language and structure in organizations are distinguished and described. For the purposes of day to day organizational activity, the relevant stages are:

> *Stage 2 = "My life sucks!"*
> *Stage 3 = "I'm great, and you're not!"*
> *Stage 4 = "We're great!"*

Stages 2 and 3 are zero-sum environments and if you find yourself at Stage 2, you are a loser, and you lost to a Stage 3.

Here's why.

In every environment that is not designed otherwise, there are winners and losers. Winners always win and losers always hope. A winner in this environment is a taker, and they take from the loser, who is a giver. So, when a giver and a taker interact, the taker wins. Every time. That is the default cultural design of Stage 2 and Stage 3. It is as old as man has been a social animal and most never see that this toxic environment of, "I'm great" vs. "My life sucks" is anything other than, "That's just the way it is." But, it doesn't have to be that way. There is an insight that makes all of the difference, some get it and most do not.

The insight is: *some givers win every time.* What do they do? The answer is: *They only give to other givers.* They do not, under any circumstance, ever transact with takers.

When a person makes the courageous choice to exit the toxic environment of Stage 2 and Stage 3, they have, in effect, made a personal declaration of autonomy and have started the process of taking over the control of their own lives.

The choice begins with a realization that "we are all in this together, and therefore, we need to collaborate." The money question is "Who do we collaborate with?"

In a Stage 2/Stage 3 relationship, the collaboration is always in favor of the Stage 3 individual or entity. It is a set-up as old as time, and, if you are in the Stage 2 position, you lose. Thankfully, there is a way out of this vicious trap. The way out is not through Stage 3 having some sort of "epiphany." There is never a reason for Stage 3 to ever change.

Everything is working perfectly for Stage 3. The design of the zero-sum game is that Stage 3 always wins. Stage 3 will lie, cheat, and steal to maintain the unnatural advantage of their position. "Epiphany" is not in the Stage 3 lexicon. The way out is for Stage 2 to have their epiphany, and realize the Stage 3 is *always* a taker. The way out is to partner with other Stage 2's who also realize that they need to transact with other givers. Stage 2 is the access to Stage 4.

Really. Imagine that... "My life sucks!" is the access to, "We're great!"

At Stage 4, several (minimum of three) individuals have consciously decided and designed a partnership that ensures that they all win. Life does not have to be a zero-sum game unless you think so. At Stage 4, it is posited that life can be a non-zero-sum game with a positive outcome for everyone involved.

It is actually possible, and successful people are doing it every day. It means giving up a 'need' to beat the other person and take on the commitment to be an authentic partner in a process that is designed for everyone to win. And then, looking in the whites of the other's eyes and seeing that they are up to the same outcome. These are the people you want to consider playing with.

Frankly, most people are playing far too small to operate effectively at

Stage 4. Therefore; for most people, this means taking your game to a much higher level and playing for much higher stakes. Obviously, Stage 3 is only interested in personal gain and domination of Stage 2.

Stage 4 collaborations are interested in group effectiveness, stable partnerships, and group gain. Stage 3 is in it for the event. Stage 4 is in it for the process. Stage 3 is in it for the win. Stage 4 is in it for victory. Stage 3 is about the battle. Stage 4 is about the war. Stage 4 is a non-zero-sum environment, and where the possibility of win-win outcomes actually exists.

Why?

Because givers who give to other givers will always triumph over takers who only take. A championship team will always beat a team of individual champions. Be a giver, but, only give to other givers. It will simplify, enhance, and light up your life.

Takers who pretend to be givers

"Beware of the taker and beware of the taker who is masquerading as a giver."

— JOHN KING, CO-AUTHOR OF TRIBAL
LEADERSHIP

Should men pay for first dates?

APPARENTLY, there is no rulebook for this answer but from my experience—what I will share below works very well for me, and perhaps it will work for you too.

First off—there're all the interpretations and meaning that we put toward what it means or doesn't mean to pay for a first date. If those are head games you play with yourself, stop it. The impact is uncertainty and you not being confident or trusting yourself in your decision. And if you're a woman, it will impact the experience of you being contributed to.

Either outcome won't feel right. It's also manipulative as the generous act of paying for a first date will degrade into a manipulative tactic to force some kind of outcome. People can see through that shit.

HERE'S WHAT I SAY:

1. <u>Always Pay, period.</u> If you're a man, most of the time the woman you are with will have a positive reaction or a reaction such as "you don't have to pay." This reaction will be a function of her not wanting to feel it's creating some kind of expectation, because they don't want you to feel you *have* to,

or simply because they aren't into you and they'd feel bad having someone who they've known for a short period of time and who they already know they'll never see again treat them. However, none of that matters. If you take on the point of view that you are treating someone for the love of treating an amazing human being out for a fun night and get pleasure and joy in that very process itself, you treating her will make you feel good which in turn ends up creating better outcomes for everybody over time.

2. If you are the one that asked her out, then *absolutely* pay. Pay for the pleasure of her being generous with her time and her presence. There's just an authentic level of respect coming from that space or context. Regardless of the outcome, it feels great. Now if she genuinely insists on splitting the check, you can always make the suggestion that she pay for drinks, dessert, or coffee afterward. Don't use this as a line but something along the lines of, "Hey I really am enjoying my time with you and treating you, so it's my pleasure to treat you. If you truly insist then how about you pay for our dessert or how about we head to a bar and you can get drinks." This shows you still honor and respect her while at the same time you're honoring her choice that paying in full is not an option.

3. Keep it fun and light. Nothing kills the mood more than getting all weird and serious about something like the check. Have fun and be authentic. If she gets weird and says that you shouldn't pay—then like I said before—be fun and light and offer her the option to pay for something else later on in the night. Or while she's in the bathroom, just simply pay for the check anyway and then reassure her that you simply enjoy her time and company and it felt good for you to treat this time (even if you know it's possible it may be the last time). Set the intention that she gets the communication and gets that you're being authentic.

Surrounding yourself with people who give into your smallness

ONE OF THE things most important to me in life is non-stop expansion and creating environments that will harness and nourish that. The best athletes in the world have coaches and are always honing their craft. They also have an environment that won't let them get away with playing small. This is huge.

One of the greatest inauthenticities for people who say they are committed to huge things in life is to create an environment that won't hold them to account and take a stand for their greatness and their own integrity when they claim to be committed to huge things in life. An environment that will let you get away with things is entirely inconsistent with that. Part of this also gets into the trap of life categorization. Like you can be this way in your professional life but then when you go back to your family, friends, kids, your health, your diet, your communication with people you aren't currently speaking to—then all of a sudden it's magically okay because there's some magical line that gets created. While you may try to categorize life, the universe doesn't give a fuck about your imaginary categorical line. How you do anything is how you do everything.

If you start breaking agreements with your family, with your health, with yourself—or you start resenting others and withholding communication—that *will* show up in *all* of the other areas of your life—sometimes in ways you can see and mostly in ways you can't unless you really start looking and doing the work.

It would be like if you decided to take a stand for world peace while holding grudges against your parents. It would just get in the way and not be very workable. It's *very* easy to find people who will listen for your *reasonableness* in life. The vast majority of people will. And if you surround yourself with people who will uphold your reasonableness while you attempt to make a large impact in the world—your environment standing for your own reasonableness will get in the way and impede on your effectiveness.

What you should be doing is the opposite and to surround yourself with people who won't sell out on you when you start getting reasonable and start to make excuses.

Being fluent in the extremes

WHEN YOU'RE comfortable with the extremes at the level of expression your authentic Self—as opposed to expressing a script being played out by your identity—it makes for very rich interactions.

HERE ARE TWO ANALOGIES:

1. If you're a guitarist who can play the scales you'll rarely or never use—you'll be much better at playing improvised guitar solos than someone who only knows how to play the scales they actually use.
2. If your an artist who can paint all kinds of crazy shit that you wouldn't ever think about selling—the artwork in your sweet-spot will be better than if you only knew how to pain the kind of art that you were comfortable with.

Surround yourself with great people like your expression depends on it

YOUR SELF-EXPRESSION IS a function of the listening of others. Therefore, surround yourself with people who will listen for the expression you're committed to expressing in your life. That takes courage as it will take a real willingness to let go of those who don't listen to you from that space. That doesn't mean resent them or invalidate them. It means just give them space and don't resist them or engage with them. Just let them be and focus on what you're creating with others.

You will know when something is feeling forced. It's unworkable when you're committed to being in integrity with a certain Self-expression and you can see the gap for what it is. When you aren't clear about this, you may feel uneasy, but you may not see this gap.

If your expression is constantly being invalidated or made wrong vs. being heard or being lifted higher, then I would assert that isn't the kind of relationship you're committed to with someone. You can only fix and change something to a point. Most of the time if you feel the need to constantly fix and change, there's probably an attachment to something and something is being forced. You're also being a jerk for thinking you can alter where someone is at without their consent to be coached. That doesn't work either.

Your intuition is a very powerful force. There will be people in your life where anytime something doesn't work or there's a discomfort, you can share and talk about it, and move through it. When don't have the space to move through it, listen to your gut.

Continuing to hang on to those kinds of people is almost rooted in some scarcity conversation. Maybe it's something like: *there are not enough people who would be right for me.* If that's you, then you know deep down that's beyond bullshit. Don't sell your Self out to keep others around. That benefits no one.

Those people who are a match for you—just take a look at the people in your life where you have that. Think about what that feels like. Think about the impact it has on your life. Consider that you can commit to *only* creating relationships with people from that space.

Set the conditions and see who shows up to the party. Be that, and commit only from that space, and the right people will join your party. And when someone doesn't fit, kindly show them the door or don't lock the door when they naturally walk out themselves.

The three stages of sexual relationships

DAVID DEIDA'S *Three Stages of Relationships* is a very powerful distinction. There are many ways to talk about them and I believe there's only so much you can understand about them intellectually without experiencing them. Eivind Figenschau Skjellum, who is an expert in the field of masculine psychology, wrote an excellent description of the three stages on *masculinity-movies.com*.

This is not to be confused with the *5 Stages of Culture* outlined in the *Tribal Leadership* work which is a completely different set of distinctions.

Stage 1: The submissive housewife and the macho breadwinner

This stage has been the predominant stage globally up until quite recent times. It is characterized by strictly defined and rigidly upheld gender roles. The man is out in the world bringing home the food and the woman is at home caring for the children. The man dominates the woman with threats of physical violence and withholding of resources and the woman dominates the man with threats of emotional violence and withholding of sex. Intimate partners acting out of DD1 use their lover/spouse as a means to satisfy their own needs, selfishly manipulating the other to get what they desire. They tend to judge themselves by external factors, be it the size of their paycheck or the impeccability of their perfect household. Whenever we focus on ourselves and how we appear to others, we are in a first stage moment.

Modern caricatures of this stage are the big-spending gold digger, the too-good-to-be-true mother of 50s TV shows, the angry hip-hop gangster and the money-hungry TV preacher.

Stage 2: The working girl and the sensitive flow boy

The cultural emergence of this stage started in parallel with feminism and the gender equality movement. In the 2nd stage, people seek to become more integrated human beings. The emergence of [Stage 2] has lead to women embracing masculine values and opportunities, becoming tougher and more independent, and men have embraced feminine flow and emotions, becoming more open and relatable. Where people acting out of a first stage moment seek approval through their possessions and appearance, people in a second stage moment want to be appreciated for what they can *do*. Value is primarily determined by internal properties of the Self.

The 2nd stage is very concerned that things should be done the right and proper way, and considers it important not to rock the boat too much. We gladly accept people's boundaries, even when they wish we didn't, and try not to escalate conflict. In intimate relationships, the tension of polarity often disappears and is replaced by a withholding of depth, often felt as repulsive by both partners. In societies, second stage is expressed as an aversion to conflict and an almost suffocating political correctness. You're not allowed to judge or rank people, and everybody agrees to disagree.

The second stage individual is generally stuck in a perpetual self-improvement cycle that seems to lead nowhere, as the development often goes away from our true nature as opposed to towards. Happiness always looms on the horizon, but never quite arrives.

Modern caricatures of stage 2 are the directed female headhunter and career surgeon, and the male crystal healer and emo singer-songwriter.

Stage 3: The radiant goddess and the warrior of love

For those rare souls fortunate enough to experience it, this stage is supposedly characterized as an ongoing state of gifting yourself to the world and your partner. The woman offers her divine radiance in service of her partner and the world, opening them up with the deep flow of her awesome life force and beauty.

The man offers his unending integrity and stability, as an expression of his desire to penetrate the world with truth and love. This stage is not necessarily calm or peaceful, as the politically correct stage two prefers. These individuals know freedom and love intimately and consciously choose not to repress their true nature, which may offend those of lesser development. When a person expresses him- or herself through a third stage moment, their intention is to serve the world – or the people in it – in their opening to truth and love. Sometimes, their service won't be appreciated, but since a person in a third stage moment has transcended the need to be validated by external or internal factors, it matters little.

In intimate relationships, the feminine third stage is expressed as pure, unfiltered life energy, bursting with love, expressed as wild storms or warm summer breezes. She is an oracle, a pure expression of the feminine, of nature Herself. She serves her man by seducing him out of his narrow-minded focus on getting things done, by sexing him out of his head and into his body, by shivering earthquakes of anger through her body as she hurls hail storms at him for being less than he is capable of. The man serves her in return by remaining unperturbed, unaffected by her wild emotions, pressing into her with his presence and love, as they both melt and fuse in the throes of ecstasy.

Who knows what a society filled with individuals operating from this stage would look like.

So I ask the question—why isn't everyone in this third stage? I would assert that everyone on some level has wanted this kind of third stage dynamic at some point in their lives. What gets in the way? The spiritual teacher, Ram Dass, shares something which is literally an amazing access for *the noticing model* as a means to authentically experience yourself in the third stage if you're in the second stage or first stage most of the time.

Ram Dass Says:

"But you begin to see how you keep coming to the same place in relationships, and then you tend to stop. Because it gets too heavy. Because your identity gets threatened too much. For the relationship to move to the next level of truth requires an opening and a vulnerability that you're not quite ready to make. And so you entrench, you retrench, you pull back and then you start to judge and push away and then you move to the next one. And then you have the rush of the openness and then the same thing starts to happen. And so you keep saying "Where am I going to find the one when this doesn't happen?" And it will only happen when it doesn't happen in you. When you start to take and watch the stuff and get quiet enough inside yourself, so you can take that process as it's happening and start to work with it. And keep coming back to living truth in yourself or the other person even though it's scary and hard."

So here's the noticing model as outlined earlier on in the book:

Noticing

1. Notice that you are opinionating.
2. Notice that you have an opinion of your opinionating.
3. Notice that you try to control your opinionating.
4. Notice that your opinions don't care, and keep flowing anyway.
5. Notice that you are not running the show, your opinions are.
6. Notice that you are not your opinions, rather, you have opinions.
7. Or, Notice that your opinions have you.
8. Notice that this is going on 24/7 in the background.
9. Do not attempt to correct or fix the condition – simply Notice.

AS YOU NOTICE you'll naturally *dissociate* (part 2 of the *Model of Transformation or MOT*) from what Ram Dass is pointing to and have the experience of *transcending* what you've dissociated from (part 3 of the MOT). Then, you'll have that space where you'll see whole new ways of being, thinking, and acting in line with your authentic Self-expression. And if you're attracted to that third stage, but there's just something that seems to keep holding you back or keep getting in your way every time you attempt to go there—you'll start to see those new behaviors, thought patterns, emotions, and even body sensations correlated to that third Stage. It's a natural reintegration process hence why the fourth step to the MOT is called *reintegrate.*

This is the difference between Change vs. Transformation. It's not magic. It's not woo-woo shit. It's actually pretty straightforward. Change is always based off something in the past. And what you get is something more, better, or different than the past. Whipped cream on shit is still shit. Change is just shoving more whipped cream on shit.

The first follower

OFTEN WE THINK of leadership as being this central figurehead that everyone follows.

However, you can also see it as empowering other leaders around you. You can also see it as creating an environment where some vision or noble cause shows up in action.

One access to that is getting up under people's projects. Helping support them and enrolling others in *their* vision that you can get up behind.

Be their first follower.

The costs of efficiency

PEOPLE WHO ARE COMMITTED to ruthless efficiency at the expense of value-centric partnership actually are missing out on profit.

One of the biggest mistakes I've made in the past was choosing to collaborate with people purely based on their skill-set. Essentially, creating transactional relationships with people. After I read the book *Tribal Leadership*, I saw how much I was limiting myself and saw how much I could increase my effectiveness by *only* working with people who I could relate to on a value-centric level or at *Stage 4*.

So now when I look for someone to work with—even if it's something very simple, I know first and foremost I want to choose someone I could see myself having a beer with, who I genuinely enjoy talking to, who is able to think big and give me the space to share my ideas—someone who isn't a fearful stiff-ass, and someone who is wildly passionate and proud of their work.

Being committed to this is incredibly rational if you're committed to high performance in the workplace and in your life.

If you truly cared

THERE'S this belief about how people who truly care will always stick around no matter what. It's also a load of crap. The more you live your life from a space of *possibility*, the more you'll leave others feeling threatened who are taking actions out of *survival* and they'll have some energetic charge to what you say and leave your life.

Sometimes they'll come back and sometimes they won't. However, the common thread won't be that they don't care—that's just the justification people use to mitigate the pain or upset.

People who have some weird or intense reaction to you typically care a lot. People rarely react to other people, circumstances, or ideas that other people talk about when there's no energetic charge there.

For example, if someone says that they think abortion is wrong, you may have a positive or negative emotional reaction to that statement. However, if someone says that the way cheesemakers in Switzerland make Swiss Cheese is dumb, you probably wouldn't have any kind of reaction to that statement unless you were a cheesemaker or had strong opinions about the best Swiss cheesemaking practices.

Wanna be a kick-ass boyfriend?

YOU WANNA BE A KICK-ASS BOYFRIEND? Right on. Read this for yourself
or share this with your boyfriend or husband (even if he's already kick-ass
which I'd hope he already is).

Below are some basic principles that have worked for me. These are
not truths or a system and don't believe a word I say. The intention of
sharing this is to distinguish some ideas and principles to give you an
opportunity to think in new ways and open you up to new possibilities in
your romantic relationships which hopefully are already awesome.

1. <u>Listening.</u>

Being a kick-ass boyfriend starts with listening. Listen to your girlfriend's needs, wants, and upsets. Listen because you want to and not
because you have to. It's an awful experience to try to express yourself
because you need to talk about something important to you and the
other person is not really listening to you...or listening from their own
point of view. Listen from their point of view. Don't come from a place
of trying to fix the situation—just hear her out. Also, give up being righteous or justifying why she's wrong. She's coming from somewhere, even
if it may not be obvious to you where she's coming from at first. Instead
of being dismissive, truly listen from her point of view and talk about

what she's going through from her point of view and fully get into her space and embrace her world. Come from a place of love, compassion, and empathy. When you can do that and give up your own point of view in the process, truly and authentically listening to someone is a powerful experience.

Consider that your communication to others is a correlate of your listening of others. If you listen to others strictly from your own point of view, from your way of seeing things, that's not really listening, and you can bet she won't feel heard. And the more she vents around you, the more disempowered she will feel. On the other hand, when you're truly listening to her and getting into her world, she'll really appreciate you being there for her—even if it's just an ear and for you to be someone in her life who really conscious effort to get her world...fully and completely.

2. Being Present

Being present with a woman is another way of saying "being in the moment." The deep connection that becomes possible in that situation is indescribable unless you're in it. If you are not deeply connected with your lover, it's very easy to put the blame on her. No, cut your goddamn bullshit and see how you're causing the barrier. At the end of the day, your lover aches to connect—and if that connection isn't there, take the lead and create the space for her—stop waiting for her to come around. Now many men may think there's some kind of system or technique to create a connection. In fact, it's rather the opposite. Consider what you can *give up* in the moment to create that oneness with a woman who means so much to you. Perhaps that means giving up your tactics, manipulations, trying to impress her or look good for her, your strategizing of the situation, or your analyzing of the situation. Give up your points of view, give up your justifications of how it should or shouldn't be, or perhaps you're withholding some communication and then you should give up withholding. When you give up what's in the way of your natural connection—you may be surprised how deep you can get in such a short period of time.

. . .

474

3. Celebrate Her Femininity

Many guys may compliment their girlfriend or the girl they are dating because they feel they have to. I'm sorry but that will be so see-through and transparent, and you are better off not wasting your time. Celebrate what you love about her, her feminine energy, what you find beautiful about her, what you love about her, not because you have to but because you truly want to, and complimenting her in the moment just feels right. When it does feel right to acknowledge her, don't be stingy. So many people feel they need to somehow play it cool, keep to themselves, and are too scared to say what they mean in the moment. When you with-hold your communication, you are out of integrity with yourself and with her. If you think her ankles are the most beautiful ankles you have ever seen in your life...say it. And don't say it because you're reading this or you think you should say it but because you authentically experience her ankles as the most perfect ankles you have ever seen on another human being. If what calls you is to buy her flowers, buy her some goddamn flowers, but don't do it to look good or impress her. Buy her flowers because it moves you to buy her flowers.

4. Be Giving

I can not stress enough how important it is to give. And again, not to give because you feel it will impress her or somehow make you look good, but because you giving to her makes you happy—simply for the fact that you have the opportunity to contribute to her life.

5. Be Vulnerable

There's some weird unsaid narrative that goes on amongst men that men don't cry, they don't show emotion, they don't feel, and if they do, it's somehow not masculine. Forget trying to be masculine. I see men all the time who put in so much time and energy trying to be masculine when underneath it all—who they are being is fearful and scared. Just let go, open yourself up, don't be afraid to take action, and give up looking good in the moment. Emotion is natural to human beings. Resisting your emotions will get in the way of you truly experience the woman that you are with and life itself. Just be present with all your body sensations and everything around you—your natural masculinity will shine through that without you having to try to be masculine. Trying to be something—isn't being it. Do you get that?

6. Embrace Her Storms

When your lover is having a shit day and just wants to unload, who better to unload on emotionally than you! That's right I said it...you! Just be with her emotions, fully listen, and be completely unmessable with. Let her act out as much as she wants around you. Allow her to be the way she is around you without you constantly throwing judgment at her. The more you allow her to be however she is around you—without telling her to stop being whiny or stop being emotional—and just allow yourself to be with her fully—that will create an enormous amount of freedom for both of you. A woman wants a man who can be with her emotions and can have someone to vent to knowing she won't be criticized in the process.

7. Be Supportive

Is your girlfriend or wife working on some new project? Well—how can you be of support to her to empower her to create possibilities for herself she may not have even thought of. There's a difference between being attached to what she's up to and contributing to what she's up to. Doing things to help her because you feel you are supposed to, or because you think it will get her to like you more or whatever your reason is does *not* work. You will feel emotionally drained, and she will feel overwhelmed by your presence. See it as win-win. You empowering her life and forwarding what she's up to while empowering and forwarding yourself is one awesome and very powerful dynamic to consistently be creating.

8. Allow Her to Love You

It's an awful experience for a woman to give her heart fully with you and completely love you with every ounce of her soul—only for her to find you being standoffish or resistant. Allow yourself to be loved.

. . .

9. Allow Her to Be

People will be the way they are. I know that is a stupidly simple statement, but it's true. You can open doors for others but at the end of the day it's up to the other person to walk through the door, you can't do it for them. If your lover resists the new doors you open for her and stays in her box—you can either choose to accept that and embrace it or let her know that doesn't work. That might mean letting her go and ending the relationship. Trying to fix it and make it work will probably leave both of you with an experience of settling for less.

10. She's A Goddess

Your lover is a goddess—treat her as such. Allow her to move you so deeply. Love her, ravish her, spoil her, give everything you have to give with who you are being in the moment with her—and do it because you want to as opposed to a technique to force some outcome.

11. Let Yourself Go In The Bedroom

Be an animal. Allow your primal instincts to take over. You'll have some of the most amazing sex of your life and so will she. Explore each other's sexuality. Always seek to deepen your physical bond. Be fearless. Communicate. Don't be afraid to try new things. Be responsible for her pleasure in the bedroom and be responsible that she has the space to explore with you and share her fantasies with you in a way that won't leave her feeling judged.

Emily from xojane.com in an article titled, *"Why I Like Facials (The Dirty Kind)"* writes:

"I started Googling intellectual feminist analyses on the topic while writing this piece and nearly psyched myself out of writing this, but you know what? Fuck it. I'm not the only dirty bitch out there who likes to push the boundaries during sex and as a grown-ass woman, I shouldn't have to be ashamed of whatever kind of sex I like to have. When I interviewed artist Marilyn Minter for this site, she wore this awesome shirt she'd had made up herself, reading 'There are no politically correct fantasies.' I'm sure there are women who are lucky enough to be turned on by erotic, lady-empowering lovemaking, but there are a hell of a lot of the rest of us who want to get cum shot in our faces sometimes and who have rape fantasies. And that's one of the things I love about sex— done well, with someone you trust, it's a boundaryless Never Never Land where cool, smart, and careful melt into sheer sensation. I don't care if your fantasies revolve around fisting or sibling role play—exploring them together, crawling into each other's weirdo sexual psyches, is half the fun. My orgasms are a politics-free zone."

UNFORTUNATELY, most women in our culture continue to be inhibited by some disempowering conversation they were born into around sexuality which has been around since patriarchal conversations to control women were invented. While much of this has gone away, there are lingering aspects of this conversation that still remain prevalent in American culture today. And while there are women who coach other women in owning their own sexual power and sexual energy, many more women have emotional blocks that get in the way of their own sexual power which can lead to all kinds of dysfunction that bubbles up to the surface in nonsexual ways. If you can be the kind of guy that can really make sure she feels safe to share and explore herself sexually with you, that will be a never-ending journey of exploration and growth for the two of you. For every Emily out there who actively explores her sexuality to the fullest, there are many more women that are disempowered in some way or have energetic blocks and dysfunction in their body. You can help her free herself from that and help take her to new levels of sexual mind-body awareness and consciousness.

12. The Power Of No

Be responsible for creating an environment in which your lover knows she can fully and completely say something you won't like hearing and feels safe to do that. Allow her to tell you what does and doesn't work for her. At the same time, stand your ground—tell her when something doesn't work for you. It keeps the baseline for integrity in the relationship sound. The more you become "fine" with a certain set of circumstances, the more the relationship will dull. Don't be okay with being fine. Being fine is just a way of getting by and coasting. You don't want to be on your deathbed and think you were just fine.

13. Allow Her to Be A Contribution to You

Us men instinctively love to feel they can provide, supporter, and be a hero in a relationship. That's great and completely valid, but it's not one-sided. She will want to be a contribution to your life in her own unique way. Allow it, welcome it, embrace it. It will only empower her further, and at the same time, it will strengthen your partnership with each other.

14. Stop Trying to be Masculine

Many men try to be masculine and try to act strong. But if you are trying to be something, you *aren't* being it. Giving up all that bullshit will allow your own masculinity to come out naturally. Women can see right through men who are trying to be masculine. It wreaks of fear. Other men can sense it too.

15. Communicate

It's so important to be in communication with your lover. If she's left in a situation feeling disempowered—be responsible for creating a space where she or any human being is left better than you found them. If you take that view in life—not like as the truth, but as a powerful place to think from—it will impact your romantic relationships and all of your relationships. Make sure you are always on the same page and that both of you are clear on where you are at with each other. Communication is also the foundation for creation. Create new visions and goals with each other. Create projects, create empowering dynamics, create games worth playing, and be each other's partner in crime. The possibilities are endless, but they can't be done without you speaking about it and making it real for you both. Also, communicate your wants and needs, and be responsible for an environment where she feels comfortable communicating that to you. Consider that your communication is not *just* what you say to her but what she communicates with *you*. What I mean by that is if your lover is resistant, emotionally shut down, etc., instead of placing blame on her, look to see where you are responsible for that and causing her to react like that around you. That doesn't mean blaming yourself, invalidating yourself, or selling out on your Self to appease her.

16. Honesty Without Intentional Upsets

Being honest is great. What there is to be responsible for is how your word lands with others. It's not about what you say, but how others listen to what you say. Not intentionally causing upset will go further than mindless radical honesty and transparency just by itself and not really caring on how your word lands with her. What comes along with that is taking responsibility for creating a space where she is comfortable letting you know when something you say doesn't work for her or that she has the space to say she feels upset so that it gets communicated out and gets complete without any blame or invalidation. That way you can still be honest and transparent, and any reactions to your honesty can be talked about so they aren't being held inside which can lead to all kinds of unworkability down the road.

17. Create Futures Together

Imagine your life together as a drawing board or a book with blank pages. Create what you want together and then work your ass off as a team to make it happen. That could be anything from a context such as having an incredible partnership together to a goal such as writing a book together or throwing monthly dinner parties and building new *triads* together.

18. Context

The context for our romantic relationships often goes unnoticed. Context is for human beings as water is for fish. There are two distinct contexts that very prevalent for relationships. There's the dynamic of "you complete me." This is almost always a struggle, will consume energy, and will constantly need compensation to keep the relationship alive. The alternative is one where the relationship is already perfect the way it is and the way it isn't, and now I have the opportunity to ask myself— how can I be a contribution to this already perfect relationship?

19. Quality vs. Quantity

A woman will appreciate 30 minutes of the most incredible and connected time with you more than 3 hours of disconnect and a lack of you being present with her. Make sure you give her the gift of your time and your presence when you're together. You'll both be happier because of it.

20. Safety

If you are someone who disregards the importance of creating a safe space for the women you're with—you can almost guarantee that her having to constantly hold the space will lead to her feeling stressed, tight, and the diminishing of her natural feminine radiance, essence, and power. Just imagine—it's the evening, and you're all dressed up at a nice rooftop bar. You're wearing a white v-neck shirt, blazer, and jeans and she's wearing a red dress that exposes her neck and shoulders and makes her feel sexy, radiant, and beautiful. You're both hanging out at the bar when a guy walks up to her and starts making crude comments towards her. Now imagine if you just stood there and watched as this sleaze-ball continued to humiliate your girlfriend in public. Now maybe you don't speak up because you know she's mature and can handle it herself, or maybe you're feeling nervous and scared. Whatever the reason is—for any woman to experience something like that with her boyfriend who is supposed to be there for her—to just watch—will create a high probability of her feeling unsafe around you. She may not even know why she feels that way as this is evolutionary hardwiring that tends to be politically incorrect to talk about these days. She may not have the words to say it. Or she may have some reason she comes up with to justify why she's turned off by you. But underneath it all, it's a deep-seeded biological mechanism to run away from danger and stay around people that will keep her safe. And yes, women don't "need" a man to feel safe, and yes, "feeling unsafe" can often be a perceived threat as opposed to a real one. So by any means, this is only a pointer to what's true, not the truth in it of itself.

21. Make Her Feel

If she's feeling numb around you, if her radiance is dampened, if her powerful feminine energy is not in full bloom around you, then make her feel. This is not to put some kind of onus on you. That's not the point. It's a matter of taking 100% responsibility for any relationship you're in. So it's not "your fault" when she's feeling numb nor is it some excuse to let your girlfriend get away with anything. Responsibility isn't about blame or fault even though it often gets degraded into such. It's a place to think from and act from to give you access to the results you want to produce regardless of your circumstances. Blaming others seldom works. There's no right action for this. However, an example I'll use to deepen this distinction is the "you not sticking up for her at the bar" situation mentioned above. Let's say you actually did that. You could say, "I'm sorry I didn't stick up for you at the bar. I was scared and feeling angry. I'm sorry I wasn't there for you when you needed me." Something as simple as acknowledging that can make all the difference in the world. She won't expect perfection, so merely being honest about where you're and leaving nothing unsaid and letting her express any impact it had on her until she's complete brings your relationship back to a space of completion and wholeness again.

22. Stop Trying To Fix Things

If you're like me, when someone is complaining to you, the automatic response is often to want to fix things. Yes, women feel great when they feel safe, and men feel great when they can be the hero. And even though we know it's possible to transcend these at times when we need to, it's still powerful to have these structures in place to support our biological machinery and give us the most support and power we can have to foster our own masculine and feminine essence. So next time she's complaining—she may just want you to listen, not to try and fix it which could lead to an upset. And yes, I know—it doesn't make sense to us guys sometimes, but we're just not usually wired like that.

23. Love All Women

If you are a guy who is stingy with their love, women (and men) will pick up on it. The way you treat other women will just be picked up by other women. If you truly appreciate all women and really allow yourself to experience yourself as a lover of women and of human beings, women will pick up on that naturally and it will feel really good for others who are in our space regardless of if they're men or women and sexually attracted to you or not. It's just a pleasant space to be in when you're around someone who genuinely loves people at their core.

Now does that mean you'll have a great relationship with every woman you meet—hell no. What it means is even with women who you have nothing in common with, who are spiteful towards you, who come from a place of survival and manipulation with you—that you will still treat them how you would any other human being and always create an environment where if that woman were to reach out to you—no matter what happened in your past—that you would embrace her and welcome her into your space all while not violating your own boundaries or sweeping things under the rug in the process.

The Presence Gap

I TAKE the position that any behavior I don't like in a lover is rooted in a gap between the quality of my presence and can be corrected by filling that gap with my loving masculine essence.

I choose a lover whose vision of me is so inspiring to me that I would give up my own comfort, temporary feel-good happiness, and even my own attachment to what I believe my life is about in the pursuit of bringing my lover into being.

Reoccurring conversations

THE REASON that people keep saying the same things to you over and over again is because you don't truly listen to them. This is the principle of the reoccurring conversation.

Perhaps you listen to another from your point of view. However, that won't leave the other with the experience of being gotten.

You know when people are listening to you but are listening from their point of view, and you're left with the experience of not being gotten? Don't be that person.

If you are willing, be the kind of person that experiences others getting that you get them and choose to be responsible for creating that. Notice the conversations and complaints that simply disappear from taking that on as time goes on.

What's in the way of partnership

WHEN YOU TAKE ON A PROJECT, there's something you can ask yourself: Are the people that are working with you inspired and empowered around their work? Are they your partners or are they just doing a job? Are *they* experiencing that partnership?

When there's a gap between your commitment to them and their experience, there's *always* something you can be responsible for and somehow where you're getting in the way of that.

Some other places to look from to see what's in the way of the experience of partnership is to locate yourself and your environment on the cultural map, building triads, and using the flow model.

Pushing away others

PEOPLE WILL OFTEN THROW out others that don't fit into their paradigm of reality. If they're run by fear—they may very well throw you out of their life if you're a space of love for them. If they constantly break their word with people—they may very well throw you out of their life if they know you'll hold them accountable for their actions.

Being out there with others

IF YOU CHOOSE NOT to get people, you will notice more and more people will stop getting you. Enter other people's worlds and more and more people will enter yours.

An attachment to people getting you will get in the way of them getting you too.

It's not a matter of if you can or not. Every human being can. It's simply a matter of if you're willing to or not. It's an unwillingness that will stop you—being incapable of doing so is a justification to avoid being responsible for your choice of unwillingness.

Everybody is capable. Not everybody is willing.

Trust vs. Merit

NOBODY HAS to earn my trust. Conversations, like "earning my trust" and "breaking my trust," are interpretations of actions mixed with feelings. Trust conversations are also somewhat ineffective places to come from in relationships with others. Once trust is broken within the context of a trust-based relationship it is rarely recovered.

There is a myth taught in business schools that building trust and trust-based relationships are crucial to being effective. They aren't. Merit-based relationships are.

The late Warren Bennis, who is credited for bringing the field of leadership into academia, had this to say on trust:

"Trust is the lubrication that makes it possible for organizations to work."

This is the one thing Bennis has said that I believe he is flat out wrong about. Now I actually feel I need to make a disclaimer here. I love Bennis. He is one of the most significant contributors to the field of leadership ever. He is also not alive anymore so we can't have a discussion about this. So in no way do I want to do anything to diminish the contributions he has made to the field of leadership. I merely think he's got it wrong about this trust thing. In my experience — getting people stabilized at Stage 4 and getting those people into working triads based on merit will be more effective than focusing how to build trust over time.

I have a friend. I will not use his real name, but we can call him Johnny. Now Johnny has a problem. A major problem. He has a problem with handling money.

When I first met him, I didn't know this about him.

However, what I did know was the following:

1. He has huge visions
2. He is a gifted orator and incredibly effective at having others buy into his vision (one of the best I've ever seen in fact!)
3. He's fun to be around
4. He's incredibly open and can see big picture ideas very easily which makes it easy for me to be around him since my mind works like that too
5. He was a great wingman to me when I was single
6. He has a huge heart

So we got into a business relationship where we were going to do some consulting work for some political campaigns. It was a ton of fun working with Johnny at first. We traveled to Rhode Island to meet with a potential client out there. However, we landed our first client in New Hampshire. We charged him $500 to do some website work for him.

I was managing the account and doing the basics while Johnny took care of the technological side of things. It wasn't hard.

Here's where things got fucked up. It's one day before our project deadline, and Johnny is not returning my calls. And there are certain things I was not able to complete based off my role on the project. Johnny never came through. When I told him that we needed to refund this customer all his money, give him free services, and complete this project, Johnny started getting defensive and starting blaming the customer. I could not believe it.

This fucking asshole had such a distorted view of what happened that he couldn't even keep his integrity with a simple project. So I refunded the money out of my own pocket to the customer as an act of goodwill, issued an apology, and left Johnny for good.

I told him that in the future I would never work with him again unless there was a contract in place that was structured in a way where if he didn't come through that I was protected. I also made it clear to him that if he didn't honor that contract, I would take him to court. Now since I'm not interested in taking a friend of mine to court nor doing business with someone that I'd even have to be worried about that, I never did business with him again.

Now it's turned out that Johnny has a problem with not completing projects and deadlines and also has a problem with not paying people back the money he owes. He's in nearly six-figures of debt and has a history of not completing jobs he was paid for. He has many people very angry at him and for a good reason.

I could easily go into the whole "he broke my trust" shit. However, all that happened if we get past the story or interpretation was that he said he would do something and he didn't. And the impact was that I needed to pay out of pocket or risk hurting my business reputation.

Now here's the facts. All six things I shared above are still valid. There is merit to all those six things, and there's also no merit to loaning this guy money or putting him on a project where he is in control and managing it. I would also never hire him to do any kind of web-based work for me as he a has a history of not completing projects on time.

So when I talk to him—which I still do on occasion—there's no weirdness there for me. There's nothing incomplete. And he's always great to be around when I am around him.

Think about ex-lovers where there wasn't merit to being in a relationship with them, but there may have been merit in other areas. When you can focus on the merit of a relationship and not on this all-encompassing trust story, relationships become a lot cleaner, smoother, consist of less drama—and usually no drama unless you get dramatic about it (which is also your choice)—and you become all around more effective in your relationships.

And don't get me wrong—feeling like you can trust someone is a nice feeling. It's just when trust becomes the foundation of your relationships that you can really run into trouble.

Of course, there's also the people who go around living life inside of a conversation called "break my trust waiting to happen" which is aligned with people with trust issues. That conversation called "break my trust waiting to happen" is *always* based on something that happened in the past and some story they created around trust.

Trust feels good, and it's just a story and interpretation. See it for what it is, and it won't be what makes the relationship nor what destroys one.

Coming from love

Choose to *be* loving even when you are feeling closed off. Love conquers all. And yes, the phrase "love conquers all" has degraded in the culture into some bullshit motivational phrase that typically makes no difference to the quality of one's life or is used as a coping mechanism when you aren't feeling very loving.

At the end of the day—the friendships and relationships you will have from coming from that place will be incredible, and the ones who don't will never be able to give you a reason to diminish your own expression in order to defend or protect something because you feel hurt or resentful.

Everybody wants to be gotten

EVERYBODY WANTS TO BE GOTTEN, have the space to be fully Self-expressed, and be loved. When this is missing for a sustained period of time, most people become resigned to that experience and end up accepting it as reality. Give someone the experience of being gotten, of being loved, and the space to be fully Self-expressed. Not only is it possible that you will make a difference in their day, you may very well make a difference in their life.

The "right" people

YOU WILL ONLY EVER BE AS great as the people you surround yourself with, so be brave enough to let go of those who keep bringing you down. You shouldn't force connections with people who constantly make you feel less than amazing. If someone makes you feel uncomfortable and insecure every time you're with them, for whatever reason, they're probably not "close friend" material. If they make you feel like you can't be yourself, or if they make you feel "less than" in any way, don't pursue a connection with them. If you feel emotionally drained after hanging out with them or get a small hint of anxiety when you are reminded of them, listen to your intuition. There are so many "right people" for you, who energize you and inspire you to be your best self. It makes no sense to force it with people who are the wrong match for you.

The one caveat is that this mindset can degrade very easily into a mentality of not take responsibility for how you feel or how others occur for you. Distinguishing your stories and your own meaning-making around a situation vs. if something is just simply not workable is something only you can ever know.

The third stage dance

INTIMACY IS this beautiful dance where two people continuously go deeper with each other. I have mentioned David Deida's Three Stages of Relationships throughout this book so I won't go into defining the stages again.

I am very clear that there are many more people on this planet who say they want what would be equivalent to a *Stage 3 Relationship* as the way Deida distinguishes it vs. actually have it. And no, I don't mean peak moments. I mean as the baseline for their relationships, marriages, etc.

Why?

It's actually very simple. The third stage isn't always comfortable. It's not predictable. It can bring up deep-rooted insecurities to the surface. It can bring up emotional blocks and walls. And sometimes it will be stormy. In those moments, you can choose to give space to all of that and work through it—which creates more aliveness and freedom and a deepening of the relationships—or, you can go to a place where *there's something wrong and I need to fix it,* and then run away while recoiling into emotional closure.

If it were easy everyone would have this kind of relationship. However, if someone says they want this kind of dynamic but they never seem to get it, don't be surprised if that same man or woman runs from you due to an unwillingness to go deeper with you. If you are truly committed to this and the other person is more committed to comfort and "safety"—yes I put safety in quotes as it's the illusion of safety which is really quite dangerous—your presence will be a threat and there will come a time when you'll want to go deeper, and they just won't be willing to match you in that dance. They'll get stopped by whatever walls or closure there is there for them.

While in that particular moment you may feel sad, it's actually great news. By going deep with someone, you'll save a lot of time on weeding out the people who just aren't emotionally there to match you. This will give you the opportunity to start that dance anew with someone who may be willing to match you this time.

Also, it gives the other individual the space to keep repeating the same kinds of relationships until they either resign themselves to "this is just the way relationships are" or they break free of those patterns of emotional closure.

The dance continues for a lifetime. There is no "end game."

Be the type of husband your wife can't help but brag about

by Gerald Rogers, *Huffington Post*

1. Never stop courting. Never stop dating. NEVER EVER take that woman for granted. When you asked her to marry you, you promised to be that man that would OWN HER HEART and to fiercely protect it. This is the most important and sacred treasure you will ever be entrusted with. SHE CHOSE YOU. Never forget that, and NEVER GET LAZY in your love.
2. PROTECT YOUR OWN HEART. Just as you committed to being the protector of her heart, you must guard your own with the same vigilance. Love yourself fully, love the world openly, but there is a special place in your heart where no one must enter except for your wife. Keep that space always ready to receive her and invite her in, and refuse to let anyone or anything else enter there.
3. FALL IN LOVE OVER and OVER and OVER again. You will constantly change. You're not the same people you were when you got married, and in five years you will not be the same person you are today. Change will come, and in that, you

have to re-choose each other every day. SHE DOESN'T HAVE TO STAY WITH YOU, and if you don't take care of her heart, she may give that heart to someone else or seal you out completely, and you may never be able to get it back. Always fight to win her love just as you did when you were courting her.

4. ALWAYS SEE THE BEST in her. Focus only on what you love. What you focus on will expand. If you focus on what bugs you, all you will see is reasons to be bugged. If you focus on what you love, you can't help but be consumed by love. Focus to the point where you can no longer see anything but love, and you know without a doubt that you are the luckiest man on earth to have this woman as your wife.

5. IT'S NOT YOUR JOB TO CHANGE OR FIX HER... your job is to love her as she is with no expectation of her ever changing. And if she changes, love what she becomes, whether it's what you wanted or not.

6. TAKE FULL ACCOUNTABILITY for your own emotions: It's not your wife's job to make you happy, and she CAN'T make you sad. You are responsible for finding your own happiness, and through that your joy will spill over into your relationship and your love.

7. NEVER BLAME your wife If YOU get frustrated or angry at her, it is only because it is triggering something inside of YOU. They are YOUR emotions, and your responsibility. When you feel those feelings take time to get present and to look within and understand what it is inside of YOU that is asking to be healed. You were attracted to this woman because she was the person best suited to trigger all of your childhood wounds in the most painful way so that you could heal them... when you heal yourself, you will no longer be triggered by her, and you will wonder why you ever were.

8. Allow your woman to JUST BE. When she's sad or upset, it's not your job to fix it, it's your job to HOLD HER and let her know it's ok. Let her know that you hear her, and that she's important and that you are that pillar on which she can always

lean. The feminine spirit is about change and emotion and like a storm her emotions will roll in and out, and as you remain strong and unjudging she will trust you and open her soul to you... DON'T RUN-AWAY WHEN SHE'S UPSET. Stand present and strong and let her know you aren't going anywhere. Listen to what she is really saying behind the words and emotion.

9. BE SILLY... don't take yourself so damn seriously. Laugh. And make her laugh. Laughter makes everything else easier.

10. FILL HER SOUL EVERY DAY... learn her love languages and the specific ways that she feels important and validated and CHERISHED. Ask her to create a list of 10 THINGS that make her feel loved and memorize those things and make it a priority every day to make her feel like a queen.

11. BE PRESENT. Give her not only your time, but your focus, your attention and your soul. Do whatever it takes to clear your head so that when you are with her you are fully WITH HER. Treat her as you would your most valuable client. She is.

12. BE WILLING TO TAKE HER SEXUALLY, to carry her away in the power of your masculine presence, to consume her and devour her with your strength, and to penetrate her to the deepest levels of her soul. Let her melt into her feminine softness as she knows she can trust you fully.

13. DON'T BE AN IDIOT.... And don't be afraid of being one either. You will make mistakes and so will she. Try not to make too big of mistakes, and learn from the ones you do make. You're not supposed to be perfect, just try to not be too stupid.

14. GIVE HER SPACE... The woman is so good at giving and giving, and sometimes she will need to be reminded to take time to nurture herself. Sometimes she will need to fly from your branches to go and find what feeds her soul, and if you give her that space she will come back with new songs to sing.... (okay, getting a little too poetic here, but you get the point. Tell her to take time for herself, ESPECIALLY after you have kids. She needs that space to renew and get re-

centered, and to find herself after she gets lost in serving you, the kids and the world.)

15. BE VULNERABLE... you don't have to have it all together. Be willing to share your fears and feelings, and quick to acknowledge your mistakes.

16. BE FULLY TRANSPARENT. If you want to have trust you must be willing to share EVERYTHING... Especially those things you don't want to share. It takes courage to fully love, to fully open your heart and let her in when you don't know if she will like what she finds... Part of that courage is allowing her to love you completely, your darkness as well as your light. DROP THE MASK... If you feel like you need to wear a mask around her, and show up perfect all the time, you will never experience the full dimension of what love can be.

17. NEVER STOP GROWING TOGETHER... The stagnant pond breeds malaria, the flowing stream is always fresh and cool. Atrophy is the natural process when you stop working a muscle, just as it is if you stop working on your relationship. Find common goals, dreams and visions to work towards.

18. DON'T WORRY ABOUT MONEY. Money is a game, find ways to work together as a team to win it. It never helps when teammates fight. Figure out ways to leverage both people's strength to win.

19. FORGIVE IMMEDIATELY and focus on the future rather than carrying weight from the past. Don't let your history hold you hostage. Holding onto past mistakes that either you or she makes, is like a heavy anchor to your marriage and will hold you back. FORGIVENESS IS FREEDOM. Cut the anchor loose and always choose love.

20. ALWAYS CHOOSE LOVE. ALWAYS CHOOSE LOVE. ALWAYS CHOOSE LOVE. In the end, this is the only advice you need. If this is the guiding principle through which all your choices is governed, there is nothing that will threaten the happiness of your marriage. Love will always endure.

IF YOU ARE READING this and your marriage isn't what you want it to be, take 100% responsibility for YOUR PART in marriage, regardless of where your spouse is at, and commit to applying these lessons while there is time.

MEN- THIS IS YOUR CHARGE: Commit to being an EPIC LOVER. There is no greater challenge, and no greater prize. Your woman deserves that from you. Be the type of husband your wife can't help but brag about.

It's (almost) never personal

JUST BECAUSE PEOPLE do shitty things to others or even people who do awesome things doesn't mean they aren't crying themselves to sleep, upset, or feeling constrained inside. It's easy to use people's shitty behavior and take it personally – but it's almost never personal. And you become more of a toxic and shitty person yourself when you start disrespecting others at their core for it. You forward bullshit, and you become part of the problem when you're simply in reaction to others. You allow others to give you a reason to dishonor yourself in the process. When you can be a space of love in the face of anything—nothing has any power over you and people's bullshit has a higher probability—not guaranteed—of disappearing in your space or they simply won't talk to you because who you are being is a space they simply can't handle for where they're at.

People's disempowering and undermining bullshit has a way of disappearing in a space of unconditional love and tends to get perpetuated in a space of judgment where they feel the need to get positional and defensive about something.

The Top Of The Mountain

THERE'S this really nice sounding saying in our society that "it's lonely at the top" and it's a load of horseshit. How do I know? Because anyone who says that hasn't ever been to the fucking top. Do you really know what it means to be at the top? I sure as hell don't and I've been trained in The Landmark Forum, Landmark's entire curriculum for living, have interviewed pornstars on the radio, built 4 companies, built a project that was funded by a billionaire, and was able to make 6 figures while only working a few fucking hours a day and have a lifestyle where I can be anywhere in the god damn world and am still millions of light-years away from the top. There is no top. The top is an illusion. The moment you believe you're at the top of the mountain, you're stumbling down again. If you don't get what I mean by that, sleep on it.

What Losers Say

But in reality, you can't know what it's like to be "at the top." However, losers LOVE to say this phrase. They adore and cherish this phase as it is some fucking sacred cow. Why? They get to bask and justify their own dissatisfaction and mediocrity in life. You don't hear Buddhist monks talking about how fucking enlightened they are so therefore it's lonely at the top. It's a pity party conversation and it's for losers.

The Three Stages Of Growth

Here's how it goes when you start actually developing yourself. I've been through it first hand and know hundreds of others in my circles who have as well and it kind of goes like this. There are three stages. These stages are not to be confused with the five stages of culture in Tribal Leadership or the three stages of relationships within the context of David Deida's work.

STAGE #1

People will be all for what you're up to. You're going to do The Landmark Forum to develop yourself.....nice!!! Good on you....I hope it works for you!!! You're going to clean up your diet and get your fitness straight.... sounds awesome!! People will cheer you on while underneath the surface be cynical and doubt you'll actually make changes. The Landmark Forum sounds like you'll get a lot out of it ....and then their thoughts are (sounds like some super scammy bullshit where they motivate you and tell you shit you could easily learn in a book and mostly common sense). Wow you're going to clean up your diet (he'll never stick to it but glad he's trying)....you know, some cynical bullshit like that.

STAGE #2

Now you actually start getting trained and developed and having actual shifts in the way reality occurs for you after doing Landmark's Curriculum. You start getting complete in your relationships, start building community projects, stop making others wrong, have access to Self, you start eating clean, looking sexy, fucking more, feeling better about yourself and others. All the shit, literally. However, all those people who were rooting you on all of a sudden go MIA. You don't hear from them anymore. They stop liking your sexy Instagram posts of your bangin' new body and stop liking your Facebook posts of all the fucking amazing breakthroughs you've been having over the past 6 months since you finished a transformational leadership program. In fact, these same people start to cynically question your motives and start to look at you in a bad light. You've changed they will say....(whether they actually SAY it or it's what being UNSAID). In reality, your way of being is a threat to them. You don't fit into the box they put you in anymore. They will attempt to dominate you back in the box. We have all experienced it who have shared this experience. It's just what happens. Your lifestyle and way of being is literally a fucking threat to their own existence. The world of possibility is always a threat to those committed to survival.

STAGE #3

Once a few years go by and these massive shifts become the new reality (you know like when people wake up to the fact that 10 years later after your fucking Advanced Course with Landmark that maybe you aren't on a one-week long motivational high....Jesus Fuck!)....these same people who were secretly or outwardly hostile towards you are now being very public about them associating with you. They'll want to tag you in shit on social media. They'll tell their friends how awesome you are or name drop you. People will randomly be wanting to catch up with you. However, these same people will privately say shit about you like there's something wrong with you living your life as art....playing in fucking possibility. Your aliveness is literally a threat to their own reality.

True Friends

These people are NOT your fucking friends. They were NEVER your friends. They were just people that happened to be around you. Real friends support you openly, authentically, and without condition regardless of what stage of your journey you're in.

The Art Of Possibility

Those committed to the art of possibility, the art of living....are growing. You're always fucking growing unfolding that underlying commitment. With that growth comes higher expectations from the people around you. (Sorry, just how it fucking is.) As you go through these stages your original group of peers will start to shift naturally. You don't have to find your tribe, your tribe will fucking find you.

You can never TRUE FRIENDS...real connections at the level of your fucking soul. Those are the people who are pulled to your way of being and nourishing those connections only brings you more fulfillment and a better life both internally and externally.

It's not lonely at the top. It's not lonely at Stages #1, #2, or #3 either.

There are billions of people on the planet. Keep creating relationships from Self. Keep staying present to what you discover through inquiring from these principles laid out in this book. Whatever you discover, DO NOT USE IT. Let what you discover USE YOU. The moment you take what you discover and turn it into a technique, you will undermine its power. When you do that, you now are back to exactly where you're at before starting this book but with lots of really sexy jargon and principles to justify your own bullshit. The different between operating from Self and being present to what you discover and operating from your identity and your identity using the principles will make all the difference between *Principles Of Power* and *Principles Of Sounding Like A Manipulative Asshole*.

So keep creating and living life from Self.

There's no need to *find your tribe*.

Your tribe will find you.

Acknowledgments

I want to thank my parents, Debbie and Charlie, for always supporting me, and loving me, and providing me the space to explore my passions in life. While they did attempt to guide me, they never told me how I should live my life. I believe that being hyper-focused on my authentic interests, knowing what I wanted to do with my life at a young age, and living my life in a way that fulfilled me, while possible, would have been psychologically much more difficult without their support. Thank you, mom and dad, for always loving me, being there for me, and being my most significant source of stability and encouragement in my life.

I also want to thank my brother, Zach Schleien, for being persistent in telling me that I should write a book. Other than me being my harshest critic, my second harshest critic is my brother, and he is tough on me. I'm grateful for him and his honesty. I love you, Zach.

I also want to thank the woman I was dating at the time I wrote this book, Amanda, who was in the same room with me while editing much of this book. Feeding off her energy was intoxicating and electrifying for me, and her very being continues to inspire me to my core to this day. So to her, thank you for being you, for your unconditional support, and for all the different beautiful ways you express yourself, express your love, and express your playfulness. My life is more abundant and more vibrant having met you.

I also want to thank my investors at my company. While I can't legally name names as it would violate my privacy policy, what I can say is that I am grateful for all of you. You have been the first group of people to support me financially with a company that I have dreamed of creating since I was a teenager, and, I wake up every day feeling grateful for your support. And yes, I mean that: it's an "everyday-phenomenon" for me. Being able to communicate investing principles with you and learning to articulate them in a way through a process where I take often complicated concepts and simplify them into general frameworks and principles has been an incredible learning practice for me as well as an incredible experience enabling me to become a better articulator of my ideas. You've all really taught me the value of building authentic relationships that can lead to transactional business as opposed to building commoditized relationships where the point of the relationship is the transaction, as opposed to the transaction naturally deriving from the relationship in it of itself. It's one thing to talk about that and another thing to live that every day.

About the Author

Eric Schleien has been featured in Forbes, The Wall Street Journal, GuruFocus, and Warren Buffett's Biography, *Of Permanent Value*. He has coached thousands of individuals including board members of public companies as well as several Fortune 500 CEOs. He specializes in organizational culture and has become a leading authority on organizational culture in the investment industry. He is the founder of Granite State Capital Management, Wyoming Warehousing & Safe Deposit Co, Transformational Leadership Associates, and ProxyActivism.com. He also is the host of The Intelligent Investing Podcast. Eric currently resides in Philadelphia, PA.

Made in the USA
Coppell, TX
10 December 2020